COMMUNIST
DAZE

To the readers of my
favorite book
With best wishes
Author: Vladimir Tsesis

12/25/2017

COMMUNIST
DAZE

The Many Misadventures
of a Soviet Doctor

VLADIMIR A. TSESIS

INDIANA UNIVERSITY PRESS

This book is a publication of

INDIANA UNIVERSITY PRESS
Office of Scholarly Publishing
Herman B Wells Library 350
1320 East 10th Street
Bloomington, Indiana 47405 USA

iupress.indiana.edu

Manufactured in the
United States of America

*Library of Congress
Cataloging-in-Publication Data*

Names: Tsesis, Vladimir A., author.
Title: Communist daze : the
  many misadventures of a soviet
  doctor / Vladimir A. Tsesis.
Description: Bloomington, Indiana :
  Indiana University Press, [2017]
Identifiers: LCCN 2016050900 (print) |
  LCCN 2016052661 (ebook) | ISBN
  9780253025944 (cloth : alk. paper) |
  ISBN 9780253025869 (pbk. : alk.
  paper) | ISBN 9780253025890 (e-book)
Subjects: LCSH: Tsesis, Vladimir A.—
  Health. | Pediatricians—Soviet
  Union—Biography. | Pediatricians—
  United States—Biography.
Classification: LCC RJ43.T754 A3 2017
  (print) | LCC RJ43.T754 (ebook) |
  DDC 618.9200092 [B] —dc23
LC record available at
  https://lccn.loc.gov/2016050900

1 2 3 4 5   22 21 20 19 18 17

Dedicated to victims of the Soviet public health system.

Contents

Preface

———⟨⚭⟩———

September 1964

It's a bright summer morning in glorious Soviet Moldova. Once again, I find myself racing across dully colored hospital grounds in pursuit of a decidedly earnest, righteously dedicated Communist who also happens to be my new boss. Lyubov Evgenyevna Oprya, specialist in obstetrics and gynecology, is the Gradieshti Rural Medical District Hospital's chief doctor. Though dressed in a doctor's uniform of white gown and cap, she resembles a typical rural village dweller. Lyubov Evgenyevna cannot be called beautiful—short, practically without a neck, and sporting sharp gray eyes, a low forehead, and a large, round, moonlike face with weathered skin carrying the unmistakable scars of adolescent acne. The fat on her body is remarkably uniformly distributed, which, in combination with the absence of a neck, gives her the unfortunate appearance of a rapidly walking meatball.

Lyubov Evgenyevna is a no-nonsense but personable woman known for her fierce, unswerving belief in the Communist Party and an unabashedly uncomplicated approach to life. The fresh-out-of-school young doctor trying to keep pace with her is, I must confess, quite different.

On that summer morning, as we march forthright across the grounds, Maria Tuliu, the hospital's chef, stands at the door of her kitchen, waving. Known for her borscht, or beet soup, and portions of butter, eggs, or meat when she can get them, Maria is young and tall, and she always seems happy. Today, her smile is not diminished by the dullness of her attire: a peasant shawl, simple country clothes, and a battered, once-white apron.

Her wave reminds my boss of something important, and she doesn't hesitate to act.

"Good morning, Maria!" shouts Lyubov Evgenyevna without breaking stride, voice booming throughout the yard and deafening, I bet, more than the handful of people now scurrying away from us. "Nice to see you! All your blood tests look absolutely normal, except the Wassermann test!" The rules require all hospital employees—including those in the hospital kitchen—to have periodic checkups, which include the Wassermann reaction test, a blood test for syphilis that often gives a false positive result.

"What is that Wassermann test for?" yells Maria back, still smiling.

"It's for syphilis! The test shows you probably have syphilis!"

"What's that? What did you say?" shouts Maria, leaning forward, now a bit puzzled. "What do I have?"

"SYPHILIS! YOU MIGHT HAVE SYPHILIS, MARIA!!!" screams Lyubov Evgenyevna at the top of her voice. The scattering crowd moves hastily.

Maria bursts out laughing, having no idea what syphilis is and not realizing her reputation has just been publically besmirched by her boss—and physician. But then again, none of the remaining handful of stragglers on the grounds seem to understand, either.

Horrified, I glance at my boss, who's looking down at her clipboard and already moving to the next item on the day's order of business. Maria's delighted chuckling follows us into the outpatient clinics, where wait, as always, leathery-skin peasants and their dehydrated children from the surrounding countryside.

Welcome to three years in strange and wonderful Gradieshti. Welcome to medicine, good ole Soviet style.

Acknowledgments

First, I am most grateful to my wonderful wife, Marina, who is always my best friend, precious adviser, and inspiration.

By a stroke of destiny, I was privileged to meet Gary Dunham, my publisher and editor at Indiana University Press, who found in my book—to my sheer luck—exactly what I wanted to express. In him, I encountered a kindred soul in perception of reality. His personal work on the manuscript is beyond any praise and description. I am very grateful to him for his friendship and unfailing optimism.

I am deeply indebted to Laura De Santo Wagner who did an excellent job as an editor of the manuscript before it was submitted to the publisher.

COMMUNIST DAZE

A listener asks Armenian Radio whether the Soviet Union would ever surpass the United States economically.

Armenian Radio replies, "No comrades, the Soviet Union cannot surpass America because the entire world might notice the holes in our pants."

Beginnings

---⊗---

Let's call it, Gradieshti, shall we? An elliptical riot of twisting, unnamed, muddy alleys and streets caught between hills swarming with brush, the rural village could be found, if one looked long enough, about ten miles from Tiraspol in the Moldavian Soviet Republic (today the Pridnestrovian Moldovan Republic). When I stepped off a dilapidated bus on August 1, 1964, Gradieshti was home to some five thousand souls and an assortment of chickens, ducks, goats, sheep, pigs, cats, and dogs, including a most agreeable three-legged mutt whom we will meet in a while. Stepping over a stray dog lying sprawled and still in the heat, I set on the ground two small pieces of luggage—one filled with medical books, of course. Taking a deep breath, I looked around at my new home.

A huge Communist propaganda poster, faded by time and weather, gazed down on me. Welcoming me to Gradieshti was a large, radiantly smiling peasant woman with hands raised wide and dressed in Moldovan folk costume. Seemingly endless wheat fields rolled into the distance behind her. The bottom of the poster proudly proclaimed, GLORY TO THE HANDS THAT SMELL OF BREAD.

Rolling my eyes, I took a few steps, squinting in the bright sunshine and hoping for a glimpse of the real Moldovan village where I had been sent to serve and practice.

Well . . .

Under a scorching noon sun, color seemed to have fled Gradieshti, like most Soviet villages, long ago. Most streets and public areas were bare of vegetation. Thatched, one-story adobe dwellings made from a mixture of muted local clay, water, straw, and horse manure crowded rutted unpaved streets. Some houses were sheaved with just branches and twigs coated with clay on both sides. Primitive fences made from rough unpainted boards or branches and twigs struggled to hold in gardens that, I soon learned, oozed thick black mud after rain. Every now and then I heard the unmistakable sounds of small livestock in a handful of backyards, signaling those lucky enough to enjoy meat and eggs, which were rarely available in our stores.

Lacking street numbers and resigned to gray, the venerable houses of Gradieshti were jumbled together around a centrally located public center plaza, where stood communal buildings housing the village council, the collective farm management, the rural post office, a small pharmacy, a milk kitchen, a dental office, a large two-story high school made of bricks, and the Village Cultural Center, which boasted a library and a spacious assembly hall. (The church on the plaza had been destroyed decades before.)

There was nary a person or car in sight, though I did spot a few horse-drawn carts and heard the puttering of a motorcycle. Shaking my head and sighing, I picked up my bags and began trudging along the two-lane asphalt road on the outskirts of town. Somewhere beyond the exhausted dogs and cats wandering in the heat were the village hospital and my new job.

My journey toward that little gray village had begun months earlier, before graduation from the medical school in Kishinev (now known as Chişinău, the capital of the Republic of Moldova.) As a Russian Jew, I had not dared to think of becoming a student there—Kishinev had long been a hotbed of antisemitism. My dear parents, however, had used all of their life savings for a bribe that opened the door to my highest dream. I was so happy, having long yearned to become a physician and to practice the most meaningful profession. Among the books from my childhood, many romanticized the field of medicine, and I wanted to be a part of it. I especially wanted to help children.

It was so exciting to start those six years of tuition-free medical school! My time as a student began with service to the state—required work "for the glory of the Socialist Motherland," as our saying went. On the day before my first year began in August 1958, we newly fledged students were informed that we were being "entrusted" with "a high honor" of helping *kolkhozniks* (farmers) harvest the cornfields of Sarata-Nova, located about forty-two miles southwest of Kishinev.

This order was not uncommon. An abiding socialist practice of the Soviet era was the massive use of urban populations as seasonal workers in agriculture, mostly for harvesting crops during fall seasons. During harvest, an army of high school, college, and university students as well as workers and employees from countless enterprises were transported to the country to help the farmers bring in crops. Every late summer and fall, present and future professors, engineers, doctors, teachers, musicians, and humanitarians from all over the country spent two to eight weeks harvesting corn, potato, carrots, apples, and grapes. Although students were hardly ever paid for this work, workers and employees continued to receive their regular salaries.

The official reason for the yearly mass exodus of urban dwellers to villages was always the same, each time I heard it: "This year it was a surprising bumper crop (*Gasp!*) and there is no way, dear comrades, for the local residents to gather it by themselves!" I didn't really mind this time, being in good spirits about starting medical school and accustomed since high school to being sent to the country to harvest corn and grapes.

A fleet of buses soon delivered us first-year college students to the village of Sarata-Nova. We were lodged in classrooms of a local school: women on the first floor and men on the second, about twenty students to a classroom, all sleeping on mattresses strewn on the floor and stuffed with the highly lauded "best-quality" straw. As running water was absent inside and outside of the building, we washed up using water brought in a cistern. On each floor stood a water tank, complete with spigot and attached copper mug, from which everybody drank. A special treat awaited us out back—a decades-old brick outhouse without partitions between the holes. Undoubtedly built way back during the October Revolution, this most attractive facility accommodated up to fifteen of us students on full display at the same time, putting into practice the Russian expression "От общества секретов нет," or "There are no secrets among community members."

Young, heady, and exuberant about the opportunity to fight hard for my medical career, I worked steadily in the cornfields and, yes, sang with loud gusto for four weeks. I really enjoyed toiling in the fresh air under the generous warming rays of the Moldovan sun, surrounded by green fields and feeling the tender touch of wind gusts. Against my will—probably because of my enthusiasm—I was soon appointed to be a звеньевой, or field-team leader. Unfortunately, I was never good at telling people what to do, especially in situations like this, where my commitment to work exceeded the other team members. They had been admitted to the medical school easily and without problems, and now, restless and full of energy, most wanted to have a good time rather than harvest corn for the state. My desire to be a role model and to inspire my field-team failed utterly—everyone else seemed to work faster, without songs to motivate them—but the effort did not go unnoticed.

One day, as usual, I was enthusiastically cleaning corncobs and adding them to the large pile on the ground. Full of zeal, I was singing my own words to the melody of a popular song "Rio de Janeiro":

> To village Sarata-Nova
> I came to harvest corn,
> And now I am sure
> That here I was born

Two of our notables suddenly stepped out from a thicket of tall corn plants to my left. The Komsomol (All-Union Leninist Young Communist League) leader Petru Sarakutza, recently discharged from the army, and one of the Senior Students (староста,) Kolya Chernenko, had been observing my fired up labor. They walked past, speaking to each other and ignoring me completely.

"I told you, Kolya," insisted Sarakutza, "even though he is a Jew, this guy, Tsesis, works like a horse."

Pausing for a moment, the Senior Student shrugged as they strolled away. "OK," he muttered, "we will see how he will behave in the future."

Apparently, the Senior Student was never fully convinced. During a general meeting of students some time later, a classmate sitting next to me asked whether we would be paid for our daily work. This question, for some reason, made Chernenko very nervous.

Piercing me with his eyes as if I was the one who had asked the question, he snapped, "To those like *you*—and everybody understands what I mean by *that*—let it be known, that the rest of the students are here to help our brothers and sisters in the village. Unlike *you*, they are not thinking about material rewards."

This was nothing new. Acquired by birth and not by choice, my ethnicity, as always, worked against me. I had heard hate speech during my younger school years, and now the cancer was surfacing again in medical school. Initially hurt by such contemptuous manifestation of a sick mind, over time, I—more or less—had developed immunity to it. Now, it made me even more determined to work hard and do what I wanted: become a doctor.

A few months later during my first year in medical school, I crossed paths again with the other notable, the Komsomol leader, Sarakutza. It seems the army veteran was struggling in chemistry, and so the professor asked me to tutor him. One day well into the course, I was explaining the concept of valence by referring to the structure of atoms. Looking very puzzled, my pupil lit a cigarette, leaned back, and casually inquired through a cloud of smoke: "But what is ... an 'atom'? "

Petru Sarakutza later went on to become an instructor in the Department of Biochemistry there, another bright Communist future guaranteed. It figures.

Let's fast forward through years of dedicated schoolwork and getting married to my lovely wife, Marina. About five months before graduation, it was time once again for me to work "for the glory of Socialist Motherland." I was asked—well, instructed—to become a military physician. During a short interview with an army colonel, I firmly refused to sign the army contract, since doing so would have forced me to serve in the military for twenty or more years, like my father, a career officer. Lowering his voice, the colonel told me that if I did not sign, he had official orders to prevent me from passing all my graduation examinations. Perhaps a bluff, maybe the truth, but I had no choice. I signed the contract and became resigned to continuing the family tradition. Marina and I braced ourselves for the nomadic and unpredictable life of an army medical officer, but months passed with no word from the military. Finally, confused about what was going on, I went to a military representative for an explanation. To my immense relief, I learned that "the Moldavian Republic currently has a critical need for pediatricians, and therefore, you cannot be drafted into the army."

Whew.

I soon realized that there was a shortage of pediatricians everywhere during that time, and there was a good reason for it. So many of my classmates at medical school who came from rural areas stubbornly insisted on being transferred from pediatric to internal medicine specialties. It was all because of politics. The catastrophe of child mortality in the Soviet Union was so bad and widespread that it could not be hidden from the rest of the world. All attempts to reduce its prevalence were unsuccessful. Child mortality, as an indicator of the overall quality of medical care, was constantly under the microscope of the party functionaries responsible for public health care. Politicians harassed medical professionals about the necessity of improving the statistical data. Childcare providers were called to meetings and seminars where they were reprimanded if child mortality was high in the locality under their responsibility. Thus rural areas were badly understaffed with pediatricians. Few physicians were willing to work in the countryside where they would be paid less, work longer hours, lack adequate backup by specialists, and wrestle with poor laboratory and medical imaging capabilities.

So, my services were desperately needed.

Two months before graduation from Kishinev Medical School in 1964, all of us last-year medical students gathered at the grand auditorium for orientation about our future employment. The key speaker for this important occasion was the Minister of Public Health of the Moldavian Soviet Socialist Republic, Nikolai Andreevich Testemitsanu, a former surgeon, born and raised in a Moldovan village.

"Most of you will be sent to work in the country," he announced. "The Motherland provided you with a free education. Now it is time for you to repay your Motherland and help people in rural areas by providing quality medical care."

In exchange for six years of free professional education at the medical school, graduates were required to work in underserved areas for three years. To ensure the mandate was carried out, we graduates would receive our diplomas only after fulfilling that obligation.

Naturally, there were special exceptions to the rule. A diploma was immediately given to male students drafted into the army, to women who were married and pregnant, and to a privileged group of students who were awarded well-paid research and teaching positions at the Kishinev Medical School itself. Those elite few were children of the party elite or indigenous Moldovans whose fellow villagers or relatives already occupied teaching positions in the medical school.

Some in this select group were shockingly undereducated. I remember my classmate Vitale Istrati, a nice-looking fellow with a childish face, who simply could not remember the cornucopia of terms in the course on anatomy and failed it repeatedly. Due to his high-level connections, he was not expelled but was permitted to take the same anatomy course three years in a row until finally passing the test. Of course—you guessed it—after graduation, Vitale became a teacher in the Department of Anatomy and later even went on to chair the department at another medical school. Apparently, the nominating committee had concluded that three long years of studying the same damn material had produced a brilliant expert on the subject.

Vitale's story is not unique; I would come to discover that such shameless nepotism in the medical profession was typical of the entire country, undermining the professional capabilities of generations of Soviet doctors. Privileged students with minimal education and training invariably were permitted to finish medical school and become physicians to whom patients entrusted their lives. Time and again, I met and worked with representatives of the honorable medical profession—ignoramuses with a doctor's coat and stethoscope—who just were not appropriately prepared to provide qualified help. It is thus not surprising, but such a national disgrace, that the level of medical research was of such low quality that research papers then were rarely published outside of the Soviet Union.

Not having connections like the esteemed and most learned Dr. Istrati, I was appointed *kustovoj pediatr*, which can best be translated as "provincial pediatrician," for the rural village of Gradieshti in the Moldavian Soviet Republic. At the young age of twenty-three, as a fledgling specialist, I also assumed responsibility for the health of a large population of children living in five smaller, surrounding hamlets. In such places, medical care often rested in the hands of *feldshers*, medical or surgical practitioners, who lacked full professional qualifications or status (something like physicians' assistants in the United States). I was not unhappy with the assignment, as Gradieshti was relatively close to Odessa, where Marina was attending the Meteorological College and living with her mother. We would be able to meet from time to time, especially on weekends.

Well, it sounded like a good, simple plan to see each other regularly. Actually getting there and back sometimes proved to be, as you will see, quite . . . interesting. As was my mother-in-law.

So, there I went, and here I was now, stubbornly plodding the asphalt road outside of gray Gradieshti, caught in the sweltering glare of noon sun. Eventually, I reached the hospital grounds and the relief of shade: Unlike the rest of the village, the hospital grounds boasted generous, lush old trees and bushes that flourished along paved alleys, free of mud and ruts. I followed one of them to the hospital's main building—decades old, L-shaped, single-story, sheathed in brick, capped in iron, and sporting a row of double-framed windows on each side. A woman orderly, dressed in a white gown, directed me to the office of the hospital's chief doctor. (In small rural hospitals, the hospital's chief or senior doctor combined their administrative duties with the responsibilities of a regular physician and were paid correspondingly more money.)

Opening a large door painted way too many years earlier, I stepped from bright sunlight into a dimly lit, long corridor with a linoleum floor. Temporarily blinded, the first sensations of my new life were smells and sounds. The typical odor of a hospital—a mixture of chlorine, camphor oil, carbolic acids, and tincture of valerian root; a soft undulating wave of voices rolling in from hospital rooms and nursing stations.

In the doctors' lounge, I spotted a woman in her mid-thirties, dressed in white gown and white cap, sitting at a desk hastily writing notes on a large stack of patients' charts. The Gradieshti Rural Medical District Hospital's chief doctor, Lyubov Evgenyevna Oprya, set down her pen, stood up quickly, pumped my hand enthusiastically, and introduced herself as my new boss. (You've already briefly met her and born witness to her neckless meatball proportions.) Chief Doctor Oprya did not hide how happy she was to have an addition to her medical staff, because a pediatrician had recently left. I soon learned that she had grown up in a peasant family, graduated high school in Gradieshti and then Kishinev Medical School, and eventually had returned to her hometown as an obstetrician-gynecologist. After two years of working at the hospital she had become the chief administrator. Later I discovered that my boss's appearance and excessive weight were partially due to thyroid insufficiency, which she had suffered from for several years. Despite this, she was quite an agile, energetic, and active woman.

In what would become an all too familiar abrupt shift from exuberant proclamation to a crisp, no-nonsense business tone, Oprya cleared her voice and went on. "You will be provided with an apartment free of charge, but it is not ready yet, so temporarily you will be sleeping in one of the hospital rooms."

Turning away, she sat back down and resumed writing on the charts. "Have a good rest and tomorrow you will start fulfilling your duties. There is plenty of work to do here with the young people of our village."

Standing there, not knowing if I had been dismissed and bursting with eagerness to make a good impression at an actual, real job in medicine, I stammered out the first thing that came to mind. "I will do my best to be useful!" I earnestly assured her. My new supervisor stopped writing, looked searchingly at me, nodded, and went back to her work.

Idiot. I came to regret on many occasions the blurted promise. Whenever Chief Doctor Lyubov Evgenyevna Oprya criticized my work performance during the next three years, she always—and I mean always—dragged us both back to that vow.

I was immediately put in charge of all eighteen beds on the pediatric floor. During cold seasons, the floor would be fully occupied, but during the summer months, not more than half of the beds were filled. There were three shifts on the pediatric floor, and each was served by a nurse and an orderly.

Three days after arriving at the hospital, I moved into a renovated apartment, located in a small building on the hospital grounds. Besides me, three other families lived in the same small building: the families of the two hospital internists and the family of a nurse, Alexandra Petrovna Kondratyeva, a Russian woman who, together with her husband and son, came to work in Gradieshti all the way from the Russian city of Ivanovo, northeast of Moscow.

Walls painted with lime and complete with wooden floors, my new home was typically small but comfortable, most of the time. An entryway served as the kitchen, and I lived in a medium-sized room furnished with a second-hand Russian-style spring bed, a small table, a side table, and an étagère, all provided by the hospital. A furnace that burned wood and coal warmed the apartment well enough. Well, except during windy, strong rainstorms, when water would flood into the room through gaps between two large window frames and the wall. Those windows did afford an excellent view of the neighboring yard, which belonged to the Muntyanu family. The father was a good craftsman, but the family was legendary for their utter poverty and large number of children. The dirty faces and bodies of the ten Muntyanu children could not distract from their youthful charm, which constantly entertained me in games and conversations.

A pity what happened to that nice family. We'll get to that in due course.

My meals I heated on a small electric stove—when power was available. Like in other villages, electricity was notoriously unpredictable in Gradieshti. Low voltage and frequent outages resulted in kerosene lamps lighting most homes. Furthermore, a minor thunderstorm or strong winds could bring down one or more of the electrical poles linking Gradieshti and Tiraspol. A popular expression, authored by Vladimir Ilyich Lenin and known to every Soviet citizen, stated that Communism is Soviet power plus electrification of the entire country. It was logical to assume then that socialism temporary ceased to exist during bad weather in the village of Gradieshti.

The unreliability of sufficient power also meant that radios—when they could be afforded—were a very rare commodity. But never worry, dear reader, as the Socialist Motherland made sure to take care of all of our information and entertainment needs. Each household possessed a major propaganda state-provided tool: the so-called *radiotochka*, a small wired radio set, which received broadcasts made from 6 a.m. to midnight. We enjoyed the officially sanctioned version of local, country, and international news, mixed with classical and light music, and topped off with songs dedicated to patriotism, love, and friendship.

That little apartment was particularly remarkable for having running water—a great luxury in the village. Plumbing in the village was available only for the lucky ones; the rest used water from wells. Before you get to thinking too highly of my living arrangement, however, keep in mind that, like nearly everywhere else, my apartment had no sewer system and so I used an all-season toilet located outside in the yard. Indoor toilets in Gradieshti were a rare privilege. For the rest of us, our outhouses were hastily constructed shacks, some made from wood, others from bricks, but most from cheap unpainted plywood. Some advanced models were equipped with homemade toilet seats, allowing a sitting position during use. Most unfortunately required assumption of the eagle position, a challenging task for older people in the village.

Well, I can't mention our predilection for outhouses without raising the delicate subject of toilet paper, one of the pinnacles of civilization invented in 1857. OK, I'll just say it—the nation that launched Sputnik and built a nuclear arsenal capable of destroying life on this planet did not manufacture toilet paper. It was imported only for the party elite. People instead used pieces of paper, usually from newspapers, rubbed between their hands to make it soft. I kept a big stack of them all the time in the ramshackle outhouse in my backyard.

A popular joke going around that I used to tell all the time went like this:

> Armenian Radio is asked, "Which is more useful—newspapers or television?"
> Armenian Radio promptly replies, "Newspapers, of course. You can't wipe your ass with a TV."

Read the state-fed news, than wipe with it. But wouldn't you know it? This necessary practice became a form of suspected resistance. Informers accused some of wiping themselves with a piece of paper that had a picture of Stalin or another Communist Party leader. Such "latrine disloyalty to Communism" might be punished with imprisonment, exile, or worse.

A permanent outhouse in one's backyard created its own problem: what to do when it filled up and was no longer usable? Most villagers I knew destroyed the outhouse, covered the pit with a layer of earth, and automatically built another elsewhere in the same yard. They had to be careful where they dug the new pit, though, as the yard served as a dumping ground for other refuse as well. The people of Gradieshti collected solid and liquid food and household waste in buckets, carried them outside, and emptied the contents into an uncovered cesspit. When that pit was filled, it too was covered with soil and a new one dug.

Between the outhouses and cesspits, it is not surprising that yards became a breeding ground for swarms of flies transmitting intestinal diseases. During my three years in Gradieshti, flies were ubiquitous and unrelenting companions. They were everywhere and in everything. To get rid of them indoors, various methods of control were tried, few of which actually worked and none of which dealt with the root cause of the problem festering in one's own backyard.

The village leaders did come up with one solution to the ever pressing sanitation problem: they built a public lavatory to discourage those seeking trees and bushes to satisfy natural needs. This "comfort station" was nothing more than a small outhouse without running water or plumbing facilities, but everyone seemed proud of it because the other villages in the district lacked that luxury. What I remember most about that public facility was one morning helping a determined young boy rescue his kitten from one of the holes filled with communal waste, down which his drunk, angry father had thrown his son's pet.

Gradieshti's challenges with sanitation were a microcosm of a widespread, unending Soviet problem. The Communist Party and the Soviet government ignored the fundamental human need for public and personal hygiene, a neglect contributing to, as I discovered as a doctor, a high level of gastrointestinal infections in town and country. Like millions of my compatriots, I grew up in a medium-sized city, in a little house with a backyard outhouse and without a sewer line, shower, bath, or hot water. With all that, my family was very lucky in comparison to people in rural areas, many of whom confronted worse sanitary conditions. Even in the large cities, finding a toilet—even the most primitive and foul-smelling—was a difficult task.

When I was fifteen years old, I visited Moscow for the first time, following the national tradition of pilgrimage to Lenin's mausoleum. A kilometer-long line led to a wax figurine that was supposedly an "eternally alive" immortal leader. After the pagan worship, I left the mausoleum and came out on Red Square, looking for a public toilet. It was located in a most unique and symbolic location: below the ground level of Red Square at the Kremlin wall. For the first time, I saw a large public toilet shining with cleanliness and without a hint of stink. White wall tiles, marble floor, running water, urinals, stalls—a veritable museum of human needs. That bathroom would not have surprised a newcomer from the West, but to me it was a marvel of technology. Looking at the straight line of people standing in front of the urinals, I thought then that Stalin, if he was still alive, could accuse them all of trying to hose down the sacred ground of Red Square.

Such difficult life conditions, but we in the Soviet system were too busy, too disorganized, and most importantly, too afraid to protest. There were exceptions, though. I remember at medical school that none other than our teacher of Marxism-Leninism hinted at how much she disapproved of the outrageous sanitary situation. The lecture, as usual, rehearsed the inevitable crises and death of the capitalist system. She—

most probably after a recent failure to find a toilet (not a decent toilet, just a toilet)—had had enough. Momentarily relaxing her political vigilance, she suddenly put down her book and told us that society must respect basic human needs. She went on to insist that the proletariat leader Vladimir Ilyich Lenin himself had written that the best way to judge the state of a country is by the condition of its roads and its lavatories.

Brave, forthright words; our teacher knew well she could be reported by someone in the class. We students simply stared at her and remained silent, knowing too well the truths she spoke but too wary to agree openly.

Lacking a shower, bath, or hot running water, one of the ever-pressing issues of my life in Gradieshti soon became where to bathe. A free public bathhouse operated far away in the center of the village, but it was open only one evening a week. I made the mistake of visiting it once. Old and dilapidated both inside and outside, the bathhouse was little more than a small hut crowned by a thatched roof. A stuffy and damp dressing room boasted dirty floors and no individual lockers; people bathed in a dark, drafty basement. Cold and hot water trickled intermittently from faucets operated with oversized wooden handles. The available soap was unpleasant smelling and harsh on the skin. Unsurprisingly, as I left that public bathhouse, I felt dirtier than before I went.

Another bathing option seemed promising at first. Because my pediatric services were made available to the maternity ward of the hospital, I was awarded the privilege of taking real hot showers on its premises. Water for the shower was warmed by a coal or wood water heater. Thanks to this amenity, the village and peasant women admitted to the maternity ward to deliver children had the unique opportunity to take what was perhaps the first and possibly the last shower in their lives.

Taking a shower there, I immediately was assailed by a new horror. Due to lack of the space, the shower room was also used as the ward's latrine. In the corner stood a large communal bucket from which emanated a most disagreeable stench that seemed to worsen as the steam thickened. All you could do was try to hold your breath and wash as fast as possible.

Eventually I was left with one choice—try to bathe at home. I warmed up water in a big pan on a Primus stove, a portable but noisy kerosene cooking stove popular in rural areas and for camping. My system of bathing was elementary. After the water heated, I poured it into a basin, which I placed either on a stool or on the floor, depending on which half of the body I was washing. When my wife Marina visited, she stood up on another stool and simulated a real shower by pouring the pleasantly warm water over me through a kitchen strainer.

One evening, refreshed and happy after taking a hot, homemade bath, I strolled along the gravel road admiring the view of the moon and countless stars. I could have enjoyed that night vista from nearly everywhere in Gradieshti, as street lights shone only from the public center plaza. Everywhere else at night, we villagers gingerly traipsed the rutted, muddy streets in deep darkness, carrying flashlights—if batteries could be found to power them.

That night, I was accompanied by a midsized dog, whom I had named Дружок, or "Little Pal." Friendly and generous, Little Pal had suddenly appeared in my yard shortly after I moved in, and for the next three years stayed outside but close by. Although his right front paw had been amputated, he could still run fast when needed, and inevitably joined me when I left the apartment.

After half an hour or so, Little Pal and I came across my boss, Chief Doctor Oprya, and her husband, Grigoriy Sergeevich Oprya, the hospital's epidemiology technician. The couple were returning from visiting their old friend and on-the-spot marital consultant, the First Secretary of the district Communist Party, Mirtcha Gerasimovich Mukutsa. Guided by the infinite wisdom of the party, Comrade Makutsa had quickly restored harmony after a(nother) major family fight. Now husband and wife were walking hand-in-hand, discussing the day's events. Without her hospital cap on, my boss's long, luxuriant braids hung on both sides. We greeted each other and they invited me to join them.

We had a pleasant walk under the light of the stars and moon. For some reason, Little Pal stayed close to my boss, seriously interested in sniffing her. Busily chatting, the chief doctor seemed not to notice.

After a while, I shared with my sojourners what pleasure I had gotten out of that evening's bathing. "It's a great thing to feel clean and refreshed after a long day at the hospital," I concluded simply.

"Oh, as a woman, believe me, I understand you, Vladimir Abramovich," my boss responded in a warm friendly manner. She then cleared her throat, and continued on in the usual clipped, business tone. "Which reminds me—it is time for me to take a shower as well. I've been so busy with hospital business that I haven't taken a bath in probably a month and have only changed my underwear."

Eyes now very wide, her husband and I exchanged glances and fell silent. We continued on into the night, my dear three-legged dog, lost in olfactory overload, never leaving her side.

A man explains to the Soviet authorities that he has to go to the United States to help his sick uncle.

The representative of the authorities replies, "Why would not your uncle come to the Soviet Union? You can take a better care of him here."

The man answers, "I said that he is sick, not stupid."

Potemkin Profession

———— ⚜ ————

I t wasn't long before I got caught up in the rural rhythm and routine of the days, weeks, and months at Gradieshti Hospital. Each weekday morning began with a briefing session for all of us; every day would end with one unlucky physician stranded on call for night duty. In between? A repetition of examinations, treatments, and paperwork, punctuated by occasional urgency and sometimes just downright craziness. And through it all slithered the bureaucratic ineptitude of a troubled national medical system that time and again was seen as a grandiose Potemkin illusion conjured by our own country for the world to believe.

Each working day in the hospital started with *pyatiminutka*, a mandatory briefing session attended by all physicians, head nurses, and representatives of various maintenance divisions, including the housekeeper, laundress, groom, chauffeur, and cook. Although *pyatiminutka* in Russian means "five minutes," the meetings usually lasted for at least an hour. They were moderated by the chief physician, Lyubov Evgenyevna Oprya. We all regarded my boss as a competent physician (by Soviet standards) and, most of the time, pleasant to work with. At the same time, we all understood without talking about it that she lacked the busi-

21

ness and organizational knowledge to run the hospital, which frequently reminded us of a rudderless ship that lacked even sails.

The morning briefing sessions could go on and on down many side roads, but I always found them spirited and democratic. Anyone present could participate in the discussion, which was supposed to produce, so to speak, a cross-pollination of minds of the people working in the different areas of the hospital. Besides the current conditions of patients, other subjects would be raised—the difficulty of buying a carburetor and tires for the hospital's sole car, the necessity of buying fodder for horses and an axle for the horse-pulled cart, what in the world to do with the ominously growing pile of horse manure, why a new washing machine was desperately needed, a snag with the supply of onions and cooking oil, a shortage of pillow cases, the impossibility of buying new mattresses, and so on.

As I said, a good cross section of the hospital attended the morning briefing session. Let's peek in on a typical meeting and get acquainted with some of the people I worked with over three years.

Sitting over there in a corner, far from my boss and contributing only occasionally, is a plain-looking man, dressed as always in a simple gray baggy jacket and pants and sporting a cap. Grigoriy Sergeevich Oprya, the epidemiology technician, is the same age as his wife, our chief doctor, with whom he has fathered two children. At the time I arrived in Gradieshti, one child was five years old and the other three. The children are taken care of mostly by Lyubov Evgenyevna's mother, who lives with her daughter's family but in a separate room. The Opryas live across from the hospital, separated from it by the two-lane asphalt road, a distance of at least seventy yards. Unlike most of us, they reside in a sturdily built, urban-style house, enjoying a living room, three bedrooms, and a kitchen with running water and a sewer line. Nonetheless, an outhouse still stands in their backyard.

The Opryas being quite hospitable, I was a frequent guest at enjoyable, friendly dinners and gatherings at their house during the first year in Gradieshti. I could not help noticing, however, that the window panes in their wooden doors were always broken. During one visit, when the hostess was in a complacent mood, I asked her the reason for the problem with the door windows.

"I am glad you noticed this, Vladimir Abramovich," Lyubov Evgenyevna volunteered without hesitation, all in a brisk, businesslike manner. "At work I am the boss of my husband, Grigoriy Sergeevich. He obeys me during working hours and never questions my orders. He is also quite good at home, but you should see him when he is drunk." She shook her head and sighed. "At such times that man becomes a real animal."

Given that Grigoriy Sergeevich was always sober and lucid on the job, I didn't believe her at first. Soon, however, while taking a walk down the asphalt road one evening, I witnessed a melee between them that took place within and outside their spacious house. Presumably lacking anything else to break inside, the spouses suddenly burst through the door and raced across the yard toward me. Lyubov Evgenyevna sprinted ahead, her short legs pumping and braids flying behind while closely pursued by her husband; her mother, gesturing wildly, brought up a distant rear. In the sudden storm of screamed grievances, all three of them loudly appealed for justice to each other and to me, accidentally caught in the crossfire. (Fascinatingly, no one swore.) Reaching the other side of the road, Grigoriy Sergeevich finally caught up with his wife and grabbed her braids. Later on, when sober, the epidemiology technician explained that at work he obeys his high-placed wife, but at home he is the boss and uses her braids as a brake to prevent her from running away from him.

I am sorry to say that the Opryas' many wild arguments, with Grigoriy Sergeevich inevitably in drunken pursuit of his fleeing wife, were exceedingly entertaining for the hospital patients. Dressed in plain grey pajamas, they liked to sit on sunny days squatting in front of the hospital's brick fence opposite the chief doctor's house—front row seats for the conflict sure to come. Between deep drags on their cigarettes, they would hotly debate the cacophonic clash of medical powers unfolding in front of them. The frequent personal outbursts by respected hospital staff were unsettling, but we can take comfort that the inquisitive ears of their patients never caught a curse word rising out of the fray between husband and wife.

Next to Grigoriy Sergeevich in the morning briefing session is a tall, lean man who glared at me when I entered the room and now refuses to meet my eyes. Gregory Mokanu is the chief hospital car driver, known to be quite a ladies man. Two days ago, he and I nearly exchanged blows over an accident involving an errant dog and one of the other drivers, his cousin, Aurel Popa. The night before, Popa, who had always been friendly toward me, offered to let me drive the hospital car. As we approached the hospital, deep in conversation, a dog darted in front of the car. Popa grabbed my arm. Startled, I veered left, sideswiping the main metal gate and taking off the passenger door. I guiltily gave the driver nearly all of my monthly salary to repair the car, but apparently that was insufficient, as Popa later appeared at my door, demanding more. The next morning, all of the drivers, led by Mokanu, were waiting for me in the doctor's lounge. Mokanu was furious; with spittle flying anad fists clenched, he advanced, roaring that I had been drunk, that I had ruined their livelihood, and that they deserved more money. The chief driver stood over me menacingly, swearing in Moldovan, spittle raining down. *Enough is enough.* I rose, prepared to fight.

As we bristled nose to nose, Chief Doctor Lyubov Evgenyevna Oprya rushed into the lounge. Lips thickly plastered with red lipstick, a big smile lit her wide, round face—until she saw us.

"What is happening here?" she cried. "Why are the drivers not in the garage?" She whirled on the others. "What are you doing in the doctors' lounge? Go to work! Gregory and Doctor Tsesis, sit down! What is your problem?"

"This one got drunk and smashed the hospital car. I reported it to you already," Gregory Mokanu sputtered, poking a long finger in my chest. "He should pay for it. He was drunk."

"Stop speaking nonsense, Grisha," the chief doctor replied, rolling her eyes. "Vladimir Abramovich is a Jew, and Jews do not drink. Leave him alone and get out of the room."

"But he should pay for the accident!" Mokanu insisted. The other drivers paused at the doorway.

"Get out of here, all of you!" the chief doctor exploded. "Observe the hierarchy! He is a doctor, and you are illiterate drivers! I have many surgeries to perform and many other things to do today!"

The drivers fled, and Lyubov Evgenyevna turned to me. "Stop dealing with these men," she said, dropping into a strict, maternal tone. "If one of them bothers you again, come directly to me. They are typical men, turning into real predators when they smell money. Do not pay them a kopeck more. They have a special hospital fund for taking care of accidents and unexpected events. Forget what happened."

Well, I hadn't and, even two days later in our morning briefing session, neither had the chief driver. Arms folded, he's now glaring at me again. Perched next to him is my young nurse, Svetlana Dogaru, who is leaning forward, intent on the chief doctor's rapid-fire recitation. Svetlana is a village native who is pleasant and very intelligent, possessing a natural talent for teaching languages, which proved a lifesaver my first day on the job.

While examining my first child patient, I simply had not been able to understand what the child's mother was telling me, nor could she comprehend my confused mumbling in Russian. The villagers and peasants spoke Moldovan, the Romanian dialect in the Republic of Moldova. I had diligently studied the Moldovan language in school for years but retained little. The mother spoke again, gesturing at her boy—what was I to do? I looked frantically at Svetlana, who immediately grasped the problem. With a smile on her face, she calmly translated what the mother said and then translated to the mother what I was trying to tell her. Svetlana's bedside translations over the next three months helped me master the Moldovan language in a short time, without learning grammar or studying textbooks. I owe her a lot.

Walking hurriedly past the door to the doctor's lounge is Lydia Fedorovna Mokryak, a housekeeper who is wife to the personal chauffeur of the chairman of the "Red Sparkle" *kolkhoz* (collective farm) in Gradieshti. She's a good-natured woman with a ready smile, a hard worker who's also a master practitioner of the widespread tradition of exchanging, for personal use, the new hospital bedding for her own. The theft of public property is very simple to perform. Before the hospital stamps each new piece of bedding with its blurred, rusty hospital seal, the bedding somehow quietly slips away—for a modest fee, mind you—to employees and their acquaintances. On paper, the "old items" miraculously become the "new items." One consequence of such ubiquitous stealing is that all of the hospital's bedding is universally dirty gray, a fine match for the colorless village. Another result is that the "always new" hospital bedding is only really and truly discarded after countless washes in the hospital laundry, once it completes a long, thinning, and fragmenting journey into shapeless rags.

Lydia Fedorovna vanishes down the hall but not before I glimpse neatly folded white sheets under one arm.

Curled up in another corner off to the left of the chief doctor is a small man with brown eyes and a receding hairline. His puffy face and red cheeks and nose betray a fondness for alcohol. This morning, he's attired as usual in a crumpled white lab coat, white medical cap, and dirty soldier boots. In his early thirties and from the Western Ukraine, Eugene Rachok is our X-ray technician, which means that he's frequently roaming the hospital with nothing to do because the X-ray machine keeps breaking down. Rachok doesn't speak much, but he's a good listener, seems good natured and trustworthy, and I enjoy sharing with him the many jokes I keep hearing about Communism:

> a person comes in to a post office and complains, "These new stamps with Lenin do not stick."
> The clerk answers, "Comrade, you probably spit on the wrong side."

(Needless to say, we tell them in private.)

Sitting behind me are the gynecological nurse, Magda Petrinesku, and our other full-time physicians: internists Tatyana Grigoryevna and Maria Shtefanovna, and the only surgeon, Ilya Sergeevich Petresku. Olive complexioned, a bit short but well built, Petresku, like our chief doctor, was born and raised in Gradieshti. He speaks Russian with a slight Moldovan accent. Maria Ivanovna, his wife, hails from Ivanovo, Russia and so struggles with the village's native language.

Petresku is rather full of himself and quick to temper, but he's also fearless and loyal. I have grown increasingly fond of him and often assist during surgeries. Gradually we have become friends. Ilya Sergeevich Petresku addresses me by my first name, but taking into account his age and experience, I address him by name and patronymic.

Petresku's known for driving an IZH-Planeta motorcycle with a sidecar, which he cares for as if it is a human being. He dreams of owning a car—a rare commodity for Soviet citizens—but the waiting list for a "Volga" automobile is long, and it's a slow shuffle to the top (importing foreign cars was forbidden at the time). He's been promised one in, oh, two or more years. In the meantime, our good surgeon abides his time and dreams about four wheels while putting around on two.

It was that motorcycle and sidecar that had recently taken me on a nearly one-way trip outside the village. Petresku and I were traveling to a professional meeting at the district hospital in Slobodzeya, close to the city of Tiraspol. The seasoned driver suddenly getting the urge for a glass of wine, motorcycle and sidecar came to a screeching halt in front of the first pub in sight, a shabby little house barely held together by dirty, blue, chipped wooden walls.

While Doctor Petresku made his way to the bar to buy wine, I waited inside at the door, looking at no one and minding my own business. Many unshaven men dressed in simple clothes crowded that dark, filthy little room. Muttering in low voices, they drank wine served from wooden barrels, which helped washed down the unappetizing pub fare: stale dark bread, hard goat cheese, cucumbers, and onions.

Suddenly, one of the customers, catching my eye, put down his mug, and struggled to stand up. Tall and wide shouldered, swaying on unsteady legs, he approached and leaned in, a swollen, red face and nauseous breath now far too close. Narrowing his red eyes, the man growled loudly, "Who invited you and what are you doing here? Who invited you here? This is not your place." He turned, sneering, back to the others. "Kikes are not welcomed here." In a short time, several men surrounded me threateningly on all sides.

Someone grabbed my shirt collar; I instinctively seized his arm and the collar of a sweaty, stinking shirt. He hit me, a glancing blow, and I swung back hard. Chairs flying and fists connecting, we fought along the back wall, while the drunken mob stood back and urged us on.

"Hey, you! Leave him alone. He's with me!" Petresku's resolute and firm Moldovan voice shouted behind me as I waded in for another punch and one more fist smashed against the side of my head. "He did nothing wrong to you, so let him go!"

Blood trickling out of the left side of his mouth, my assailant paused, and looked over at the surgeon. "You better tell us what this kike is doing in our territory! Dirty kikes are not invited here."

Clutching his wine, Petresku stepped forward between us. "Forget it," he snarled fearlessly, back to me. "You better let us go!"

Luckily, we were already at the door and only needed a few backward steps to make our escape. My last view of that unremarkable excuse for a pub was the drunken bully shaking his fist at me and spitting on the floor in our direction before washing his blood away with more cheap wine.

Let's face it, nobody is perfect. My good friend Ilya Sergeevich Petresku is unmatched in confidence in his own bravery and abilities as a medical wizard. On those rare occasions when the X-ray machine is working, he performs old-fashioned fluoroscopy, where the radiological image is projected onto a screen in front of the radiologist. He never fails to mention to the patient how dangerous the radiation is for him, just so he can hear the expected words of appreciation for the considerable risks of his work.

Just last week, I had a revealing conversation with Petresku as he sat at a desk in the doctors' lounge writing on a patient's chart. Putting down a pen, he leaned forward, beckoning me closer.

"I'm sorry, Volodya, that you were not available this weekend. I operated on a patient who had a perforated appendix with symptoms of peritonitis. Very difficult case, believe me."

As always, I nodded and murmured sympathetically. On cue, he continued, straightening up in his chair and voice rising. "The surgery was successful, and now, three days after the operation, he has significantly improved. I think his improvement is related to the *perfect* antibiotic coverage I provided for him. Just look at his order list! It enumerates *all* the antibiotics I've ordered for him." Full of pride now, the surgeon handed me the patient's file.

Oh, goodness. I could see that my friend had ordered for his patient nearly *every one* of the antibiotics available at that time from the hospital's pharmacy.

Knowing my colleague's hot temper, I didn't dare outright contradict him. "Ilya Sergeevich," I interjected humbly, not meeting his eyes, "maybe you've ordered too many antibiotics for your patient. There are six of them. You forgot almost none of the antibiotics we have in our pharmacy."

"Oh, Volodya! It is so obvious that you're a recent graduate who doesn't know much about the practice of medicine," he replied with a victorious smile, grabbing the file. "Just look: penicillin will cover almost all possible infections. Levomycetin—the same way, but it will enhance the action of the penicillin. Streptomycin is ideal to cover lung complication, which we want to prevent. Terramycin by mouth covers gastrointestinal infections and something else. Neomycin will add to this effect, and colimycin is good for peritonitis." Looking at me intently, he handed the file back. "Are you clear now?"

I couldn't help myself. "But so many antibiotics might somehow interact and be a little bit difficult for the patient to take," I pleaded.

The surgeon's response was triumphal and dismissive. "Are you kidding, Volodya? Do you imagine that *I* did not think about possible complications? Indeed I thought about possible side effects and to prevent them, I've ordered nystatin for my patient."

"But nystatin prevents only fungal infections," I protested. "There are too many other possible interactions—"

"Let me tell you, other interactions are not of interest to me," my friend interrupted, coloring slightly. "What *I* follow is my surgical intuition. Medicine is not all science; it is an art as well." He shook his head, looking disappointed. "You should know it without my having to tell you. But you are a baby doctor. You cannot understand such simple things."

That concluded our discussion, as Petresku resumed writing on the chart. I walked away, fervently hoping that that his brilliant artistry wouldn't kill the patient.

Yes, my friend the surgeon can be a bit, well, arrogant, but gosh darn it, I can't help but be fond of him. Chief Doctor Oprya is not. Interestingly, their houses stand next to each other, facing the hospital. That's about as close as they get. Every morning at our briefing sessions, the Chief Doctor and the surgeon do not sit near each other, and only rarely do they exchange glances. So far this morning, they have studiously ignored each other.

That's because Lyubov Evgenyevna Oprya is engaged in an unending cold war with our village surgeon, who graduated from medical school at around the same time as she did. Ilya Sergeevich Petresku is jealous of the Chief Doctor's career success and never misses an opportunity to hint at his intellectual superiority. No doubt, Chief Doctor Oprya could have found a thousand ways to get rid of Petresku, but he was the only available surgeon in Gradieshti and a replacement would have been extremely difficult to find. So, she wisely tolerated him—up to a point. I did my best to remain neutral and not ever to take sides in their never-ending conflicts.

My strategy worked well until near the end of the first year. One day, Lyubov Evgenyevna Oprya informed me in confidence that the district hospital had finally approved the new position of Deputy Chief Physician for our hospital. She insisted I accept it. I congratulated her on the great news, but, trying to be fair, responded that I was too much of a novice in the hospital to assume such a responsible and honorable post and that this position rightfully belonged to the hospital surgeon, who had worked in the hospital for six years.

Big mistake. My boss's face became pale and her hands began to shake. Shaking her head and saying nothing, she simply waved me away. Eventually, the deputy position was accepted by an internist, further gouging the open wound between my boss and my friend.

Sometime afterward, Doctor Petresku attended a medical conference and returned four days later than expected. On pay day, he discovered that the chief doctor had refused to pay him for the days not spent on his professional development. The surgeon protested, claiming that he deserved to be paid anyway for all the extra hours he spends in the hospital operating. Chief Doctor Oprya refused to yield.

Two days later, after assisting Ilya Sergeevich with three surgeries, I joined him, as I often did, at his house for a snack and a glass of homemade Moldovan wine. He remained unforgiving, revisiting a long litany of complaints against our boss.

His loud voice dropping to a whisper, he glanced toward the rooms where his wife and children slept. "You know, Volodya," he hissed, clenching his fists. "This time I will not forgive this woman. I intend to avenge myself with an exclusive method of revenge so that pig will remember it forever."

Displeased with the crude description of the Chief Doctor, but not wanting to contradict one of my few friends in the village, I responded vaguely and noncommittally. He paused, waiting for me to inquire about this "exclusive method of revenge." Shrugging my shoulders and mentally rolling my eyes, I did just that.

"Very simple," he whispered, smirking. "I am going to seduce her and have sex with her."

I hastily took another sip of wine and looked out the window. In the house next door, a kerosene lantern spilled yellow oily light through a broken pane.

Yes, the staff of Gradieshti Hospital gathered around me at the morning briefing session are a complicated and curious bunch, aren't they? Let me assure you that, although we squabble, sometimes steal, and, heck, even tend to fisticuffs now and then, we are united in approaching our patients with the best of intentions. What gets in our way is ... ourselves. Our biggest obstacle to treatment is the Soviet Union's own stunningly inadequate, state-supported free medical system. The Soviet practice of medicine is built around improper and inconsistent training, shortages in equipment and medicine, and brilliantly incompetent and illusory bureaucratic policies and procedures. The Socialist Motherland, however, keeps insisting to us and to the rest of the incredulous world that all is wonderfully otherwise.

By the 1960s, the Soviet system had become a grandiose global show for all those who preferred wishful thinking to reality, demagoguery to truth, and preferred to swallow lies spoon-fed by a well-funded and powerful governmental propaganda machine. Gullible visitors from the West were shown "Potemkin villages," complete with model hospitals brimming with pleasant rooms, modern equipment (most of which was decoration and did not work), and beautiful smiles from the staff. Each Potemkin hospital room held only two patients. Toilets were large, clean, and did not smell.

The reality we faced every day was so much different. While the country bragged incessantly about its free medical care and presented itself as the moral compass of humanity, most Soviet hospitals in fact provided substandard medical care, on the level of third-world countries. Typical hospital rooms housed between eight and sixteen patients. In rural Gradieshti Hospital, only four inside toilets served patients in fifty beds. Lacking hot water, showers, or baths in the main building, our patients

were unable to take appropriate care of their personal hygiene and re-
sorted to wiping themselves with wet towels. One of the biggest difficulties for me during morning rounds in the hospital rooms was enduring
the smelly and stale odors from dozens of unwashed bodies.

Our nurses' station was a dimly lit room equipped with table, chairs,
and unsophisticated medical equipment, consisting mostly of metal
boxes full of syringes and needles darkened from frequent sterilization.
The needles were reused, and were never sharp or small enough. All syringes were made from glass and were reused until they broke.

Though it was common knowledge how blood-borne infections were
transmitted, none of our medical instruments were disposable. Like
other hospitals in the glorious but now perished Soviet Union, we used
those instruments repeatedly. After surgery, each surgical instrument
was meticulously washed, cleaned, and then autoclaved; such well-inten-
tioned practice, however, did not prevent the spreading of blood-borne
diseases such as infectious hepatitis. To deal with this problem, local
hospital commissions around the country periodically checked syringes
and surgical instruments for occult blood. The medical unit where an
inspection was next planned, however, was always notified beforehand,
giving them an opportunity to be prepared. Cleaning the equipment of
possible residual blood was performed with all available chemical means
by nurses on duty. Such measures served no purpose other than acting
as a smokescreen that to suggest something was being done to prevent
the transmission of blood-borne infections.

When I arrived in Chicago in 1974, I worked as a translator for a large
medical company producing IV infusion equipment. The first time I
encountered the word "disposable," I didn't know what it meant, even
after consulting an English-to-Russian dictionary. When a coworker told
me that syringes and needles, so precious in my understanding, were
intended only for one-time use, I thought he was joking. I simply had no
idea that disposable medical instruments had been a mandatory norm
in the West for over a quarter-century.

How were we to reliably treat our patients in a safe manner at that
rural hospital? Because of the lack of double-blind studies to prove scientific data, treatment of the patients was arbitrary and often chaotic. The

absence of an established system of peer review allowed Soviet physicians to treat patients with unproven and potentially fatal drugs. I have already mentioned that the X-ray machine rarely worked. When it did, we didn't always have film for it. A machine for electrocardiography, promising a new epoch in diagnosing cardiac diseases, finally arrived at the hospital during my third and final year. Unfortunately—wouldn't you know it—the dawn of the amazing medical era was delayed due to the repeated breakdown of the electrocardiogram (EKG) machine and the absence of an EKG technician, whom no one had thought to hire. Two anesthesia machines decorated the operating room, but neither of them worked either; even if they had, we lacked an anesthesiologist or anesthesiologist technician to operate them.

Complicated surgeries had to be referred to the city of Tiraspol, while common minor surgeries, such as appendectomies or gallbladder removals, were performed under local anesthesia, using a Novocain solution. For rare, selected cases where the patients continued to be sensitive to pain after local anesthesia, we provided a very primitive, dangerous general anesthesia. A nurse, under the guidance of the surgeon, dripped an ethyl chloride solution from a brown glass vial onto a gauze mask, which was then applied to the patient's face. The dosage was calculated using the trial-and-error principle, based on the minimal amount of ethyl chloride necessary to keep the patient asleep. Fortunately, as far as I can remember, no one died under those circumstances.

"Glorious" Soviet medicine also was catastrophically behind the West in appropriate systems for starting and maintaining an IV, especially when the patient was severely dehydrated. A set for intravenous fluid infusion consisted of a needle and two glass reservoirs connected with rubber tubes. Unfortunately, the rubber tubes became swollen and spongy from repeated sterilizations; they were thrown away and replaced only when they finally became sticky. Solutions for intravenous administration were poured into open-top glass reservoirs. A nurse then put a piece of sterile gauze on top of the reservoir, supposedly to prevent the solution in the reservoir from contamination by such environmental elements as dust, small insects, and microorganisms. Even when the IV system was started and running on a patient, without intravenous pumps (which were unknown to Soviet medical professionals), the IV became clogged. When all visible veins were perforated and nothing else was available, doctors used an ancient method, forgotten in the West, of fluid injection in the subcutaneous tissue of the thighs. The clinical effect of this inadequate procedure produced large, slowly resolving swellings on the inner surfaces of the thighs.

The hospital could not find a lab technician for a long time, so the diagnostic lab did not function until my second year in Gradieshti. The new lab technician, Nastasia Gremina, a pleasant and bright young woman from Odessa, was qualified to perform only a complete blood count, hemoglobin level, erythrocyte sedimentation rate, urinalysis, and stool analysis for ova and parasites. I must admit that even those five tests were enough to improve our diagnoses dramatically.

Another factor that continually affected our ability to treat patients was poor lighting, due to the electrical grid's low voltage in Gradieshti. Most nights, the incandescent bulbs did not provide enough illumination for an adequate examination of the patient, much less for performance of surgical and gynecological procedures. When the electric lights dimmed or went out, we treated and operated by kerosene lamps and sometimes even by hand-held flashlights.

Inadequate medical training, equipment, and facilities were compounded by a surreal adherence to bureaucratic policies and procedures that buttressed the state-driven Potemkin illusion rather than facilitated the actual treatment of patients. A superb example of the latter was the manipulation of statistics to hide the high infant and child mortality in the Soviet Union.

As a member of the World Health Organization, the USSR was obliged to present critical statistical data on the quality of medical care in the Soviet Union. The rumors were damaging enough, but if the actual figures on infant and child mortality in the USSR had been disclosed, they would have documented a monumental, ongoing disaster. Such international scrutiny encouraged political bureaucrats to systematically punish medical workers and administrators for poor results. Consequently, those responsible developed countless ways to manipulate the statistics. In rural areas like Gradieshti, one solution to "improving" rates of infant and child mortality I witnessed was brought almost to perfection and ingenious in its simplicity.

The law of the land required parents to be provided with a child's birth certificate during the first month of their life. After the newborn was discharged from the maternity ward after the first seven days, the happy parents took their baby home without the birth certificate. At the end of the baby's first month, the parents were required to visit the head maternity nurse of the hospital. If the newborn was still alive and well, the head nurse wrote in the medical statement "healthy newborn." If the child had died for any reason, the head nurse's statement would read instead, "fetus" or "late spontaneous abortion." The parents would then go to the *selsoviet*, the village council, where the clerk would enter a record relying on the documentation provided by the head maternity nurse. Thus, the wolves were sated, and the sheep remained intact. The Soviet rulers proclaimed their great achievements, the so-called fellow travelers in the West applauded with delicate hands the advantages of socialism, and the superlatively unblemished medical community remained without blame for high child mortality.

I ran headlong into the labyrinth of illusory statistics very soon after starting work at Gradieshti Hospital. One morning, Chief Doctor Oprya handed me a sheet of statistical forms regarding pediatric service in the district. She announced that I was expected to fill these forms out within a week.

One week? A quick glance revealed that there simply weren't enough data to provide the necessary information.

"No problem, Vladimir Abramovich, no problem," my boss cheerfully replied, opening a drawer in her desk and handing me several additional sheets of paper. "You are nervous because you have no experience. Do not worry. I will let you see the last few years' statistical forms. They will help you."

All I could do was stare at the yellowing papers in my hands.

"You see how well-organized I am," she sniffed, ignoring my widening eyes. "Please, do not forget to return all these materials to me."

"But these forms are years old," I exclaimed. "How in the world can I find out what has happened since?"

"I do not understand what you are saying, Vladimir Abramovich," the chief physician replied, now slightly indignant. "I graduated medical school ten years ago and you—just recently. Your knowledge of statistics should be better than mine." She turned away, calling over her shoulder, "Be flexible, use your own imagination and intuition, but we need the forms filled out."

My boss was absolutely right. How could I be so naive as to forget that I worked in a country of universal make-believe? The deception of invented statistical data was so ubiquitous that even members of the Central Party Committee frequently had no idea what the truth was. Generally speaking, the Central Statistical Bureau provided the Communist rulers with data that fit what they already expected and believed about their country.

Thumbing through the population statistical data forms from previous years, I quickly realized that the information presented in them did not make sense. Digging deeper, I discovered that many questions simply contradicted each other and were illogical. Confused, I went to the Gradieshti Village Council to obtain at least some general information about the child population. A clerk there refused to cooperate, informing me she did not have the authority to divulge confidential data. Everything was a state secret.

Not knowing what to do with forms that I could not fill out, I made my way by hitchhiking to the Tiraspol Rural District Hospital in Slobodzeya, where I was scheduled to present my report along with other pediatricians. In a meeting hall there, I discovered to my great relief that others also had problems with their forms. Surprisingly, the more experienced colleagues seemed not to be concerned. Puzzled, I shared my frustration with a friendly looking elderly pediatrician.

"Stop worrying about that trifle, doctor," he smiled at me and winked. "Wait a little and your problem will be solved."

Soon the deputy to the chief physician of the Tiraspol Rural District Hospital, a man in his thirties, entered the room with a spritely step and an optimistic smile. In his hands he carried a pile of older statistical forms.

"Let us start our job, my friends," he said, spiritedly. "We should be done with your reports within the next fifteen minutes."

Now, just wait a minute. At twenty-three years of age, I didn't understand how the world really worked. So, young Doctor Tsesis raised his hand.

"Arthur Petrovich," I said earnestly to our common savior, "if we use the imprecise data from the reports of previous years and now add approximate information from the present year, this will only double the possibility of mistakes. Besides, some of the questions asked by the forms are illogical."

The deputy's knowing grin in response was matched by my fellow pediatricians. "Very good, doctor. If you have precise information, please, provide it, but your colleagues do not have such a luxury."

Nothing left to do but follow instructions. He assumed his place at the table, calmly smoking, as we participants of the meeting as obedient schoolchildren, one after another, approached him. When it was my turn, he consulted my hospital's previous years' statistics and, arbitrarily adding and subtracting from the thin air, very quickly manipulated the statistics to a desirable outcome. Within half an hour, all the statistical forms were filled out and the issue "was resolved."

Despite all my efforts over three years, I was never able to learn the true population data in the district where I worked. Not a clue.

Another run-in with the Potemkin statistical mirage occurred six months after I began practicing in Gradieshti. Chief Doctor Oprya informed me that in two or three weeks a commission would be visiting to check on how we provided health care to the schoolchildren of the village. Because Gradieshti High School had no nurses on its staff, the physical examination and medical supervision of the students became my responsibility, in addition to my main hospital duties. If a child was diagnosed with a medical problem, the parents were notified and the child brought to the ambulatory for further evaluation.

The pending arrival of the commission made my boss nervous. "Are you done with the physicals of all the schoolchildren?" she demanded.

When has there been time? "So far, I've examined four or five classes," I answered, looking at her steadily.

"That's only a drop in the bucket," she snapped, pointing at me. "It is *your* responsibility to finish examining all the students in the school within the next two weeks. The letter from the district hospital says that for each child you should have a special form on which you have recorded weight, height, pulse, blood pressure, temperature, your diagnosis, and the disposition of the patient."

"But it's impossible to do that in such a short time, Lyubov Evgenyevna," I objected. "It is a big job. This is the first time I've heard about these forms. With how busy I am in the hospital and ambulatory, I need at least a month to finish the task."

She sighed loudly, clearly exasperated that I was not grasping the obvious. "Vladimir Abramovich, please, do not think it is only you who is going to be reprimanded if we do not submit the necessary documentation. As the chief doctor, I am just as responsible for it as you are. And, just like you, I do not want to be reprimanded for not providing the necessary materials regarding the health of the schoolchildren. Do you realize that the hospital will not get a bonus if we do not satisfy the requirements?"

"But where I am going to find time for this work?" I appealed, digging in my heels a bit more. "It's a big school with many students, and we have only one day a week allocated for work outside the hospital. Plus, I do not even have transportation to reach the school."

Seeing me so distressed, the Chief Doctor, who was not unkind, softened her tone. "You should not be so worried," she continued. "All you have to do is quickly check vital signs when you examine the class. Nobody is demanding precision from you. All the commission wants to see is documentation of a physical examination. Listen to their lungs and heart, check their skin, check their teeth for cavities—hardly anybody doesn't have cavities, by the way—then briefly register your findings, and that's it."

She shrugged. "That's how the system works. I will teach you how you can examine a student in one or two minutes. It is very simple. The most important part of the process is to enter information in the medical form."

"But I do not even have these special forms!" I insisted, raising my hands in frustration.

"Yes, we never received them," the Chief Doctor replied, smoothly, her expression now inscrutable. "But from now on we are going to have a special ten-page notebook for each child. You will line up all the required graphs, and that's all that is necessary. The hospital will provide a personal ruler for you, but the pencil should be yours."

She paused, looking at me searchingly. "Why isn't it clear to you that all they want to see is the documentation that the work was done? In the end, I am sure that, with due diligence, you will receive a beautiful certificate of commendation for exemplary work in creating the medical form for schoolchildren, which you can display on the wall of your office."

"But I don't give a damn about this certificate! Give me a month, and I will do a good job instead of assembling this window dressing."

"Listen to you! 'Window dressing!'" my boss exclaimed, shaking her head. "*Everybody* must do this, and we are no exception!"

She sighed again, this time rolling her eyes. "To make you happier, for the next two weeks you are totally excused from work in the clinic. I will make all necessary arrangements. Nobody is asking you to be precise. Just make a short entry in each student's notebook. Your handwriting is not too bad, so it might make a good impression on the members of the commission. And cheer up! I would not worry about it at all. You must remember that practically all our schoolchildren are healthy anyway." Her mind now clearly moving on to other things, the chief doctor turned and marched away.

I so wish she had been right.

Every day at Gradieshti Hospital ended with night duty, for one of us. One week each month, a physician in our medical group, including the chief doctor, was on call during the evening. All physicians lived in proximity to the hospital, which was ideal because nobody—including the Chief Doctor Oprya—had a telephone in their residence. In case of an emergency, the physician on duty was summoned to the hospital by orderlies, who usually came in pairs. When they arrived at my apartment or at one of the other physicians' houses, they would knock loudly at the door and shout that a physician was needed. It was useless to ask the reason for the call—they never knew.

I do not know the other physicians' thoughts about being on duty, but for me it was almost always a source of painful anxiety. The patients admitted and hospitalized during the night could be of any age and of any pathology. Running to the hospital, I would almost shake with fear, not knowing whether I would be competent and experienced enough to manage their cases. The on-call physician was greatly discouraged from transferring patients elsewhere, so I became responsible on the spot for finding a solution to sometimes unsolvable problems. In the case of surgical emergency cases, I could ask for consultation from Doctors Petresku and Oprya, but they were frequently not available. I invariably had no other choice but to perform the functions of whichever special-ist was required. During emergencies beyond my experience, I would dive into medical books, ask for advice from a nurse if they had treated something similar, or, when the telephone occasionally worked, seek help from a specialist in the city.

Such medical emergencies at night were enormously stressful, as I was not always sure I was doing the best for patients. My elder brother, visit-ing me once, advised me that in challenging circumstances, when I was the only one helping a critically ill patient, I should behave as if I were a captain on a ship. I tried from that point onward—as best as I could—to remain resolute and calm, not betraying a scintilla of panic regardless of what was happening in front of me.

Sometimes it worked.

One evening during my first year in the fall of 1964, I was on call, sit-ting on steps in front of the apartment complex, listening to the radio, and petting my faithful dog, Little Pal. Suddenly, Little Pal stiffened and sat up, and I heard a woman's cries from the hospital.

Two orderlies sprinted toward me. Not understanding what was going on, I ran toward them and quickly learned that a child was dying on the pediatric floor. When I reached the procedural room, I saw the patient, Dorin Negrel, a four-year-old boy I knew. His mother was not present. Dorin sat on the examination table, trying to breathe, his chest moving strenuously but failing to take air into his lungs. His eyes were popping out of his head, and his skin, especially at the naso-labial triangle area, was turning blue.

"Dorin is choking!" one of the nurses blurted, stuttering from excite-ment. "I was giving him a sweet vitamin in the shape of a ball, and he choked on it. First he was choking just a little, so I brought him to the procedure room right away. The vitamin is stuck somewhere in his throat."

Given the child's critical state, not a minute could be lost. With a large steel tongue depressor, I opened Dorin's mouth, but spotted nothing suspicious. Knowing the relatively large size of the vitamin on which the patient choked, it was reasonable to assume that it had become lodged in the area of the laryngopharynx. It needed first to get into the esophagus, then into the stomach. The situation could become even worse if, instead of going down the esophagus, the vitamin ball dissolved and slid down the trachea and into the lungs.

"Do something, doctor!" yelled one of the nurses, not hiding her panic as she watched me thinking about how best to help the patient.

Think think think. In 1964, the Heimlich maneuver was still unknown. I asked that the tracheostomy kit be prepared and meanwhile tried other less invasive measures. First, trying to expel the object, I used back blows, which did not produce any effect. Dorin continued to try to gasp, unable to produce a sound. Suddenly, the hospital internist dashed into the procedure room. With the same tongue depressor, she tried to do what I had already done—locate a foreign body in the pharynx. Nothing could be seen.

Time was running out; soon the boy would lose consciousness due to hypoxia. After the tracheostomy kit had been prepared, I remembered something I had learned in medical school as a historical fact. At the end of the nineteenth century in France, for cardiopulmonary resuscitation, they used a tongue-stretching procedure. This procedure, as I recalled from a class years ago, consisted of holding the victim's mouth open while pulling the tongue forcefully and rhythmically. Praying silently for a miracle, I approached Dorin, opened his mouth, unclenched his teeth, and wrapped his tongue in gauze hurriedly given to me by a nurse. Energetically and rhythmically, I began pulling his tongue and letting it go. Wonder of wonders! Before letting the tongue go another time—to the amazement of everybody present, me included—I heard Dorin deeply inhale like the first breath of a newborn. He then continued to breathe on his own as if nothing had ever happened. Before long, the recently choking patient became more and more pinkish, and the blue tinge vanished.

Overwhelmed with joy, I embraced my patient and left the room, triumphantly imagining that—as it is usually portrayed in movies and theater—Dorin's mother, with tears in her eyes, would throw herself on my neck and express deep gratitude for saving her son. Alas, nothing of the sort. I could not even find her. An orderly pointed me to the porch, where a group of women stood talking.

Never aware that her child had been on the razor's edge between life and death, Dorin's mother was involved in a vivid conversation about nothing. Still flush with victory, I walked quickly up to her, and loudly proclaimed that her son was alive and well. My grand reward was a confused hush from the women and a bewildered look from the mother. Why not? She had been standing out there the whole time, thinking her child was just getting a checkup and "a big sweet vitamin in the shape of a ball."

Sometimes night duty was more about the downright weird than the miraculous.

Case in point. Once, when surgeon Ilya Sergeevich Petresku was on call, we were enjoying a sumptuous, riotous feast following a typically colorful Moldovan wedding. We sat at the table in the middle of the hall with all the hospital's physicians and their spouses. For hours, everyone ate and drank, with many, many toasts offered and counter offered. I as usual drank only a small amount of wine, and my friend Doctor Petresku limited himself to a single glass.

Around midnight, one of hospital drivers ran into the hall. Looking back and forth frantically, he raced over to the table of the only still sober people at the feast.

"Ilya Sergeevich! They need you at the hospital right away! Come with me right now!" he shouted in one breath. Without asking any questions, Ilya Sergeevich left quickly with him, beckoning for me to join them.

A grocery store clerk, Anya Gorban, lay on a couch in the hospital admitting room, pale and eyes closed. Her husband jumped up and, looking somewhat sheepish, confessed to Ilya Sergeevich Petresku that an hour ago his wife had swallowed . . . a fork.

"A fork? Swallowed . . . I never heard such nonsense. What you are talking about?" snapped the surgeon, disdainfully. "Do you realize you took us away from a wedding? Let's go back, Volodya." My friend resolutely turned toward the entrance. Then, we heard the very quiet, pleading voice of the patient.

"Doctor, I swallowed not only a fork, but a beetle as well."

"A beetle? What else are you going to say?" Ilya Sergeevich said, mimicking the patient. "Are you crazy, Anya, or what?"

Slowly drawing herself up on one elbow, the patient looked pained but now decidedly annoyed. "Do I look crazy? No, I'm not crazy. I was preparing for the audit so I came home from work late. I cooked mamaliga and brought a spoonful of it to my mouth, but then out of nowhere a bug flew into my mouth. I could not help it and choked on the insect. The insect got stuck in my throat. In my hand I had a fork. I did not have time to think. I was so frightened, I went after the bug with the fork. I reached too deep, and completely accidentally, I suddenly swallowed the fork. I do not feel the beetle, but the fork I feel in my stomach somewhere here." The clerk pointed with her finger on the epigastrium.

"Looks like we need to operate. Call for nurse Xenia," muttered the surgeon, shaking his head and giving orders for the patient to be taken to the operating room. Xenia quickly arrived, and we prepped for surgery. As usual, Doctor Petresku watched me like a hawk to make sure I scrubbed my hands according to all the rules of his much self-lauded surgical artistry.

The patient was transferred to the operating room, and the operation was performed under local anesthesia with novocaine. Gradieshti's only surgeon worked in complete silence while I assisted by holding retractors. The stomach was quickly reached and opened. Ilya Sergeevich Petresku, to the general excitement of all present, pulled out with great flourish not only the unfortunate fork but a semidigested bug as well. Both objects were rinsed and cleaned for public display.

That night, I witnessed a surgeon become a local legend. Although this operation was no more complicated than hundreds of others performed by Ilya Sergeevich, it brought him fame for many years to come in the little village and beyond. *Everyone* always talked about it whenever his name came up in conversation. Even the main newspaper of the Moldavian Republic published a long article about the infamous surgery, complete with a photograph of the surgeon and his retractors-holding assistant.

Why, might you ask, did that one operation take such hold in the mythos of Gradieshti? To be sure, the notoriety of the much-passed-around extracted objects played a role. But as important was the simple fact that the skilled remover of those strange items had become a wondrous, almost deific being to the villagers—no one in living memory had ever remained so sober that late into a Moldovan wedding feast.

Four dogs—Mexican, American, Polish, and Russian—are discussing their lives.

The Mexican dog says, "The servants used to leave meat out for me, but now I have to bark for it."

The American dog says, "You have servants in Mexico?"

The Polish dog says, "They feed you meat?"

The Russian dog says, "They let you bark?"

Hard Lives and Few Choices

---❖---

After one month in Gradieshti, I received my first pay as a doctor—ninety-five dollars, all in hard cash, as personal checks for private citizens were unknown in the Soviet Union. My pocket full of hard-earned salary, I joined a late afternoon conversation among the physicians in the doctors' lounge. Next to me sat a physician who, prior to my arrival in the village, had performed the duties of pediatrician in Gradieshti. He was just visiting the hospital today, and was eager to hear how I liked the job so far.

My enthusiastic satisfaction at being a country pediatrician brought a knowing smile and nod.

"I liked to work here too," he replied, carefully, now looking regretful, "but the one thing that made my life miserable here was diarrhea. I am glad I do not have to work as a pediatrician anymore. The dehydrated children drove me absolutely crazy." He paused and looked away, dropping his voice to a murmur. "I still feel very guilty that I was unable to help them."

I nodded slowly in return, not really understanding what he was talking about. That all changed over the following weeks, as I began more and more treating the sick children from the collective farms.

Collective farms, or *kolkhoz*, were the economic and political corner-stones of life in the Moldovan countryside during the 1960s. Seraphim Mikhailovich Namashko, the chairman of Gradieshti's "Red Sparkle" *kolkhoz*, was a former KGB officer and the highest executive power in our village. The *kolkhoz* was run essentially like a feudal fiefdom. The peasant farmers, or *kolkhozniks*, who toiled on the collective farms were all hardworking representatives of the socialist system who could not leave because their IDs (internal passports) were kept under lock and key by the Village Council. When a peasant needed to be away from the *kolkhoz* for a short time, they were required to receive a statement from the Village Council certifying permission. Only a small number of peas-ants—those drafted into military service, or going away for professional or higher education, or marrying nonresidents—were able to get their hands on an internal passport.

For the *kolkhozniks* of both sexes it was critically important—espe-cially in the summer season—to work on the *kolkhoz* for the maximum number of workdays (*trudodni.*) Those workdays were the main, vital source of income for the farmers. The number of workdays accumulated determined how much they received in payment in kind at the end of the year: agricultural products produced by the *kolkhoz*, such as sacks of wheat, corn, and potatoes, and a small monetary reward. The collective farmer could then either keep the produce for personal use or sell it in the city markets.

For three years, I treated the children of the ever-toiling *kolkhozniks* mostly at Gradieshti hospital and clinic, and when it was necessary at their homes, or at school and in tiny villages. All over the country, on every Wednesday it was customary for physicians, after making their morning rounds, to dedicate their working day to patient education and visiting medical ambulatory clinics in rural villages. We would spend the hours consulting with local patients at the rural medical posts man-aged by *feldshers* (medical assistants). House calls to treat the farmers' children were rare, as many roads were often inaccessible, and none of us physicians owned personal cars.

Most of the time, I enjoyed speaking with the *kolkhozniks* about their children, whom they loved and provided for as best they could over the course of their difficult lives. The parents were simply too busy and poor to bring their children to the ambulatory for medical problems that seemed less than life threatening. I found the parents almost always to be highly intelligent but, with little leisure time, surprisingly uninformed and uninterested in the world around them, despite the proximity of the city. My attempts to communicate in rudimentary Moldovan with village mothers on issues other than the health of their children were invariably unsuccessful. Outsiders like me were never fully accepted into their community but were regarded rather as benevolent aliens.

So, what did those trips to the rural medical posts and examinations at school reveal about the general health of the *kolkhozniks'* children? Let's just get to the point—I bore witness to the ongoing national catastrophe, child mortality, which took thousands of children's lives around the Soviet Union. In a socialist country with a self-proclaimed world-class medical system and free health care, the health of children especially in rural areas like Gradieshti was absolutely abysmal. Soaring child mortality levels from gastrointestinal infections prevailed, a result of wrenching poverty, lack of transportation, illiteracy, poor equipment at the hospitals, and a scarcity of critically needed medical personnel. Because the conditions of life in rural areas were much more difficult than in cities, village children were two or three years behind their urban peers in both weight and height. Lagging physical development was just the beginning of their challenges, which included an abundance of skin, tooth, hair, ear, and eye pathology. Hearing loss was common, partly because parents did not pay the necessary attention to their child's ear infection, but also because we physicians lacked the proper medical equipment and medications. Even if a patient with an earache visited the pediatric clinic, an infection could only be diagnosed empirically; portable pocket otoscopes and audiometry were not available. Reflector otoscopy, which could be performed only by an ENT specialist, required a special trip to the city that would cost at least one precious workday at the *kolkhoz*. Especially shocking were dental cavities, which ravaged the teeth of most of the schoolchildren. Dental care was limited to treating tooth-related problems, not to their prevention. No one ever added fluoride to water to prevent tooth decay.

Widespread, neglected infections of the upper respiratory tract among village children included tonsillitis and pharyngitis. When combined with the near-universal tooth decay, untreated tonsillitis, often caused by streptococcus bacteria, led to the enlargement of lymph nodes in the cervical area. Streptococcal infections caused many cases of rheumatic fever among children in Gradieshti and the smaller villages and were invariable accompanied by serious complications such as valvular heart disease and neurological disorders.

Such streptococcal infections were widespread, but we lacked the means and training to aggressively treat them. Despite a worldwide abundance of accepted scientific data, Soviet medicine did not use simple antibiotic therapy that could potentially have prevented countless debilitating complications, such as rheumatic fever, kidney damage, and chorea, a disease of the nervous system. At the time, it was the universally established practice in developed countries to treat streptococcal tonsillitis with antibiotics for not less than ten days. In the USSR, the commonly accepted dogma was that acute tonsillitis and pharyngitis were caused by various viruses and atypical organisms other than the dangerous hemolytic streptococci; therefore, they did not require treatment with antibiotics. The physician's diagnosis was even harder because the laboratory test for streptococcus, which was so widely available elsewhere, was very rarely used in the Soviet Union. Together with the lack of reliable laboratory testing, this led to a situation where many dangerous streptococcal infections were overlooked and not diagnosed by me and my colleagues.

But there was an overwhelmingly even worse affliction among the children, as the previous pediatrician at the hospital had admitted to me—dehydration. I have never, ever seen such catastrophically dehydrated children as I did in Gradieshti and the surrounding villages. In textbooks, it is written that in cases of severe dehydration—more than ten percent loss of body fluid—a child presents with symptoms such as lethargy, sunken eyes, fast and deep respiration, and decreased skin turgor. But the severely dehydrated children I encountered at least once a month in Gradieshti looked like small skeletons tightly covered with skin. For three years, I treated little clones with dry, parchment-like skin that was sunken practically everywhere. It was so damn painful and traumatic to see the last sparks of life glimmering in these children. My utter inability to help severely dehydrated children drove me crazy and poisoned my career as a pediatrician. With every new dying child, part of me was dying as well.

Looking down at a dying little boy or girl in Gradieshti, I would always wonder how difficult living conditions must have been for the families who had waited such a long time to bring their children to us for medical care. And some parents' struggle for daily survival was so extreme that they were forced to leave their critically ill child alone in the hospital.

If the mother stayed, she always insisted on taking the sick child into the hospital bed with her. Inevitably, the very deep sleep for recovery required after such a severe illness would panic her. I remember so many times a distraught mother bursting into the doctor's lounge, thrusting a still infant in front of me, and shrieking that the baby was dead. Although all-too familiar with the situation, I must admit that every time it happened, I shook inside until my examination proved the child lived.

Once these severely dehydrated, very sick children arrived, what could we treat them with? They desperately needed controlled fluid and electrolyte replacement. In addition to the lack of proper intravenous equipment, which I have already described, our treatment of severe dehydration was unsettlingly primitive. At a time when medical laboratories in other countries were able to determine the blood electrolytes and blood gases of patients, we didn't and couldn't. We treated them empirically, frequently given them solutions whose composition may or may not have been appropriate for the type of dehydration they suffered. Furthermore, the composition of the intravenous fluid itself could be inadequate or even dangerous. In the 1960s, pharmaceutical companies distributed solutions for intravenous rehydration in the West. In the Soviet Union, those solutions were prepared at hospitals and at small pharmacies, where they were reliably sterilized but, because of insufficient technology, were not appropriately filtered. In such a solution, numerous microscopic particles of dead microbes and organic corpuscles could abound. When the solution was administered intravenously in a relatively large amount, it sometimes caused fever in children and fever and psychotic reactions in adults.

A final challenge in treating the children was simply keeping them in the hospital bed. Given the bonded servitude connecting farmer to *kolkhoz*, where every workday in the summer was extraordinarily critical to their wellbeing, it should not be surprising that I found it very difficult to keep the *kolkhozniks'* children for long at the hospital. After a child was brought into our hospital by horse-drawn cart or on foot, the decision about when they could be discharged was mostly in the hands of the family, not the pediatrician.

Tough choices. Time and again, I witnessed the immediate needs of their hard lives clashing with the recovery rate of a child patient as well as the dogmatic medical rules of the Socialist Motherland. Because the overall funding for our hospital, like others, depended on the average annual number of bed-days for patients, I was constantly pressured to keep patients for the number of days officially established by the state for that type of disease. I did my best to persuade the parents of hospitalized children to let the child stay until they, according to the state, were "fully" recovered. The mothers never ever argued with me, but the next day, during morning rounds, I frequently discovered that one or more of my recovering patients had disappeared from the floor. Both parents desperately needed to return to work in the fields, and reasoned on their own that their child's health had sufficiently improved to bring them home. If the vanished patient had been running a fever, or had a cough, diarrhea, rash, or significant headache, I did what I could to visit them in the surrounding countryside—by hospital car, by horse-pulled cart, and even on foot. Most of the children were still recovering acceptably. On those occasions when I demanded that the parents return their child to the hospital, the parents rarely argued.

Most of the time.

I remember one afternoon receiving a call from the Tiraspol City Children's Hospital about a baby, Sofia Batrinescu, whose mother had taken her home against medical advice. A special baby, Sofia had been born a couple of months before with congenital defects, including a significant heart defect, and had been transferred by me to the City Hospital. In the process of hospitalization, other problems arose, and Sofia's condition worsened. For some reason, her parents had abruptly removed this very sick child from the hospital and had taken her home. I was asked by the child's attending physician in Tiraspol to persuade the mother to return the child to the City Hospital.

Driven in the hospital car, I arrived at the Batrinescu house. A high wooden fence kept at bay two very large dogs growling and running in the yard.

Yeah, well, I think I'll juuuust stand out here.

At the fence gate, with it decidedly closed, I yelled until the mother opened the door. She looked like most of the other peasant parents I spoke with—face, neck, and arms so dry, red, rough, and wrinkled, all the result of a hard lifetime's exposure to the sun, wind, heat, and cold. She might have been 20, 30, or 40, I could never tell.

She stood in the doorway, defiant, holding Sofia tight in her arms as I asked her in broken Moldovan to please take her baby back to the City Hospital. Like all infants, Sofia was swaddled—tightly wrapped in a rectangular cloth diaper with her legs straightened and arms placed along the body. (It was believed that children slept more quietly in this position, not waking themselves with spontaneous movement, and that tight wrapping of the baby's legs kept them straight.)

After I finished pleading, we both stood there, silent, the dogs now quiet, and stared at each other. She then shook her head and closed the door without saying a word.

Resolved to save the child's life, I returned the next day with a village militiaman, Nikanor Usov. Usov was a tall, good-looking, middle-aged man who clearly liked to polish his military boots. After we had knocked and yelled over the now-familiar growling dogs for some time at the gate, the mother stepped out of the house. Usov, whose Moldovan was much better than mine, repeated what I had told her the day before. The mother remained silent, hands on hips, and not even looking at us. Finally, she cut off the militiaman by raising her right hand and shouting "No!" as she slammed the door behind her.

Usov turned to me and shrugged. "Well, that's it. We cannot do anything else." We turned and began walking back to the car.

"But this child is very sick," I protested. "She could die if we do not take her to the hospital. You're a state representative. There should be a way to persuade the mother."

The militiaman stopped and put his hand on my shoulder. "Take it easy, doctor. I know this woman. Her husband visited me at my house this morning. He said they gave enough time to the doctors to help her get better, but the baby's health did not improve. What am I to do with her? Can you imagine if I force this mother to take her sick child to a place where the baby's health got even worse? Her neighbors would throw me out of the village. They have their ways."

When we reached the car, he paused again. "Because we are alone here, let me tell you, I personally do not believe that there is a way to help this child born with so many troubles. The child is too sick and medicine has its limits, right? Leave the child alone and let time decide what will happen to her. Her father told me she is already doing a little bit better at home."

How could I really disagree with Usov? In my heart, I knew that a child born with severe congenital anomalies and no access to heart surgery would likely not survive long.

I left the family alone. Ten days later, Sofia Batrinescu died at home. Undoubtedly, the next day, her grieving mother returned to the fields for another long day under the sun.

Lest you think that I was always correct about the fortunes of a child removed from our hospital care by the overworked parents, let me hasten to tell the story of a charming ten-month-old baby named Elizabeth Zanga. She had been admitted with pneumonia, and was being successfully treated with intramuscular injections of penicillin. On the sixth day after admission, during morning rounds, I listened to her chest and was pleased that the noises were diminishing. Baby Elizabeth was active, alert, and coughing less. I told her mother that the child was recovering and soon would be discharged. Nodding her head enthusiastically, she gave me a wide maternal smile of gratitude.

The next day, an empty bed. I learned that Elizabeth Zanga had been taken home by her parents the previous evening. I became worried. For a child with pneumonia, standard procedure was to spend at least ten bed-days in the hospital; my patient had been taken home by her parents after only a week. I was concerned that Elizabeth would not finish the recommended course of antibiotic treatment.

I couldn't let it go. The same day, having completed all duties, I stuffed in my small doctor's bag a syringe with a vial of penicillin as well as tablets of penicillin and streptomycin, medications given orally for uncomplicated cases of pneumonia. I asked the hospital driver to take me to the Zanga residence.

The middle-aged driver, Kirill Zandelov, knew well who lived where in the village. He seemed skeptical when I had instructed him to drive.

"Why do you need to visit the Zangas?" he asked me on the way to the patient.

I explained. Kirill took his eyes off the rutted road and glanced at me, his expression ample testament that I was too young to understand the local life.

"In your place, I would not go there," Kirill told me, choosing his words with precision. "The child is OK, believe me. The Zangas are simple peasants, but they know how to love their baby and possess enough common sense to take good care of her. We are just wasting our time here."

We remained silent until the hospital car arrived at the Zangas' house at the edge of the village, standing on a hillock behind a cornfield. We shouted, but nobody seemed to be home. Not knowing what to do, I looked at my driver, who smiled understandingly and beckoned me towards the front door.

"Stop worrying, doctor. In the village everybody is related, so you can enter the house together with me," he assured me. "The door is not locked because, well, there is nothing to steal here."

With these words, he pushed the door, and we entered the home, a typical Moldovan hut, with a corridor separating everything into two halves. On the left was a room with wooden floors covered with handmade runners. It was used, as I came to understand, only for very special occasions and for the storage of the wedding dowry and the most valuable property. As we slowly made our way down the corridor, I glimpsed on the walls to the left embroidered cloths, icons, and photos of the dead and still-living older members of the family.

On our right was the everyday room with earthen floors topped with clay where the family lived. There, they cooked, slept, grew, and guests were received. The windows were covered with embroidered primitive curtains.

It was so quiet in the hut. The driver, Zandelov, turned to the right into the everyday room and beckoned, putting a finger to his lips. A cradle stood in the far corner of the room.

"Look who is here," he whispered. "Here is your treasure, doctor."

In the wooden cradle lay my patient, Elizabeth Zanga, tightly swaddled. She was wrapped in a clean white blanket and covered with a beautiful and delicate handmade lace coverlet. She was deeply asleep. Judging by her peaceful breathing and the rosy color of her cheeks, her condition was definitely quite good. To my surprise, the baby periodically sucked on something stuck in her mouth. It appeared to be a piece of gauze with something wrapped in it.

"What is happening, Kirill?" I whispered back to the driver. "Where are the parents? And what is this baby sucking on?"

He shook his head. "Nothing unusual," he murmured. "You really know nothing about how people live here. The parents are at this time working somewhere in the *kolkhoz* field. The baby will be here alone and safe until they come back. The iron law in any *kolkhoz* is who does not work shall not eat. After Elizabeth's mother spent several days with her in the hospital, she is now behind in workdays. The parents must make ends meet, otherwise the entire family will starve." He looked down at the infant. "I know Elizabeth's mother well. She is my distant relative. She would not leave her baby alone if it were not extremely important to do."

The driver then smiled at me. "This baby appears to be completely healthy. She is sucking on chewed-up poppy seeds wrapped in the gauze. Thanks to that, she sleeps so deeply that nothing can awaken her. The baby has a 'babysitter' in her mouth, grown in the family's own backyard. When the mother comes home, she will take away the gauze, and soon the baby will wake up."

I couldn't help but raise an eyebrow. Pointing at the door for us to go, he whispered, now a bit defensively, "My mother did the same to me when I was a baby, and as you can see, I am not in bad shape at all. Moldovan mothers are very responsible. They do not leave their children alone for a long time, and they return to them at the first possible opportunity."

"I understand what you are saying," I replied softly, shaking my head as we stepped outside. "But look—here the child, from her early childhood, gets poppy seeds that contain a large amount of opiates. What if that results in a predisposition to addiction to narcotics later?"

"It will result in nothing," Kirill retorted confidently. "You know life from books and I know it from real life."

Standing in front of the car door, the driver paused and looked at me. "Have you ever seen in our village even one drug addict? Wine is given to children everywhere like it is water, especially during celebrations, but did you ever see a child who is an alcoholic around here?"

"Okay, Kirill. But what do you say about the drinking problem in the village?"

"You are confusing apples and oranges, doctor. I have never seen a single child alcoholic in my life. Am I an alcoholic?"

To object was useless.

We agreed to keep the house call to ourselves. Nevertheless, the next day, the baby's father stopped by the hospital to tell me that his daughter continued to be healthy. The farmer then looked down and cleared his throat. "I appreciate you coming to see how my daughter was doing," he said, politely but firmly, "but I do not want you to come to our house again when we are not home. Elizabeth is our child, and we have the right to do with her whatever we want."

With that, he turned crisply and left. Rightfully chastised but relieved for the baby, I picked up the patient chart of another severely dehydrated child and began writing. Perhaps the next outcome would also let me sleep at night.

And there were the treatment journeys with the *kolkhozniks* and their children that proved, well, to be rather dangerous. During the routine Gradieshti school physical examinations during my second year, I identified many schoolchildren as seriously ill. One was twelve-year-old Nikushor Trokalov. He had a mild systolic heart murmur, slight fever, and sweating—classic signs of rheumatic fever. Nonetheless, it took me an entire week to convince Nikushor's parents to bring their son to the hospital for treatment.

They arrived, son quietly trailing behind his father, Vasile, who wore on his head an old Moldovan *kutchma*, or *astrakhan*, a traditional head-dress made from lambswool. He was dressed in an old, grayish cotton suit with old, short, and wrinkled pants. Over his right shoulder, he carried two ancient bags, one in front and one behind, connected with a strip of coarse scrim cloth.

Vasile was not happy and spoke little, motioning abruptly to me to just get the examination done. Nikushor's previous symptoms were more pronounced, and now he was also limping and looked sick—clearly, he had an acute case of rheumatic fever with heart and joint complications. He needed to be hospitalized immediately in a specialized intensive care unit in Tiraspol.

"I am taking him nowhere!" Vasile exploded, pacing back and forth. "I need to go to the *kolkhoz* farm to get credit for my workdays! I have my small piece of land to take care of. My wife takes care of our four children; one of them is only six months old. Am I going to earn a piece of bread for my family or will somebody else do it for me? You are his doctor! Treat him *here!*"

Fortunately, after much persuasion and especially after the *kolkhoz* chairman promised the Trokalov family some modest financial help, the father finally agreed to take his son to Tiraspol for treatment. I sighed with relief. Hopefully, Nikushor would improve and his systolic heart murmur would disappear.

After four weeks at the hospital, Nikushor returned to the village. Soon his father brought him to me for a follow-up visit. My patient looked healthy and the intensity of his heart murmur had lessened somewhat. His tonsillitis was gone, and the swelling of the lymph nodes in the neck had almost disappeared. Vasile was unchanged; resentful at being called away from his work and impatient for the examination to be done. Ignoring my many questions, he simply thrust into my hands the discharge forms given to him at the city hospital. I reminded him that his son would need a monthly check-up, a simple blood test, and a shot of Bicillin—long-acting penicillin. Vasile remained taciturn and Nikushor, glancing fearfully at his father, said little.

With the arrival of the rainy season, mud made walking extremely difficult, and later, during the winter, a thick layer of snow covered the

Moldovan roads. Nikushor was not able to come to Gradieshti Hospital for his regular appointments. He still managed to walk three kilometers from his home to school, five days a week. In order not to miss his next prophylactic dose of Bicillin, a visiting pediatric nurse gave him his shot at school.

A few months later, to my surprise, Nikushor's mother, Nadia Trokalova, brought him to the clinic for his monthly check-up. Her age, as with other peasant women, was difficult to determine after long years of exposure of her face and hands to the elements. At the end of the visit, without saying a word, Nadia Trokalova opened a primitive coarse straw basket and, after fumbling inside it, removed a small plate wrapped in a piece of clean cheesecloth. Putting it on the table, she removed the cheesecloth and motioned to her son. Nikushor carefully took the plate from the table and put it before me. It was fresh cottage cheese—a great treat. My sincere thanks eventually produced a small smile on the mother's face.

Nikushor was more talkative around his mother than father, so I asked him what he would like to be when he grew up. With pride and resolution he answered that he wanted to be a soldier. Knowing too well that his heart condition would prevent him from being conscripted, I gently urged him to consider becoming a teacher, agronomist, or engineer.

The boy shook his head, firmly. "No," he flatly declared. "I want to be a soldier. In the army they feed you, there's no dirt around, and they give you a new uniform."

During my last winter in Gradieshti, Nikushor arrived at the clinic with his father for his monthly preventive Bicillin shot. I immediately saw, to my dismay, a recurrence of rheumatic fever symptoms: a fever, a slight swelling in two joints, and, again, a soft systolic heart murmur. I insisted and this time his father surprisingly did not object to his readmission to the specialized unit at the Children's Hospital in Tiraspol.

Two weeks later, in the middle of a working day, a driver from the Agricultural Council dashed into the ambulatory examination room, shouting. "Get into my car, doctor! It's an emergency!" There's trouble at the school with one of the students!"

Svetlana Dogaru, my nurse, grabbed our emergency kits and we rushed to the car. Entering the principal's office in the village school, we saw teachers hovering around a couch on which Nikushor's body had been laid. It was too late. After checking my patient, I asked for a sheet to cover his body and solemnly informed all present that their student was dead.

What in the world had happened? Later, I learned that, after a week or so at Tiraspol Hospital, Nikushor's father had impulsively taken him home, against medical advice, and then had just sent him back to school. During recess, Nikushor was playing soccer with the other children on the school playground. While running on the field, he suddenly fell to the ground and let out a loud cry. His heart could not bear the excessive exertion, which resulted in cardiac fibrillation followed by cardiac arrest.

Nikushor Trokalov had barely reached thirteen years, had known poverty all his brief life, and would never escape that world to become a soldier. Four days after he died, Svetlana and I were among a small crowd at his funeral in a cemetery located on a small hill. Emotionless and silent, Nadia stood still, just staring at her son's coffin. For the most part, Vasile also remained motionless and quiet, eyes locked forward on nothing. His one brief glance at me during the ceremony, as always, smoldered in cold fury. Before the coffin was committed to the earth, there were short speeches and—yes, even in the Soviet regime— a prayer.

Following custom, all who were present at the funeral were then invited for a meal at the Trokalov house. Neither Svetlana nor I had the heart to refuse. The dining table, standing on a dirt floor, was set with a typical Moldovan feast: black bread, onions, cheeses, boiled potatoes, cabbage rolls, and bottles of homemade wine and vodka.

When it came time to drink vodka toasts, I refused, blaming my nonexistent stomach ulcer. Svetlana confirmed this condition, and I was allowed to drink wine in small quantities. When each new toast was said, I symbolically raised my faceted glass filled with wine. As Vasile downed one toast after another, he began reproaching me for not joining the other vodka drinkers. I smiled back at him, pretending I did not understand exactly what he was saying.

An hour passed, and the guests began singing sad Moldovan songs. Svetlana and I glanced at each other. The laws of hospitality precluded us from leaving just yet.

Each glass of alcohol made Vasile more talkative and menacing. Finally, when I yet again declined an offer to drink with him, he stood up with his face flushed. "What's the matter with you, doctor?" he roared. "Why are not you drinking with my family? Who are *you* to refuse? Drink together with us if you are a real friend of my family!"

Everyone stopped singing and chatting, and stared at us.

"I am sorry, but I cannot," I apologized again, carefully breaking the shocked stillness and speaking slowly so that the whole room would hear. "I have an ulcer in my stomach. The doctors will not let me drink; my stomach might rupture."

"Oh, is that so?!" the grieving, drunk father took a step towards me, gesturing to his guests. "Now listen to me, doctor! My Nikushor, who is not alive anymore, had a doctor—you. And look where your help got us. Nikushor is dead. Do you understand? Probably not, so I will tell you why he is dead." Now nearly apoplectic, Vasile stabbed his finger at me, repeatedly. "*You* are the one to blame! It is *you* who gave him the wrong medications and the wrong shots, and *you* should pay for it! Why should I care about your stomach's ulcers? "

Fists clenched and raised, he advanced, weaving slightly. Suddenly, three equally inebriated male relatives rose and joined him.

Oh, brother. One against four drunk but strong men, and no way to escape the room. I felt something cold in the palm of my hand—a large syringe with a long needle, which my nurse had just slipped me from the ever-present medicine bag. Svetlana brandished another syringe.

Four pairs of reddened eyes fixated on the long needles and syringes filled, I now saw, with suspicious white contents. The attackers paused, and the room again grew quiet. The stalemate was broken by Nadia Trokalova. The usually silent and extremely reserved woman, who had been invisibly serving food and drink, suddenly became assertive and tough.

"Stay where you are," she exclaimed, stepping between us. "You, Vasile—you forget that this doctor is one of many who told you that our son must stay at home and go nowhere. But it was *you* who insisted he should go to school. So tell me, whose fault is it?"

The four behaved as if they hadn't heard the mother, and shuffled even closer to Svetlana and me. We backed up against a wall. Only the two large sharp needles stayed their attack.

Waving her hand and shaking her head, Nadia quickly returned to the kitchen.

"You, doctor, and your nurse are killers!" screamed Vasile, grabbing a stool and throwing it at my head. I ducked and it splintered against the wall behind. Nadia then reappeared, this time carrying a large bucket full of slops.

"Everybody take your seats!" she ordered in a loud voice. "Whoever doesn't do what I say will get slop on him. You, drunkards—you are not going to have a fight in my home on the day when my son was buried! Do not touch our guests!" She turned to us and lowered her voice. "You, doctor and Svetlana, you better go home and get away from these crazy people."

With hearts beating hard, we quickly slipped out of the house, leaving behind a grieving mother just trying to endure, and a drunken father full of fury and regret. Tomorrow he would be sober, but his son would still be gone.

Propagandists in the 1960s repeatedly trumpeted the virtues of the free Soviet medical system, where patients never paid for medications when hospitalized. Well, there was a catch: many foreign-produced medications could not be bought anywhere in the country, but could only be obtained for free from a special fund at the offices of the Ministry of Public Health. The lack of ready availability of some vital medications affected us all at one time or another in the Moldovan countryside, but none more than one kind and sensitive *feldsher, the* village medical assistant.

Severe respiratory tract illnesses were not as dramatic as gastrointestinal infections but could still be very challenging for young patients. During one of my planned Wednesday visits to the small village of Zheltoye, its *feldsher,* Dimitry Onchan, asked me to look at his two-year-old son who showed signs of an upper-respiratory infection. My examination indicated that Dimitry's son probably was in the initial stages of pneumonia. On my advice, the child was admitted to Gradieshti Hospital where he was treated with antibiotics. For the next two days, the boy's condition significantly worsened. Out of options, I sought the opinion of a medical consultant from the city of Tiraspol. On the third morning, he told the parents and me that the child might benefit from a foreign-made antibiotic, sigmamycin. The problem? We had none on hand, the City Hospital in Tiraspol had none, and the only supply was at the Ministry of Public Health in faraway Kishinev, the capital city of the Moldavian Soviet Socialist Republic, where I had attended medical school.

Learning of an antibiotic that might save his son's life, *feldsher* Dimitry Onchan grabbed the prescription, nodded at us, and left the hospital immediately. I last spotted him walking purposefully north on the two-lane asphalt road.

Early in the morning of the next day, as I began my rounds, Dimitry reappeared, less than twenty hours after he had left. Without a word and clearly exhausted, he handed me the entire ten-day course of antibiotic treatment for his son. I learned that this determined, loving father had hitchhiked the sixty miles to Kishinev. There, in the late afternoon, he was able to reach the office of the special deputy for distribution of drugs at the Ministry of Public Health. Though he arrived without an appointment, the secretary, upon learning that he was a *feldsher* in a village of the republic, allowed him to wait along with other visitors to be seen by the deputy. Receiving the medicine, the *feldsher* had immediately turned around, and walked and hitchhiked all night sixty miles back to Gradieshti Hospital.

Sigmamycin did the trick, and the boy successfully recovered and was safely discharged. Whenever afterwards I would try to praise Dimitry for his amazing effort, he would just wave it off and turn away.

A couple of months later, when I was visiting Zheltoye, the Onchans invited me to lunch at their home. Their son was alive and well, playing with toys. At the table, I again told Dimitry that he and he alone had saved his child's life. Once more, Dimitry only waved his hand and said nothing.

When he left the room to bring more coal for the stove, his wife leaned towards me. "I love Dimitry and he has a heart of gold," she said softly, smiling. "My husband is very modest and sensitive, and he will never tell you what really happened. Initially, when he showed your prescription to the deputy at the ministry, the deputy gave him a couple of doses of sigmamycin, saying it was all he could help him with.

"'This type of medicine,' he had lectured my husband, 'the state buys from abroad, paying with *valuta* (valyuta), the foreign currency, and it is used only for extraordinary cases.' But Dimitry, as a *feldsher*, knew that two doses were good for nothing to help our son. So he started begging the deputy for more antibiotics. Nothing helped and eventually the deputy yelled at him to leave the room. But Dimitry did not give up. He was so desperate when he thought that our son might not recover that he fell on his knees before the deputy, imploring him for the medicine, and vowing not to leave the office without it. After ten minutes of my husband begging on his knees, the deputy, without a word, opened the safe and gave Dimitry the full ten-day course of treatment.

"Only recently my husband—a very proud man, believe me—confessed to me that on the way home, each time he recalled the humiliation he had suffered trying to save our son's life, he had started crying and could not stop."

She looked at me, her shining eyes full of tears and pride. Mine glistened as well.

Shaking her head slightly, she sighed. "I am a law-abiding citizen, but I ask you, is it fair to go through all this humiliation? It's called free medicine, but I would rather pay for what is necessary a thousand times than be at the mercy of anyone, especially a medical bureaucrat."

Dimitry Onchan then returned with the coal, and we all resumed eating. Looking down at his son, the *feldsher* ruffled his hair and smiled. The little boy, who would never know the true sacrifice of his father, giggled and continued playing with the toys.

A member of the Communist Party sees a *kolkhoznik* heavily drinking and walks up to him. "Tell us, what forces you to drink vodka every day?"

The farmer smiles and replies, "Nothing. I'm a volunteer."

Just One More Drink

———⌘———

I bet by now you've figured out that the villagers of Gradieshti enjoy a drink every now and then. Hold on to your hats, dear reader, you're going on a special, crazy ride.

There's no better place to begin than with an annual rite that marked the beginning of the homemade wine season in late summer. It's two hours into evening, and there's quite a roar from the two-lane asphalt road going by Gradieshti Hospital. Two brothers are racing each other as fast as they can up and down the road, each driving a big four-wheel T-40 *kolkhoz* tractor that's been produced for a few years now by the Lipetsk Tractor Plant. Brothers Dimitriu and Ivan Kodryanu, twenty-eight and twenty-six, respectively, startlingly resemble each other. Both are about six feet tall, strongly built with big broad shoulders and large hands and feet. Even through the thickly spewing tractor smoke around them, it's obvious that they're quite handsome, with light brown hair and oblong faces with roman noses and well-defined cheekbones and lips. Well, they're not completely identical. Dimitriu's missing two front teeth, due to a massive brawl during his late teenage years, and his younger brother's sporting a noticeable scar on his cheek from falling off a horse in an inebriated state (the horse was sober).

The brothers zoom by again, shouting wildly and gesturing at each other with bottles. As the large tractors rumble out of sight for the fifth time—with Ivan in the lead for a change—a hospital orderly and I brave the exhaust smoke to scamper across the highway.

In response to my questioning look, the orderly explains that no one really knows why the Kodryanu brothers race tractors. "Some think they are reassuring us that they are sober and easily handling the temptations of the new seasonal alcohol abundance." He shrugs, coughing from the smoke. "Others believe they are just full-of-life youngsters who are rip-roaring drunk after too much wine, and are just letting off steam."

I soon discovered that one explanation everyone agreed upon, however, is that the racing tractor brothers were continuing a family tradition. One morning after a night of tractor noise and smoke, I got a peasant father of a patient to tell me the story. A smile flickered across the weathered man, who began with, "Their father, Radu, and uncle, Liviu, used to do almost exactly the same until one day when they crashed into each other."

Well, that's a tale we better hear quick.

Apparently that collision between the Kodryanu father and uncle, which happened four years ago, had been quickly and deeply woven into the legendary lore of Gradieshti. Radu and Liviu had raced tractors for years; the difference from the present generation is that they drove *toward* each other. When they passed, one brother would throw a bottle of vodka to the other, who was expected to nimbly catch it, swallow a mouthful, and then toss the bottle back after they had turned around and were racing past each other again. Of course, being reliable and conscientious citizens, Radu and Liviu allowed themselves no more than one mouthful of alcohol per encounter. Their tractor encounters in a given evening, however, were many.

Taking into account that each tractor's speed topped twenty-five kilometers per hour, successfully catching a flying bottle of vodka was certainly an accomplished trick; from all accounts, the older generation of Kodryanu brothers were deservedly quite proud of that skill. Perhaps their fame would have spread even beyond the village, if not for the regrettable fact that one evening Liviu missed grabbing the bottle and it smashed into his head. He lost control of his powerful vehicle and fiercely collided head-on with his brother's tractor. Each brother was propelled through the air to opposite sides of the asphalt road, fortunately landing in the numerous puddles left by a thunderstorm the hour before. Radu and Liviu suffered severe trauma, but survived, escaping the accident with fractures of the ribs, arms, and legs (Liviu also sustained a head injury—not from the collision but from the flying vodka bottle).

Miraculously, the vodka bottle survived the catastrophe, and was picked up and saved by one of the many ardent admirers of the brothers' showmanship. After spending more than a month in Gradieshti Hospital, Radu and Liviu celebrated their discharge by finally emptying that bottle.

The Kodyanu brothers, senior and junior, were celebrated in Gradieshti, but in an undeniable way they were so ordinary. It's not news that the countries of Eastern Europe, especially territories of the former Soviet Union struggle even today with alcoholism. The village of Gradieshti in 1960s Moldova was not exempt. I know of many sad and heartbreaking stories that could be written about the villagers' excessive use of alcohol. Why do such interesting and useful people drink so much, voluntarily transforming themselves into pitiful and helpless creatures? But nestled even in that ongoing tragedy are small places for humor, for racing brothers on tractors, which keep us sane. Certainly, alcoholism in the village was not as obvious as in the city of Kishinev, where I attended medical school. There, drunkards—almost exclusively men—littered the sidewalks, sometimes passed out in their vomit and urine.

Alcoholism as a way of life in Gradieshti manifested in other ways, some on the surface, some not so much. As one of its main agricultural products, grapes made wine cheap and easily affordable for everyone, even the *kolkhozniks*. Wine was most abundant during the late summer grape harvest, when supply far exceeded demand. It was manufactured or pressed practically in every household. The first wine from the press was called *must* (pronounced "moost"). Its taste was sweet, so people drank a lot of it and became drunk very quickly. When homemade wine was in plentiful supply, it was common to substitute it for water, not only for consumption by humans, but also for domesticated animals.

Yes, you read that right. There's nothing like stepping around tipsy chickens and ducks when walking to work.

Rampant village alcoholism affected my practice most directly, of course, through drunken accidents. I remember the time, when I was on call, that a young musician, a trumpeter, arrived at the hospital dead from a major trauma—a broken neck as a result of a fall from the second floor in the beautiful House of Culture, which had been built by the *kolkhoz*. It seems that the trumpeter had been drinking, and then tried carrying with both hands his instrument case up the stairs to the second floor, where young local men regularly held practices for playing music at important public events. Unfortunately, the stairs had no handrails. The House of Culture had been completed for some time, but the supplier still had not delivered the railings for the stairs. After years, when they had not arrived, someone decided that the House of Culture might get along without handrails. Why bother if nobody complains?

Well, no one complained until a drunk young musician died, leaving behind a young wife and three children.

A short time later, on a warm summer afternoon, I was walking through the center of the village and spied the secretary of the local Communist organization, Comrade Zachary Ionovich Lupu. The secretary was the spiritual and ideological adviser to the chairman of the Gradieshti "Red Sparkle" *kolkhoz*, thus making him a powerful individual whose hands pulled levers for sweet rewards and severe punishments. Lupu was tall, thin, in his forties, with straight, fine auburn hair. Like many in the village, his face was round, with thin eyebrows, pointed nose, and a round chin.

Comrade Lupu appeared to be in an intense conversation with a twenty-one-year-old beauty named Camelia Kodreanu. (Before you ask, yes, Camelia was married to one of the ruckus-fueled, tractor-driving brothers—she was also the cousin of my nurse Svetlana. Yes, it's a very small place.) On impulse, I walked quickly toward them. Camelia blushed slightly and slipped away.

Ignoring the annoyed look in the secretary's eyes, I immediately asked about the death of the trumpeter. "Zachary Ionovich, something should be done right away about those handrails. The man never would have died if the stairs in the House of Culture had been equipped with them," I said, looking into his dark brown eyes directly. "Until handrails are installed, this building is dangerous for visitors. Do you think this problem could be resolved as soon as possible?"

"Railings will be available soon, maybe in a month, Doctor, but as I've told you more than once, whatever goes on beyond your hospital is none of your business," Comrade Lupu spoke calmly, looking away and fixing his gaze on the infinite distance, where he apparently saw the vague outlines of Communism.

"Yes, I understand. But this man was brought to the hospital, and that's why I am asking you about this issue."

The local party secretary turned toward me. "Do you have nothing else to do other than disquiet people with your unnecessary worries? I am sorry for what happened to the trumpeter, but it was entirely his own fault. If he hadn't been drinking, he never would have fallen. Every sober person knows he should be careful when there are no handrails."

I had to make him see this simple point. "But, Zachary Ionovich, he is not the only one in the village who has a drinking problem, and without handrails we might have another bad case on our hands in the future."

Comrade Lupu shrugged, now clearly irritated and dismissing me and my argument. "Nothing is going to happen. This trumpeter was a strange fellow, not like anybody else. That's all. Why don't you organize a campaign against drinking wine and vodka in our *kolkhoz* instead of this empty talk?" He paused, peering closely at me. "As I said before, stop interfering in things that are not your business. Next time you want to tell me something, tell your boss and she will pass it on to me."

And with that, the local party secretary began walking away. Abruptly, he stopped and turned. "Listen doctor," he said loudly, clearly for the benefit of passers-by, "anyone who gets drunk and falls brings it on themselves."

Three months later, late in the evening after a local Communist Party meeting, the highly respected local party secretary and the chairman of the *kolkhoz*, Seraphim Mikhailovich Namashko, were making their way back together toward their homes, impressively built of stone and standing side by side. Actually, it is more accurate to describe our two village leaders as weaving and rhythmically swaying their way back to their wives. Both had heartily participated in the much celebrated "item three" of the party meeting, always marked by countless toasts of wine, vodka, Soviet champagne, Zubrovka, Pertzovka, and Armenian and Georgian cognacs. (A real wife of a Communist was never supposed to ask questions starting with "why," "where," and "how," if her husband had been attending an "important party meeting.")

Long after midnight, a very drunk Lupu and Namashko shared a single flashlight to illuminate the path home in pitch darkness. Success! They reached the houses as their dogs recognized them and began barking welcome. Standing in front, for a moment they forgot their official roles and in an outburst of fraternal feelings—fueled by alcohol—the neighbors embraced each other tightly.

Suddenly, the heel of the *kolkhoz* chairman's boot skidded into a large hole, which seemed to only swell in depth as he slipped farther. Grabbing his newly affirmed brother, both fell out of sight, clutching each other. When the embracing Communists found themselves at the bottom of a fairly shallow hole and too drunk to climb out of it or yell for help, they companionably settled down in the pit. Warming each other in the balmy Moldovan night, our lauded leaders peacefully fell into a deep sleep under the glow of the moon and light of the bright stars.

It seems that their wives, impatient for a new gate to be installed, had ordered postholes dug that evening while their dutiful husbands gave it their all for the state. An hour or two later, Capitolina Artemovna, the wife of Chairman Namashko, was awakened by the dogs' barking. With the help of her own leashed dog, she quickly came upon the hole, from which thundered loud snores. Waking up Lupu's wife, Capitolina Artemovna called the personal chauffeurs of both leaders for help in extracting them from the hole and driving them to the hospital.

Guess who was waiting for them? I was on duty that night. Both Lupu and Namashko, assisted by their chauffeurs, limped into the hospital, demanding to see the chief doctor. Lyubov Evgenyevna happened not to be in the village that evening, so I was told resolutely and repeatedly that I was highly privileged to examine the patients and to absolutely keep this story a deep secret.

The type of trauma experienced by our still drunk patients usually did not require immediate attention, but taking into account their high positions, I called on the hospital's surgeon, my friend Ilya Sergeevich Petresku. He diagnosed Comrade Lupu with a muscular sprain, while the ligaments of one of Comrade Namashko's ankles were torn. Each victim was placed in a private room at the end of the corridor with elements of comfort unknown to the regular patients. Their rooms were guarded by their chauffeurs, and their food was specially prepared by the domestics at home and delivered to the hospital.

Two days after admission, the patients were discharged personally by Lyubov Evgenyevna, who had returned to the village by that time. She was happy to have the two leading village figures in her hospital. Thanks to the opportunity of their prolonged, undivided attention, she got them to promise that our hospital would be provided with construction materials, extra coal, additional food, and more feed for the horse.

As for me, I couldn't resist. The first night, after surgeon Petresku had left, I helped the chauffeur assist Lupu to his room. As the secretary groaned and settled on his bed, he caught my wide grin, which I had been trying so hard to conceal.

The chauffeur departed, and I turned out the lights. As I turned to leave, an authoritarian voice sliced through the darkness with precision.

"Doctor—"

"Yes, secretary?"

"This still won't get you those handrails."

Gradieshti's love affair with alcohol also affected my practice in another way: it made home visits protracted and sometimes downright awkward. Regardless of the season, after I had examined a child at a home and was preparing to leave, out of nowhere would appear the father. As part of the family's appreciation for my visit, he always invited me to stay a bit longer and have a little snack and a glass of wine. Even before he finished speaking, his wife would be serving us bread, cucumbers, radishes, sunflower oil, *brinza* (sheep's-milk cheese), just-prepared, delicious *mamaliga* (cornmeal porridge traditional in Romania and Moldova), and, naturally, the ever-present carafe of homemade wine.

I soon learned that refusing the treat was useless. In the first place, it would offend the parents, period. In the second, if, after such an invitation, I tried to leave the house, its master, with an understanding smile, would unceremoniously lock the door and escort me to a chair. After a toast, the established rule was to drink the entire glass of wine. Not following this custom would have resulted in the host seeing their hospitality as refused, and the guest regarded as "not one of ours." The minimum amount I was expected as a guest to drink was two glasses of wine. Only when I demonstrated undeniable signs of intoxication would a couple allow escape from their hospitality. I became good at impersonating a drunk pediatrician.

Even decades later, I still do not know why so many Gradieshti villagers inverted the rules of hospitality so that the guest was forced to do what was imposed on him by the master of the house. Perhaps it was a desire to ensure that I would spread the word about the great hospitality of the hosts; maybe they needed to be reassured about the quality of their homemade wine. It could be that the hosts wanted to prove to me and themselves that despite all my education I could still get as drunk as any peasant. Or maybe they simply needed company or a good excuse for drinking.

Once, my lovely wife Marina rescued me, however inadvertently, from a marathon drinking session after I had examined a child at home. I had been treating a severe case of pneumonia in the daughter of the local chief veterinarian, Nekulai Radescu, and his wife, Flora. A month later, after office hours, when we ran into each other at the village grocery store, the veterinarian asked that I come to his house to see his daughter, who that afternoon had resumed her cough and fever.

"I know that you do not have much time, doctor," he told me. "I have a car and will drive you to my home and then right away will bring you straight back."

After examining the girl, who was absolutely healthy with a normal temperature, I noticed that in the adjacent room the hostess had set the table with hearty appetizers and the ubiquitous carafe of wine. I insisted on going, but the parents laughed and locked the door, and so I resolved to pretend to be significantly drunk as soon as possible.

In due course, having stuffed my stomach with food and ready to consume a third, and hopefully final, glass of wine, I heard a delicate knock at the door. I prepared myself to use this interruption to disappear.

The hostess opened the door, and completely unexpectedly, on the threshold I saw my wife Marina, who was smiling. Having finished her examinations in Odessa ahead of schedule, she had decided to give me a pleasant surprise and come to Gradieshti. Unfortunately, as I later learned from her, on the bus she had sat next to the *kolkhoz*'s accountant, Viorel Gridyanu. The accountant was known to all of us was a joker and prattler, punished more than once for his brainless and sometimes malicious jokes. I had never met him before.

Marina, upon his polite questioning, told him she was my wife and that she was coming for a visit.

"Oh, I am glad you are Doctor Tsesis's wife," answered Viorel Gridyanu, a cunning smile spreading across his narrow, rat-like face. "I heard he is a good surgeon—"

"He is not a surgeon. He is a pediatrician, a children's doctor," Marina corrected him.

"All right, he is a good pediatrician," Viorel Gridyanu responded, smoothly.

"Thanks," answered Marina.

"Yes, he is a good doctor and they love him," smirked her traveling companion. "Do you know who loves him most of all?"

Marina was silent.

"Don't you understand who loves him?" the accountant persisted, leaning toward her. "Young nurses, of course, that's whom."

"Well, good for him if they love him," interrupted my wife. "And now leave me alone."

Gridyanu began apologizing, but Marina stood up abruptly and took another seat with her back to the hoaxer.

Of all the nights not to find me at home, this was not the one. Marina immediately went to the hospital and asked a driver where I was. A village has a thousand eyes, and after talking with a couple of peasants, the driver found out exactly my whereabouts and promptly took her there.

After knocking on the door in anticipation of a pleasant surprise, she entered the veterinarian's house and found me, her husband, rather drunk. Still annoyed after her encounter with the nasty man on the bus, and now seeing her usually sober husband inebriated for the first time in our marriage, she gave me an unforgettable glance full of rebuke and displeasure. Ignoring Doctor Radesku and Flora's invitation to join them, she resolutely turned on her heels, flung open the door, and soon was on her way back to our house.

My wife's departure rapidly ended the festivities. With unsteady gait, I made my way to the door. Nekulai reminded me of his promise to take me home in his car. Given that I had drunk less than half of what he had, I collected all that was left of my sobriety and somehow, with slowly moving tongue, conveyed to my hosts my deep concern about his ability to drive.

His wife immediately reassured me, sharing that her husband had been drinking since childhood and never got really drunk from four glasses of wine.

"Are you kidding? Nekulai is the father of my child, doctor," she said, soothingly. "I love him as only Moldovan women know how, and I would be the first to forbid him to drive our new car if I suspected it might be dangerous to his life. Nekulai, when he drinks, drives better than when he is sober."

Her irrational arguments somehow persuaded me, and I embarked on a most unforgettable trip home. Indeed, for the first five minutes, our car moved smoothly and confidently down the rural road. But as soon as the Radeskus' house was out of sight, the alcohol in the veterinarian's blood took a hairpin curve much too fast. We sped through the night, the driver drunk and more and more reckless, the passenger more and more sober and anxious. A peasant crossing a street barely escaped our careening car by diving past it on a sharp curve. Afraid to distract Nekulai by speaking, I remained silent like a frightened fish. Miraculously, we made it. Nekulai hospitably grunted "goodbye," shaking my hand as if I was his best friend, and then roared away.

I stood in front of my apartment door in the darkness, judging whether I was sober enough to go in yet and explain everything. Not for the first time, I wondered if the entire village itself was one high-functioning alcoholic.

Gradieshti women, as a rule, drank less than the men. Many became the victims of abuse after others became drunk. Aside from the roar of racing tractors on the asphalt road, another unmistakable sign of the late summer overabundance of homemade wine was a phenomenon that the hospital personnel called "the running woman." On the road leading to the hospital, a woman would appear, running as fast as she could toward our open metal gates, her husband in pursuit, sometimes brandishing an axe. It was a Gradieshti tradition that village women would take refuge in our hospital from their drunk, abusive husbands. During the seasonal epidemics of alcoholism, the hospital assigned at least five beds in a room for these battered married women, who were provided refuge, shelter, and, when necessary, immediate medical attention.

I sometimes visited the abused women during my evening hospital rounds. The faces and arms of most were covered with scratches and bruises from recent beatings. If I asked why they had been hurt, most of the women remained silent with wry smiles to hide their fear and embarrassment. But there was always somebody to give me shocking answers, such as a shrug of the shoulders and "If he beats me, it means he still loves me," or "That's how it is in our village." It soon became apparent to me that these women were too frightened of their husbands and of the prospect of living without a breadwinner to say anything bad about their abusers, especially in the presence of other women. Eventually I stopped asking.

The majority of the abused, running women were *kolkhozniks*, but not all—you already know that. Our own chief doctor, Lyubov Evgenyevna Oprya, fled her own drunk husband, epidemiology technician Grigoriy Sergeevich, all the time, to the great entertainment and speculation of our patients. Many times, she appealed for help to the Communist Party, in particular to the First Secretary of the district Communist Party,

Mirtcha Gerasimovich Mukutsa, whose office was in Tiraspol. In his senior position, and as a successful graduate of the so-called Higher Party School, Mirtcha Gerasimovich was well versed in how to find the most unexpected ways to solve conflicts, including domestic ones. After too many such impromptu therapy sessions, Mukutsa's solution—make the abusive husband a member of the Communist Party—yielded a domestic truce for a few months. And then one evening Grigoriy Sergeevich drank more alcohol than his reformed brain could tolerate, began breaking glasses and tableware, and then started screaming accusations at his wife the chief doctor that she was flirting with men in and out of the village. The offended wife slapped his face, dodged his return blow, and ran out of the house, thin braids flying behind. There they go again.

First Secretary Mukutsa had to dig deep down into his bag of Party tricks and try once more. Having been told over the last decade too many details of the intimate life of the hospital's chief doctor, one can only imagine his reaction when she appeared at his door again. His new idea to end the Opryas' domestic abuse? Take advantage of a Wedding Palace that had recently been built in Gradieshti and host a celebration of their tenth year of marriage there. Wedding Palaces satisfied the ambition of the Communist Party to cultivate happy socialist families. They were common in the large cities, but had only recently begun being built in the villages. The good first secretary reasoned that since the husband was now a Communist, such a party-sponsored glorious jubilee in the amazingly new and clean Wedding Palace would be the best way to remind him emphatically of his responsibility to follow the moral principles of Communism. He offered to pay for the occasion and publish pictures of the anniversary celebration in the local newspapers. His one condition: no alcohol. Well, the affair had to be *practically* without alcohol. Only one small glass of vodka would be allowed per person for the entire festivity.

Yes, it turned out to be as foolish as it sounds.

A month later, in mid-September, many guests, including me, were invited to the celebration of the tenth wedding anniversary of Lyubov Evgenyevna and Grigoriy Sergeevich Oprya. We hospital employees arrived at the splendid new Wedding Palace at six o'clock in the evening—an unusual time for traditional Moldovan weddings, which usually started in the morning and ended late at night.

We all stood in front of the Wedding Palace and chatted a bit before seating ourselves for the ceremony, which was taking place outside, since it was summer. Let me hastily inject that the "Wedding Palace" did not in any way resemble a real palace. The collective farming district could only afford a small house with two modest-sized rooms, one for the formal marriage ceremony in colder months, and another for drinks and snacks. Today, a red runner with tassels on the sides ran from the door of the Palace all the way down to a wooden gazebo. On the top of the steep roof of the gazebo was a spire from which fluttered, in all its state-inspired beauty, the red hammer and sickle.

On both sides of the road in front of the magnificent Palace, poles had been thrust into the ground, from which hung boldly-lettered slogans authored, as always, by the chief of the Gradieshti Cultural Center, Valeriu Raylyan, and approved by village Communist Party secretary, Comrade Lupu, who was already here today with us. Raylyan loved to decorate our village with propaganda, not only those sanctioned by the officially endorsed Communist Party list, but also his own earnest, exultant texts reminding hardworking peasants what a joy it was to live and work in this rural Communist paradise.

Today's posters proclaimed a certain theme. Hmm. I wonder if Grigoriy Sergeevich Oprya would get the point.

SOBRIETY IS THE PRIDE OF SOCIETY.

RESPECT YOUR SPOUSE; SHE IS A TREASURE IN YOUR HOUSE.

ALCOHOLISM, ALCOHOLISM KILLS PEOPLE'S ORGANISM.

ALCOHOL FOR EACH OCCASION CAUSES DEATH AND DEGRADATION.

GRISHA OPRYA: VODKA AND WINE BRINGS YOU TO A DISLOYAL SWINE.

COMMUNISTS ARE EXAMPLES OF SOBRIETY; THEY BUILD A HAPPY SOCIETY.

We guests solemnly sat on simple benches in front of the Palace; I joined my friend, surgeon Ilya Sergeevich Petresku, and his wife, Maria Ivanovna. The air was rich in ironic chatter about the soon-to-arrive heroes of the day and the real reason for the celebration. Three cars approached, we quieted down, and out stepped with dignity the secretary of the district committee, Mirtcha Gerasimovich Mukutsa, the hospital's chief doctor and her husband, and the chairman of the *kolkhoz*, Seraphim Mikhailovich Namashko, whose gray, fluffy moustache always reminded me of Stalin.

No, I never told anyone that.

The ceremony started with a short opening speech by the tall and slender Zachary Ionovich Lupu, the local Communist secretary whom, I had discovered, was allergic to handrails. In flourishing cadences while catching the eye of more than one of the young hospital nurses, he spoke about the role of a strong marriage in achieving the heights of Communism by the Soviet people. The heroes of the day then led the participants in single file toward the gazebo, all doing their best to avoid stepping in the Moldovan black dirt threatening to spill over the sides of the red runner. Lyubov Evgenyevna wore a shiny brown dress, low-heel black patent leather shoes, and a white silk scarf over her head, while Grigoriy Sergeevich was dressed in a black raw-silk suit with a flat gray cap on his head.

First Secretary Mirtcha Gerasimovich Mukutsa clearly relished this occasion of his making. "Comrades, we have gathered for a tremendously important occasion," he proclaimed, smiling broadly. "The leading Communist of your village, Doctor Lyubov Oprya, today celebrates a decade of her exemplary marriage to the village epidemiology technician, Grigoriy Sergeevich, of the same last name."

Taking a breath, he got to the real point. "The other reason for our festivity is that this month we are running a district campaign dedicated to the fight against alcoholism in our district. If you want your village to win against the other collective farms, you must uproot drunken feasts! Comrades, drunkenness is the scourge of our society, and our people, led by the Communist Party of the Soviet Union, will fight it until we win the final victory of sobriety in our country!" He pointed toward the road. "The excellent slogans there reflect our iron will to uproot alcoholism from our life. Look at them!

"Comrade Karl Marx and our Communist leader who is dead but miraculously (you would not even believe it) still alive, Vladimir Ilyich Lenin, were never, ever drunk. Our leader, Comrade Nikita Khrushchev, sometimes has a drink—that is true—but he drinks a little and in good company. He knows when to stop and what to eat so he doesn't get drunk. Fulfilling the will of the collective farmers of Gradieshti, after the first toast with a glass of vodka, today our drinks will consist of local water and locally produced grape and apple juices. I predict, comrades, that the entire Moldavian Republic very soon will take up your *kolkhoz's* initiative and will become the first sober republic in the Soviet Union."

The high party official turned his attention back to the happy couple. "Dear bride and chief doctor, Lyubov," he continued, smiling and raising a hand benevolently, "congratulations on your decade of being a faithful married woman. Dear groom, Grisha, we congratulate you not only as the husband of your wonderful wife but also as a Communist, and we wish you many years of sobriety and real respect for your wife. She is the chief doctor at the Gradieshti Hospital, and her husband and employee has no right to offend his wife especially if both of them are Communists. Grigoriy Sergeevich, tell all of us your promise to stop your drinking!"

The single permitted glass of vodka half drained in his hand, Grigoriy Sergeevich stood up. "I solemnly promise not to drink, and not to lay a finger on my wife, even if she annoys me to death," he obediently stated, looking only at the first secretary.

My boss sighed. "I want him to promise it as a real Communist," she asked, not looking at her husband.

"Yes, give us the promise as a real Communist," the secretary of the Communist Party confirmed.

Grigoriy Sergeevich took a sip and nodded. "As a Communist, I promise to love my wife and to pay party dues on time."

Comrade Mukutsa then pulled from the breast pocket of his jacket a sheet of paper, carefully unfolded it, signed it himself, and handed it to the couple.

"Our celebrants," he said, "now will symbolically re-register their marriage, and it is written here that they must respect each other, must not drink alcohol, and must never become violent." He went on, his voice rising to a lecturing thunder, as he sternly looked at husband and wife. "No fists, no pulling of hair, no running after each other! Understood?"

Exchanging amused glances with my surgeon friend, I reckoned that the marriage counseling days of Comrade Mukutsa were officially now in the past.

When the marriage contract was signed by the anniversary spouses and also by selected guests, the wedding party walked from the gazebo to the party room indoors, where an orchestra awaited, complete with fiddle, accordion, trumpet, and drum. Perched on chairs we all began eating and exchanging toasts with glasses filled with local juices.

Surprise, surprise, the tamer beverages did not last long. Guests became bored, disappeared for a short time, and returned with certain additional items, most not well concealed. On the tables, cut-glass decanters with fruit juices and water remained, but underneath revelers began pouring from bottles of wine, vodka, and cognac. As for the high dignitaries, the chauffeurs from their personal cars, who also served as unofficial footmen, stood by to assist with a range of discretely slipped drinks as needed.

As everyone's mood became increasingly cheerier, the anniversary spouses solemnly sat at the head table, accepting congratulations from the assembled guests.

Grigoriy Sergeevich stood up to say his own toast. "*Mulţumesc,* thank you, my dear friends," he said with a slightly faltering and tongue-tied voice, which we had heard too many times before. "I thank also the Communist Party and, personally, dear Nikita Sergeyevich Khrushchev for making me a good Communist and a good husband and father, and for allowing me to live and to breathe. My wonderful wife is the chief physician and she is my boss at work, but as you all know, at home I am the boss. We will never fight again. I will suffer like a dog, but I will not take a drop of alcohol into my mouth. Never again will I be drunk. I raise this toast to peace and understanding in my family!"

Now came Lyubov Evgenyevna's turn to make a toast. Thanking everyone for coming, she unexpectedly turned to her obviously inebriated husband. Addressing him loudly by name and patronymic, in a didactic tone she reminded him of the dangers of alcoholism to their marriage.

Well, this is going to be good. I straightened up and made sure I was sitting near an exit. Across the room, Ilya Sergeevich Petresku winked at me, while his good wife Maria Ivanovna stared at the spectacle, horror growing on her face.

Grigoriy Sergeevich seemed to nod approvingly at his wife's words until his face suddenly turned blood red. Jumping to his feet, he whirled on Secretary Mukutsa and yelled, "You bastard, stop touching my wife! Do you think I am blind or drunk? First you touched her breast, which

I ignored, but now you go for her behind! Just come closer to me. I am going to show you!"

Secretary Mukutsa sat imperturbable, his face expressionless, not even looking at his accuser.

Leaping up, the chief doctor grabbed her husband's arm. "Grisha, dear, please calm down. Nothing happened. I swear to you, I felt nothing," Looking fearfully at the First Secretary, Lyubov Evgenyevna pleaded, her adolescent acne scars now reddening and prominent. "Know before whom you stand!"

Shrugging off her grip, Grigoriy Sergeevich's rage seemed to only grow. "I do not care who he is! He touched you, and I will not forgive him for that! And as for you, Lyubov, you could not feel it because your behind is too fat!" Everyone around me burst out laughing, and the happy husband scowled at the anniversary guests as they began jeering him.

Secretary Mukutsa still remained silent and aloof. He was the representative of the unlimited power of the Communist Party, and the last word belonged to him, if he chose to speak. The tense situation was finally defused by Seraphim Mikhailovich Namashko, who stood on his chair, shaking a fist at the uproar.

"*Ajunge*. Enough. No fights today!" the *kolkhoz* chairman shouted, staring down on us all. "The wedding party will continue! If you do not stop right away, I'll give the order to close all the stores in our village. For vodka and potatoes, matches and kerosene, you will need to go to the city. Is that what you want?"

The seriousness and immediacy of his threat silenced and sobered up the guests, who continued with a more subdued celebration. Grigoriy Sergeevich fell asleep in his chair. His clearly embarrassed wife studiously ignored him, after sparing her husband one sad, disappointed glance.

At midnight, the dry anniversary jubilee ended, and everything and everybody returned to what had been. The men of Gradieshti, supported by their spouses, went home, drunkenly stumbling down the road through a gauntlet of Valeriu Raylyan's posters, still stapled to the long poles. Above them the posters triumphantly extolled the virtues of a very different life. No one believed, and no one looked up.

A listener asks Armenian Radio,
"Is there life on other planets?"

Armenian Radio replies, "On other
planets there is also no life."

Secrets

———⚭———

It did not take me long to grasp that most of the working hours of our hospital's ob-gyn physician, Chief Doctor Lyubov Evgenyevna Oprya, were dedicated to delivering babies and performing abortions. In the 1960s, abortion was the most common method of birth control in the Soviet Union. Despite its full legalization in 1955, difficulties in accessing medical care and the need for secrecy resulted in a significant number of criminal abortions, that is, abortions being performed by unqualified personnel outside of hospitals in outrageously unsanitary conditions. As a medical student, I witnessed many times the consequences of unsafe abortions during my rotation in a unit of criminal abortions at Kishinev Hospital. The beds were full of desperate women mistreated by shady characters (often illiterate women in their homes) who had tried to cause a miscarriage by introducing into the uterus sharp objects such as knitting needles or straightened wire hangers.

Fortunately, it wasn't that way at Gradieshti Hospital. Chief Doctor Oprya was very proud of the efficiency of the abortion procedure that she had perfected over the years. Usually, after the patient entered the procedure room, a nurse gave her an injection of the anesthetic Promedol (a medication similar to morphine). Promedol, like many other items of our hospital pharmacopeia, was always in short supply. Only VIP women were guaranteed to receive the full dose. The majority of patients were given only half or even less, naturally resulting in intense pain during the pregnancy termination procedure. The patient then assumed the appropriate position on the gynecological table. Lyubov Evgenyevna came in, her normal medical attire covered by a big, greenish, oily rubber apron splotched with bloody marks from recent procedures, despite repeated scrubbing. Then, using appropriately sterilized, but not disposable, instruments, she performed the abortion, which took no longer than fifteen minutes.

One of the major complications of abortion is the perforation of the uterus due to previous uterine conditions or to overzealous scraping of its inner surface with a curette. Lyubov Evgenyevna often boasted that she had never perforated a uterus.

The chief doctor liked to share her experiences of performing abortions, never missing an opportunity to tell and show me, as a young physician, the secrets of her mastery of the procedure. I never performed abortions, but the techniques she discussed helped me save the lives of women with uterine bleeding after unsuccessful criminal abortions. Treatment for their life-threatening condition was a D & C (dilation and curettage), essentially the same procedure as for an abortion.

Eventually the day came when my familiarity with the procedure paid off. I was on night duty at the hospital and Chief Doctor Oprya was out of the village. At seven o'clock on a Saturday evening, I was called to the ob-gyn floor to examine a new admission. Pelagea Makaresku was a single, thirty-two-year-old woman who worked on a cattle farm. Lightly built with short, black, curly hair and brown eyes, Pelagea's skin had weathered under the sun into an all-too-familiar dark brown with numerous wrinkles.

A *kolkhoz* car had delivered her to the hospital because she was weak and very tired and could not work. On examination, my patient was slightly pale. She stated that her regular menstrual period had started the day before. Her gynecological status, according to her, was completely normal, and she categorically denied having had any sexual contact for the last year.

The laboratory technician, whose services, fortunately, were available that night, informed me that the patient's hemoglobin level was suspiciously low—10 grams per deciliter. The test for occult blood in the stool was negative. Ruling out all other possible reasons for anemia, it was logical to assume that it had to do with her gynecological status, maybe excessive menstrual bleeding.

Palagea adamantly refused to let me examine her, quickly backing up on the examination table, closing her legs, and shaking her head vehemently. She claimed her menstrual blood loss was no different than usual, and she categorically denied any recent intercourse. Given her refusal and the absence of a laboratory test for pregnancy at that time, all I could do was to continue observing her. And wait.

An hour ticked by, and at midnight, I ordered the hemoglobin test repeated. The reading was one-half unit lower than an hour earlier. My patient was bleeding to death, and I, a recent graduate of medical school, simply did not know what was responsible for it. She wasn't telling me something, and she was dying because of it.

Pelagea spoke only Moldovan, and I wondered if my lack of fluency was preventing me from understanding her completely. I quickly called the maternity department and asked Valentina Stepanovna Vorona, an older, experienced nurse and a native Moldovan speaker who had helped me on several occasions, to assist me with my patient.

Into the night, Palagea's hemoglobin levels continued to decrease. Together, Nurse Vorona and I asked the patient about any history of trauma, and problems with gastrointestinal and gynecological status. She just kept shaking her head and responding in the negative. Her sincere tone and honest face made it impossible for me to doubt her.

What to do? Valentina Stepanovna caught my eye and motioned for me to step out of the patient's room to the corridor.

"Don't you understand, doctor?" she asked, not hiding her surprise. "Somebody performed an unsuccessful abortion on this woman and now she is bleeding after the procedure. What else it could be?"

I just didn't get it. "But she appears to me so honest, so innocent, so genuine, Valentina Stepanovna. Why would she lie if she might pay for her falsehood with her own life?"

The nurse sighed and put her hands on her hips. It was the middle of the night, and we were both tired. "Oh, how naive you are, doctor!" she scolded. "Why can't you understand the simple truth? This woman lies and she will continue to lie until she dies. She has no other choice but to lie. Over the last thirty years working here, I have seen many of these 'sainted maidens.'"

Her tone softening, she went on. "You're not from Gradieshti and do not have any idea how people really live here. She works on the animal farm far from the village. The long distance prevents workers from returning home for months at a time. They sleep there in some kind of primitive dormitory. Performing the same work every day, the people there get bored to death. There are no newspapers, no radio, no books—nothing there to entertain them except nighttime sex. If she tells us the truth, her life will become worse than death. It is not possible to keep such a secret in a village where people live all their life. Here, everybody knows each other, and she has no chance of getting married if people become aware she was sleeping with other men."

I soon understood. My patient knew well that if she voluntarily confessed to me that she was pregnant, that tomorrow everybody in the village would discuss it. Members of her own family would not leave her alone until she told them the identity of the man. If he was married, then some type of violent retribution was likely. If Palagea had lived in a city, she could have easily changed her residence and job. But here she couldn't become invisible. She was unable to leave Gradieshti because she was uneducated and because her passport was forever under lock and key at the village council. Without identity papers, without money, without education, she was chained to this place, and would thus rather die today than confess to the truth.

The nurse explained to me the simple rules of the game. The patient does not confess, and we pretend to not understand what is really going on with her. What we will do, with minimum explanation, is perform an immediate dilation and curettage to stop the bleeding and save her life.

The problem? I had heard the procedure explained, but had never performed it myself. There was no one else around, though, and we could not lose a minute. Valentina Stepanovna left to speak to the patient, prepare the surgical tools, and start a blood transfusion.

Just then, the filaments of the incandescent lamps began flickering and then dimmed. Here we go again. Good ole Soviet electricity, coming through when we needed it most. Eight years before the Soviet Union impressed the entire world with the launching of Sputnik while at the Gradieshti Hospital that night I did not have enough light to save a human life.

As we started lighting kerosene lamps, my wife Marina appeared in the doorway. I was delighted to see her, but, honestly, the last hours of bustle and stress had made me forget that she was visiting that weekend. Quickly explaining to her in a low voice what was going on, I asked her to go home as fast as she could and bring back the textbook on gynecology. She ran home and returned with reference material to refresh my memory while the patient was being preparing for surgery by the nurse and orderly.

We next discovered that the phone had gone dead, again. If despite all precautions I perforated the uterine wall, I now could not rely on outside help.

Soon, I stood in front of Pelagea Makaresku, who lay on the operating table. On the right, separated from me by a small table with surgical instruments, the nurse, Valentina Stepanovna, would assist as needed. To the left, dressed in a sterile gown, mask, and cap, an orderly, Anastasia, was also ready to help. The last member of our operating team was my wife. Marina stood close by in the corridor, holding the textbook on gynecology opened to the pages with a detailed description of the D & C procedure I was about to perform.

Right away, we had a problem—the kerosene lamps were too dim to light the operation. The orderly, Anastasia, grabbed a flashlight and held it over the patient. An injection of Promedol was given to Pelagea, and I approached her with trepidation in my heart. *Please let this be all right.*

"Stop worrying, doctor," Valentina Stepanovna murmured, leaning over the surgical instruments. "A D & C is a very simple procedure. I have assisted Lyubov Evgenyevna during this procedure a hundred times. All that is necessary from you is to be patient and gentle."

Remember your brother's advice—you are the captain of this ship. Driving away unpleasant thoughts of possible horrific consequences, I proceeded to my work.

In the operating room, all was quiet. Retractors were applied. Trying to calm my inner shaking, I dilated the uterine cervix with Hegar devices. The patient was quiet and cooperative. The lights continuing fluctuating in agony, but thanks to the narrow beam of the flashlight held by Anastasia, I could see the inner wall of the vagina. The most important step began: blindly scraping the inner surface of the uterus with a metallic curette.

I needed to be sure. The orderly opened the door to the corridor. In my sterile gown, I read for the umpteenth time the detailed description of the procedure in the textbook held by my wife. Returning to the operating room with a curette in my hand, I very carefully began manipulation. Several tense minutes passed. With animated facial expressions and gestures like Marcel Marceau, Valentina Stepanovna quietly instructed me in the best way to perform each step of the operation. Eventually, I was relieved to hear a specific scraping sound—a sign confirming that the bleeding tissues had been successfully removed. And then, to my joy and incredible relief, the bleeding practically stopped.

Pelagea Makaresku, the first patient on whom I ever performed a D & C, tolerated the procedure well. By the time she was transferred to her hospital bed, thanks to the procedure and a blood transfusion, the color of her face had improved immensely. She fell into a deep, well-deserved sleep.

The next day in the hospital room she shared with seven other patients, I looked down at Palagea, sleeping, and thought about the cost of protecting what, in the end, is all that we really have—our privacy and dignity. Rather than make a confession that could have saved her life, Pelagea had chosen taking her secret to the grave over being humiliated and disgraced. I wondered if I could have done the same.

As I turned to leave, my patient opened her eyes and looked at me. Grabbing my hand, she squeezed it briefly and let go. Neither of us said a word.

A man, about to be executed, is asked for his last wish.

The man says, "I want to become a member of the Communist Party."

"Why?" asks the warden.

"My brother-in-law will be very happy that there is one Communist less."

The Party's Party

———⚭———

It's a Saturday afternoon in late spring, and a small group of us are gathered in front of the main hospital building, awaiting a special departmental car from the Tiraspol Party Committee to pick us up. Chief Doctor Oprya, surgeon Ilya Sergeevich Petresku, gentle *feldsher* Dimitry Onchan, and myself are dressed in our finest, because we are going to a fine party hosted by the Party.

The chief doctor has been ecstatic for weeks because Gradieshti Hospital was awarded the Challenge Red Banner for achievements in the field of public health. In the Communist system, where salaries and bonuses were miserly, high achievements of people or of a collective were acknowledged by a letter of commendation and medals, and by giving the recipients special titles. An award such as the Challenge Red Banner was given only to collectives "for special achievements," and it was transferred annually from one collective to another. Our honor that year coincided with an award given to the entire Tiraspol District for the best public health results in the Moldavian Republic. A special delegation of Communist leaders were coming to Tiraspol from the capital of the republic to participate in the *partsobranie*, the Communist Party meeting, where our ceremony would take place. Party members and non-Party individuals, including me, from Gradieshti Hospital had been invited to join them.

As an ardent Communist, our chief doctor can't stop talking about the award and the upcoming meeting. Only when she mentioned last week in the middle of excited chatter that exotic, hard-to-get food was usually served at party meetings did my friend Ilya Sergeevich decide to also become a proud representative of the hospital. I am eager to go, as I have never attended one of the party meetings. They're one of the primary tools for uniting Communists, for ensuring that they understand what is required to govern party organizations. From youth, I have been very curious to see with my own eyes how this primary mechanism of Soviet rule works.

While we wait, I and Petresku stand off to the side and swap jokes.

"Vladimir, do you know what is the difference between capitalism and socialism?" asks my friend, and then blurts out with a wide smile, "Under capitalism, a man exploits a man, and under socialism, it's the other way around!"

Soon, the red-cheeked, quiet X-ray technician Eugene Rachok joins us for a bit before running off on an errand. Rachok does more listening than telling jokes, but he seems affable enough and laughs with us, his uneven, tobacco-stained decaying teeth on full display. He never comments when I joke but just intently gazes at me, which I interpret as a sign of appreciation.

Above us, another one of Valeriu Raylyan's too-large, glaring signs declares COMMUNISM IS KNOCKING AT OUR DOORS. Beneath the ominous pronouncement, it is in fact we who are knocking Communism. We're doing so in a way common across our enormous country—by telling jokes about it to each other.

Despite the incessant grind of the Soviet propaganda machine, despite the terror and huge numbers of informers seemingly everywhere, the people of our Soviet paradise always fought back through humor. Gradieshti was no different from any other place I lived. In the face of shortages, the heel of totalitarian rule, extreme poverty, and bureaucratic ineptitude, all we could do was mockingly make fun of the utter absurdity of the Communist system. Often the first thing loyal friends did when they met was to tell new political jokes they had just heard. There was even a joke about the danger of telling a joke:

> Two men are placed in the same prison cell. One asks the other why he is in jail.
> "For being too lazy, my friend!"
> "Lazy? Why?"
> "My next door neighbor told me an anti-Soviet joke. It was late in the evening, so I decided to denounce him to the KGB first thing in the morning, but he reported me the same night."

In my experience, nearly everyone repeated or at least had heard of such jokes. (Well, maybe not Chief Doctor Oprya.) Years ago, when I was a medical student in Kishinev, I also served as an emcee for our student talent shows. During one of those amateur events, unknown to us, a major of the KGB was in the audience for a routine political surveillance of what we told and performed on stage. He liked the show so much that he invited our entire collective to perform at the KGB Club located on Lenin Prospect. After a successful performance, we medical students were invited, as was commonly hospitable, to a private room on the second floor for an assortment of good food and soft and alcoholic drinks.

Remembering exactly where I was and with whom I was mingling, I tried to be as quiet as possible. Unexpectedly, in walked the KGB major, resplendent in uniform. One of the medical students, whom I had always suspected of being an informer, immediately joined him. Addressing me by first name, the major asked why, as emcee, I did not tell jokes. Turning to the other students, he offered one of his own:

> During a lecture in the House of Political Education, the lecturer says to the audience, "Comrades, I have great news: Communism is already on the horizon."
> A student raises his hand. "But what is the horizon, comrade lecturer?"
> "The horizon, comrade, is an imaginary line in the sky which is connected to the ground and which is moving away from us as we try to approach it."

The KGB major then turned back to me, expectantly. All he heard was a safe reply—I claimed I didn't know any such jokes to tell.

But, let's face it, I did. My boss at Gradieshti Hospital was always rolling her eyes and chastising me for my humor. I filled my friends' ears full of anti-Soviet jokes. I am sure my passion for them came from my father, who did all he could to make me a free thinker and frequently made cynical remarks about the Soviet rulers in my presence. On the day Stalin died, while a significant part of the country's population was (at least in public) in tears, my father danced and sang behind the closed doors of our house.

So, while we wait for the car from Tiraspol, I honor my father with every joke.

When we arrived at the Communist Party meeting, the Tiraspol city theater was already open. Enormous red slogans, banners, and bows flooded the hall, occupying every available space.

WHO DOES NOT WORK SHALL NOT EAT.

THE WHOLE WORLD WILL BE OURS.

WORK SO THAT COMRADE BREZHNEV WILL THANK YOU.

WHO IS NOT WITH US IS AGAINST US.

IF YOU DO NOT KNOW—LEARN! IF YOU REFUSE—WE WILL FORCE YOU!

IF THE ENEMY DOESN'T SURRENDER, HE WILL BE FINISHED OFF!

Well, I know *I* felt inspired. Because of the special occasion, some of the slogans and posters were dedicated to public health issues. A few have stuck with me over the years.

OUR CHILDREN SHOULD NOT BE SICK WITH DIARRHEA!

SEXUALLY TRANSMITTED DISEASE WILL PUT YOUR LIFE IN A SQUEEZE.

WOMEN, HAVE YOU TAKEN CARE OF YOUR BREASTS? TOUGHEN YOUR NIPPLES BY WASHING THEM WITH COLD WATER DAILY.

On the stage at a large table covered with a red tablecloth sat the presidium, mostly men, doing their very best to look simultaneously solemn, focused, and enlightened.

The meeting began, as was customary, with the singing of the Communist Party anthem, the "International," accompanied by a large military orchestra. The walls of the hall shook in response to the combined sounds of orchestra and the inspired and enthusiastic voices of lots of singing Communists. Everyone gave it their all, with gusto, as one could not rule out the possibility that his or her neighbor could be a potential informer.

A popular joke tells of an inspection commission visiting a mental asylum.

> To greet it, a choir of patients passionately sings lines from the "International":
> "Arise, ye prisoners of starvation! Arise, ye wretched of the earth!"
> But one woman is not singing.
> "Why are you not participating, comrade?" the head of the commission asks her.
> "I'm not crazy," she replies. "I'm a nurse here."

Immediately after the anthem, one of the delegates went up to the podium and, from a piece of paper, read the names of those who were nominated to be in the presidium. First he recommended an honorary presidium consisting of General Secretary Leonid Brezhnev and the rest of the Communist Party Central Committee in Moscow. No one objected to such an imaginary gathering. The delegate then offered an already authorized list of members for the presidium from those who were actually there at the meeting. Again, no objections were voiced, although criticism was officially welcomed. Those present voted unanimously to confirm the list.

As at any other party meeting, the first part was dedicated to eloquent reports on the mind-boggling achievements of the party apparatus in the fields of economy and social life. Such self-praise! Such eternal optimism! So many accomplishments!

Within a short time, the eyes of many around me were drooping, and they began falling asleep. One by one by one. Surgeon Petresku and I grinned at each other; the good chief doctor scowled and didn't look at us.

After an hour and a half, the First Secretary of the District Party Committee, Mirtcha Gerasimovich Mukutsa, stood up with a solemn announcement. "Comrades, now we will be greeted by young Communist pioneers!" With these words, the doors swung open, and to the beat of drums and blare of trumpets, three columns of young pioneers entered the hall. Up each aisle they crisply marched, all dressed in black and white, with red ties around their necks. The columns came to a standstill and the pioneers started their patriotic performance. Each word expressed immeasurable love for the Motherland and the Communist Party and its leaders; and overwhelming determination, should they ever have the "precious opportunity," to give their lives for the final victory of Communism. After twenty minutes, the performance ended with thunderous applause from the now-awakened audience.

When the last of the future martyrs had marched away, Mirtcha Gerasimovich Mukutsa stood up again and began reading his own report, which was the intended centerpiece of the entire meeting. The speech lasted for more than another sleepy hour. The First Secretary spoke about the phenomenal economic achievements in the district, which he illustrated by rattling off a bunch of numbers. A big part of his report was the five-year plan. "Comrades, on your behalf," he shouted, now getting really worked up, "I have promised the Central Committee of the Communist Party that we will achieve the results of the five-year plan in just four years or even sooner!" His pledge was met with approving applause from those still awake.

He then dramatically shifted gears, following the official slogan, "Criticism and self-criticism are the strongest weapons of our party." Self-praise was followed by the condemnation of factors that had prevented successful fulfillment of the promises he had given a year ago. Echoing what was written in newspapers and heard on the radio every day, he blamed the West, and especially the USA, for aggressions and warmongering that forced the USSR to waste its budget on defensive needs and thus prevent the victorious advance of the Soviet people to Communism. He also blamed those Soviet people who still suffered from the vestiges of capitalism. Corruption, bribery, thievery, alcoholism, and a careless attitude toward work hindered the heroic march of the people to the shiny peaks of Shambhala. A final traditional excuse given for another year of poor agricultural production was bad weather.

Although as a Communist my boss *must* have heard those excuses many times before, she nodded eagerly with each pronouncement. Soon it was her time to shine.

After the speeches, Mirtcha Gerasimovich called to the stage those who had received awards for high achievements in public health. Ilya Sergeevich and I leaned forward as our chief doctor approached the stage—

was her husband right? Would her rear be in fact touched (perhaps again) by the First Secretary? Hands clutching the gloriously flowing Challenge Red Banner awarded to our hospital, Lyubov Evgenyevna Oprya started to cry, promising through tears to achieve yet more successes in the near future. As she wept and sputtered, the First Secretary kept his distance.

After many interminable speeches and orgies of applause, at long suffering last the first part of the meeting concluded. As agreed beforehand, we four, led by our boss, raced the mob heading to the second floor for food and drink. Want to know how to guarantee excellent attendance at Community Party meetings? Feed 'em food they hardly ever saw in grocery stores—red and black caviar, lox, special kinds of sausages and fish, instant coffee, and such impossible-to-find goods as bananas, pineapples, oranges, and Bulgarian grapes.

Our astonished satisfaction at the array of eats reminds me of a popular joke about an ordinary woman who walks into a Russian food store.

"Do you have any meat?" she asks the grocer.

"No, we don't."

"What about milk?"

"Comrade, we deal only with meat here. Across the street there is a store where they have no milk."

After devouring dazzling, exotic food, we returned to our seats for the second half of the meeting. Professional musicians opened with patriotic songs and poems. Mayakovsky's poem "My Soviet Passport" was performed with such melodrama that the audience rose to its feet.

Two more never-ending speeches, and then something fascinating happened. The party meeting became a tool for settling accounts among the Communists themselves. The first part of the speech of the Third Deputy of the District Party Committee rehearsed a bland litany of economic and propaganda issues. But then the audience began waking up.

From a script prepared in advance, the speaker began throwing a torrent of accusations against the Second Deputy, charging him with immoral behavior, including alcoholism, womanizing, and neglect of official duties. Nearly bursting, the Second Deputy tried repeatedly to stand and defend himself, but was stopped every time by the First Secretary and the members of the presidium before uttering a single word.

I didn't dare look at my boss.

"Comrade Pilipenko!" yelled the Third Deputy, pointing at the accused, "We know all about *you*. Do not think that the party is blind! Our party has ears and eyes! Communists who know you personally complain that you come to work drunk and that you are on your way to becoming a real alcoholic. You, a married man, must be ashamed that you use your position to force women to please you with lewd, bourgeois behavior. Even more unforgivable is the recent news that you have an illegitimate child, which you have hidden from the eyes of the party all this time. How are you going to respond to these undeniable facts?"

Finally allowed to speak, the Second Deputy leaped up and cried, "It is *you* who are an alcoholic! I never drank at work, but you did! Instead of throwing vile accusations against me, you'd better prove it." The accused turned to the presidium, gaining some composure and confidence. "If you think I will be fired from my position and you are going to assume my job, let me assure you, I have high connections too. And stop your lies—I never had an illegitimate child. Prove it first!"

"Oh, you want proof? We will show you the truth," the Third Deputy shot back in a prosecutorial manner, nodding indignantly. "You can hide nothing from the all-seeing eye of the Communist Party. Let the innocent casualty of your bourgeois carnal pleasures step in."

The back door of the hall opened wide and a woman rushed in past us, clutching a baby about a year old in her arms. Everyone gasped. While the baby howled, the young mother raised one hand and pointed an accusatory finger at the Second Deputy. In a dramatic voice, loud and clear for everybody to hear, she leveled her verdict. "Andrey, you are the father of this child, and you will never go away from us! You betrayed me and you betrayed your own child!"

"Lies, lies!!! Comrades, believe me," the deputy shrieked, "I swear to you on my mother's grave this is the first time I've ever seen this woman." He ran towards the mother, hands gesturing wildly while sweat poured down his face. "The child is not mine. Look at him. He does not look like me at all. This is a conspiracy against me!"

Suddenly, well beyond the point of no return, we from little Gradieshti were remembered. Jumping quickly to his feet, the usually unruffled First Secretary swore and stared at us, clearly shocked. Beckoning frantically to assistants, he loudly yelled, "All the guests should leave this meeting, and I recommend that you forget what you just saw and heard!"

All of us were completely silent on the ride back to Gradieshti. I and the *feldsher*, Dimitry Onchan, found much to interest us in the surrounding countryside, although we were speeding through the middle of the night. For his part, surgeon Petresku also kept quiet, although he couldn't help stealing a few smug glances at his rival, who sat motionless, head down and arms wrapped around the prize.

The driver stopped the car in front of the gates of our hospital. The chief doctor still did not move. Awkwardly, we disembarked and waited. After a minute, the chief doctor sighed heavily and then got out of the car with great dignity, the Challenge Red Banner clutched tightly. Holding it out and up before her, the proud Communist began marching resolutely across the hospital grounds. We medical martyrs glanced at each other and, without a word, fell into line behind.

A Communist is a person who read *Das Kapital*.
An anti-Communist is a person who read
Das Kapital and understood it.

The Longest Shortest
Parade in the Soviet Union

———— ❧ ————

One morning, Comrade Zachary Ionovich Lupu sprang up out of bed with an amazing idea. The local party secretary immediately ordered his chauffeur to drive him to the hospital so that he could share it with the rest of us.

It was about two weeks before May Day, 1967. A handful of physicians were in the doctors' lounge, filling out patient charts and chatting about our plans for the upcoming socialist holiday. Unlike the urban areas in the Soviet Union, there were only rarely walking demonstrations—parades—to commemorate May Day in small villages like Gradieshti. Usually a small public assembly of some type occurred, followed by parties with relatives and friends. I intended to forego such festivities and visit my wife, Marina, in Odessa over the holiday.

Not so fast, Vladimir.

Stepping purposely into the lounge with a broad smile on his thin face, Lupu came to a halt in front of our chief doctor. Flustered, she stood up quickly.

"What is wrong, comrade?"

Still smiling, the secretary motioned her to sit down. "Lyubov Evgenyevna," he announced grandly, opening his arms to take in the rest of us, who by now had stopped writing and were watching curiously.

"I gave a pledge that this year we are going to have a demonstration on May Day like in the city. Instead of a rally, we are going to have a real demonstration of *kolkhozniks* and intelligentsia in the center of our village. All members of your collective must be involved, Oprya—no exclusions. That's an order." He stared down at her, and grew serious. "We *will* celebrate the holiday with dignity and excitement!"

We found out later that Lupu wanted the administrators in Gradieshti, including us, to participate in a May Day parade in order to impress the new Communist boss in the district. The problem? None of us had ever organized or marched in a village parade before.

Yeah, this was going to be a good idea.

"Your hospital," the secretary continued, addressing all of us in the doctors' lounge, "should be an example of good preparation and exemplary discipline. I brought you instructions from the district as well as the slogans, posters, and flags that your collective is required to carry during the demonstration. Can I rely on you?"

The chief doctor's jaw dropped and moved silently for a moment before we heard words. "But Comrade Lupu," she finally gasped, "we were both born in this village, and we have never had such demonstrations here. I have no idea how to organize this event. It is totally unplanned. I have thousands of other things to do!"

"Do not even start your baby talk, Oprya," Lupu snapped, his suddenly sharp tone all too familiar. "Our *kolkhoz* is one of the best in the district, and we should set an example for everyone of our devotion to the spirit of May Day!"

"But there's only two weeks left, Comrade Lupu. I do not even know where to start!" At this point, I became concerned for the skyrocketing blood pressure of my boss.

"You are probably not serious, Lyubov," the secretary of the local party replied, a little less harshly. "Are you a mature Communist or a peasant woman? You ought to know what to do without additional explanation. Do not worry—the District Party Committee and I, personally, will help your organization."

Deciding the conversation was over, he turned smartly and walked away, taking with him our holiday plans. All a very worried chief doctor could do was stare at his tall, thin retreating back.

The grand preparations for Gradieshti's first ever parade started the next day. We brainstormed ideas and began preparing propaganda material on the hospital grounds. A truck from the District Communist Party office brought us piles of bellicose slogans and posters, all dutifully authorized, of course.

"Comrades, employees," Lyubov Evgenyevna addressed us at the next morning briefing session, "everybody should be ready to celebrate May Day. Everybody must be on time at the center of the village behind the office of the *selsoviet* (village council) at eleven o'clock sharp."

The chief doctor stood up tall on her short legs, and looked at us sternly. "I am personally responsible. So if somebody does not show up, expect a reprimand in your labor book." In the Soviet Union, each worker had a labor book where all the pleasant and unpleasant information about his or her working activity was recorded.

Not at all happy at being forced to cancel our holiday plans at the last minute, my coworkers began shaking their heads and muttering to each other. Someone even complained out loud that they had planned long ago to attend a niece's wedding in Soroki.

Chief Doctor Oprya would have none of it. "OK," she spat. "*You* want to attend a wedding, and because of *you* I will receive a reprimand from the party? Is that what you want?"

None of us dared to look at her at that particular moment.

"No exclusions. Each collective will be controlled by appointment to make sure we have excellent attendance. Is this clear?"

Taking our silence as affirmation, she went on to the next order of business.

On the morning of May Day, our medical personnel gathered—right at eleven o'clock of course—at the required location, which was an open space behind and next to the village council building. It was a pleasant morning. Nature was waking up after a long winter, the sun was bright, and a gentle wind caressed all who were participating on a voluntary-compulsory basis. Having two weeks to get used to the idea, people seemed to be in a festive mood. Everybody was dressed in their best clothes; some carried flowers from their own gardens. Red flags, slogans, and flowers covered a temporary podium in front of the village council building, from which the dignitaries would view our parade.

Above us in every direction hung the new, colorful fruits of Valeriu Raylyan's creative mind, all soon to become propaganda classics.

REMEMBER THE COMMUNIST PARTY LINE. DO NOT DRINK TOO MUCH WINE.

STOP ABUSING YOUR WIFE, YOU MIGHT NEED HER FOR BETTER QUALITY OF LIFE.

MOONSHINE AND WINE WILL TURN YOU INTO A SWINE.

Although busy organizing us demonstrators, Lyubov Evgenyevna Oprya could not resist pointing out the last sign to her husband.

Smoke-spewing *kolkhoz* trucks squealed into the square, bringing people from the far corners of the village. Some I had never met before— workers from animal and poultry farms, drivers and technical personnel who serviced agricultural equipment, and clerks from every obscure office. The largest column was made up of Gradieshti middle-school students. Judging by the number of us there, I assumed the celebration was not supposed to last long.

It was time to assemble and march. Some of the participants had seen enough May Day parades on television to figure out a rudimentary formation and marching sequence that seemed to make sense.

Next to the podium, ten musicians from the village amateur orchestra began loudly playing wind, brass, and percussion instruments. A recognizable tune didn't escape their cacophony, but nobody cared. Most important for us was the mobilizing beat, produced by a middle-aged man who enthusiastically banged on a drum and by his son who loudly crashed cymbals, one against the other.

On a sign given by an organizer, we shuffled forward, coming first around the corner of the village council building and then advancing slowly toward the podium. Everything was going well. The advanced technology of the *kolkhoz* led our parade: three tractors, a combine, and two trucks smothered with portraits of Lenin, Marx, Engels, and current members of the Politburo. Some residents walked behind the *kolkhoz* vehicles.

Behind them was a large truck towing a flatbed from the animal farm. Two exemplary cows stood on the platform of the flatbed, chewing their cuds with almost revolutionary enthusiasm and passively staring ahead. The cows were being groomed by three peasants. Slogans were attached

to both sides of the flatbed, one of which read, MILK AND NATURAL
FERTILIZERS HELP ACHIEVE HIGH COMMUNIST GOALS.

Our hospital's moving display was next. Dressed in a new, white,
starched doctor's gown, Lyubov Evgenyevna Oprya, with a very large
portrait of Lenin in her hands, marched proudly in front of a truck.
In the bed of the truck was a display designed personally by the chief
doctor. Her husband, Grigoriy Sergeevich, lay covered by sheets on a
firmly attached gurney. Next to him bustled two nurses, pretending
to perform a medical procedure, and each carrying big syringes with
long needles. With stethoscopes around their necks, they listened to his
chest. An IV infusion had been set up next to Grigoriy Sergeevich. The
sides of the medical truck were decorated with slogans calling for the
further success of public health in the name of the future paradise on
Earth—Communism.

I and the rest of our hospital delegation slowly followed the truck.
Behind us swarmed the middle-school youngsters, bringing up the rear
of the parade.

Soon the parade of glorious farm vehicles, cows, and pseudo-patient
reached the podium, where sat the deputy secretary of the district party
committee, the chairman of the *kolkhoz*, the secretary of the local party
organization, and two agriculture foremen. Judging by the oily glances
and smiles glued to their faces, it was clear that those on the podium
were not sober. They greeted the demonstrators with raised hands and
shouted the names of people they recognized marching. Those in our
parade eagerly shouted and waved back.

"Cordial greetings to Communist Lyubov Evgenyevna!" Comrade
Lupu yelled, as she and her enormous Lenin poster passed in front of
the podium.

"Happy holidays! Long live May Day!" Lyubov Evgenyevna screamed
in delighted response.

"Long live May Day!" the people on the podium shouted back to her.

Grigoriy Sergeevich suddenly decided to slip out from under the
sheets and stand up. Ignoring the nurses' pleading to get back in bed, he
lifted his hand and hollered at one of the foremen on the podium.

"*Buna diminyatsa.* Good morning, Gutzu!"

"Good morning, Grisha!" yelled back his friend.

"Look, Gutzu, what I have!" Grigoriy Sergeevich bragged, pulling a bottle of moonshine from under a pillow on the gurney. "It is still full, my friend!"

"Be quiet, Grishka. I have more than you," answered the foremen, laughing. "Come over here as soon as the demonstration is over. We'll have fun!"

"Grigoriy Sergeevich!" his wife and boss, fully turned around and now walking backwards, was furious. "Immediately lie back down on the gurney and stay quiet there. Have you forgotten that this is a demonstration and you are not at home?"

Under public pressure, Grigoriy Sergeevich submissively returned to the gurney and crawled under the sheet, not forgetting to tuck his precious drink carefully back under the pillow.

We reached the other side of the square, as the middle-school students filed past the podium, thus concluding the magnificent May Day parade.

Well, that took five minutes.

Shrugging our shoulders, my friend Petresku and I took one long look around and then began walking away.

"Stay where you are!" our chief doctor shrieked.

She and the other organizers frantically gestured for us to circle around the village council building and begin the parade again. And so we did, passing the podium one more time while the inebriated representatives waved and called out as if they were seeing us for the first time. During my school years, I had participated twice in the same trick, called "carousel," to create the illusion of great attendance at a political demonstration. After we circled the building and passed the podium for a third time, I am sure the members of the presidium on the podium had become convinced that the village of Gradieshti boasted an unusually good attendance at the May Day celebration.

We gave up after three times. The marchers were tired from walking, the exhaust smoke was heavy and stank, and the bowels of the exemplary cows had become restless.

The good people of Gradieshti were not ready just yet to end their May Day celebration. Many began dancing Moldovan folk dances in the square, accompanied by the ragged orchestra. Some women were dressed in beautiful, colorful, traditional clothing. The dancers moved slowly in rounds, soon raising a fog of dust with their shoes.

Eventually, the celebration ended, and I walked over to the car with the other hospital staff. Our driver was passed out behind the steering wheel, and the interior reeked of alcohol. It was impossible to wake him up, so our group trudged back to the hospital on foot, kicking up dust on the road.

Our clever little carousel worked, well enough. Pictures from the event in Gradieshti were printed in local newspapers. The district party committee named us the best rural-area May Day demonstration. It also gives me immense pleasure to report that Comrade Lupu was awarded a free voucher for him and his wife to visit a resort in the Georgian Republic, where they could spend a month drinking mineral water and taking mud baths to strengthen their precious health. Even better, *kolkhoz* Chairman Namashko, who had just returned from a resort in Odessa, received a generous monetary bonus.

As for the rest of us, we woke up the next day and just went back to work. In scorching fields, poorly lit examination rooms, and offices buried by bureaucracy, we all rejoined another parade, in unending carousel, passing in front of the watchful eyes of the Socialist Motherland.

In a Soviet school, a teacher asks a
student, "Who is your father?"

"Stalin!" the child eagerly replies.

Who is your mother?"

"The Soviet Union."

"And whom do you want to become?"

"An orphan."

How Much Do You *Really* Want That Vacation, Vladimir?

——— ⚜ ———

I t seemed so blissfully simple and straightforward that morning—one last item, practically an afterthought, brought up at the end of a daily briefing session around the middle of August, 1966.

By that point in the briefing, we had all become thoroughly alarmed and unconvinced. Lyubov Evgenyevna Oprya had just concluded sharing news from the Rural District Hospital in Slobodzeya that the only plant in the country manufacturing penicillin would cease production due to a major renovation. Many of us exchanged startled glances. Penicillin was the most important of the seven antibiotics stocked at the hospital pharmacy at that time.

The chief doctor waved away our concern. "Comrades, whatever happens, happens for the good. I know how you doctors feel. Do not forget that I am one of you. I also at first started to worry how I would treat my patients without penicillin, but then I realized that—taking into account that this antibiotic was used for a long time—we can assume that many germs have developed resistance to penicillin, and therefore penicillin is not as effective as it used to be against them." She shrugged, ignoring the palatable apprehension. "So this is nothing terrible. We are going to replace penicillin with even more effective antibiotics."

Our surgeon cleared his throat. "You might not worry, but I am quite worried. How am I going to treat my patients for the surgical infections I always treat with penicillin?" His question was full of undisguised dismay.

She sighed, loudly, seeing the issue simply as the beginning of another jousting match with the surgeon. "It is a totally irrelevant question, Ilya Sergeevich," the chief doctor retorted. "I am trying to inform you what I was told officially at the district hospital. If you are not satisfied with my explanation, go and talk to the authorities yourself. You probably do not realize that mankind survived without penicillin for millions of years and nothing extraordinary happened. Period."

Her concluding tone encouraged some to stand up, thinking that the morning session had finished. But then the chief doctor took an envelope from her purse. As everyone quickly sat back down, she read a letter from the District Committee of the Party, offering an opportunity to one person from our collective to go on a cruise in the Mediterranean.

"Comrades, I never saw anything of this kind. This unusual two-week cruise will take place this coming October. To tell you the truth," she confessed, smiling slightly, "I would go there myself with pleasure—it would give me a good rest from my beloved husband—but I cannot because my cousin's wedding is during that time. Her groom is an Army officer, and it is impossible to change the date."

Now taking no notice of the frown from her treasured spouse, she looked around the room. "So who wants to use this opportunity? Whoever decides to take this offer should spend for this pleasure about four hundred rubles," she said with an ironic smile, clearly not expecting anybody to volunteer.

Shocked and silent, we just looked back at her. Never in the history of the village had anybody ever gone abroad. The people present had grown up during the Stalin years, and they knew they might be punished just for expressing slight interest in crossing the border to the West. For me, I was younger than most there and soaked through with blind optimism. I had read books about Italy and Greece, and dreamed of one day visiting those legendary countries. As any enlightened member of Soviet society, I regularly listened in secret to "Voice of America" and could not wait to see whether their claims about the West were true. At least once in my lifetime, I wanted to see how people lived on the other side of the Iron Curtain. I fidgeted and quickly thought.

Could I afford the cruise? Marina and I had been saving money for a television set and furniture for a couple of years. The package was only for one, but I knew Marina would generously not object to my traveling alone. I reasoned that when she started working after school, then it would be her turn to go abroad, with my financial support.

Raising my hand, I resolutely offered myself as a tourist.

"Put down your hand, Vladimir Abramovich," Lyubov Evgenyevna answered tenderly, maternally shaking her head. "I do not think you are making the right decision. You are a young specialist. The children of our village need you here, not somewhere on a ship."

"But I am entitled to my two-week vacation, so I will use those days," I objected softly but firmly.

Everyone was quiet, as we stared at each other. Finally, the chief doctor nodded. "All right. It is your decision."

Marina enthusiastically approved my decision, and the slow, painful swallowing by the maw of Soviet bureaucracy began. Looking back, it's clear that we were so naive. But never having traveled abroad before, how could we know that anybody—unless they belonged to the ruling class—who expressed a desire to go voluntarily through the gates of the Soviet Garden of Eden into the capitalist world needed to endure prolonged bureaucratic scrutiny first?

The cruise would take place in seven weeks, so I needed to make the arrangements right away. My descent began with a visit on a day off to what functioned as a tourist agency—the *raikom*, the District Party Committee in Tiraspol.

A petty party functionary, a humorless woman in her fifties, dressed in a crisply pressed white blouse and black skirt, sat stiffly at the desk in the waiting area. I handed her the paper given to me by my boss. She stared at it for a moment, and then intently looked up.

"Why do you want to travel, young man?" she asked, still expressionless but now with a tinge of suspicion.

"Just for leisure, comrade," I assured her, trying to smile and sound casual. "For nothing else. I have never been on a ship before."

"Then why, instead of going to the Crimea or the Caucasus, have you decided to go to the capitalist world which is so hostile to us?" demanded the woman, shaking her head and thrusting in my hands a large envelope bulging with forms.

"To tell you the truth, comrade secretary, I want to witness with my own eyes how the global crisis of capitalism looks and once again to prove to myself how happy I am to be a citizen of the Soviet Union." *Too smooth, too smooth, Vladimir.*

She didn't take the bait and kept meeting my eyes, watching closely. "This is, of course, commendable. But if you are an informed and knowledgeable member of our society, do you really need to see something that is self-evident?"

"You are absolutely right, but I also want the opportunity to support my assertions with specific facts when, on my return, I meet my friends and tell them about the dark side of capitalist society. I am sure that this way I will be much more effective in telling the truth about the rotten West." By now, condemned to follow my own reasoning, I was afraid to look away.

"Maybe you have a point," the woman replied, nodding slightly, her posture as stiff as ever, "but I still cannot understand why you do not first take advantage of our immense and beautiful country."

"Oh, I cannot wait to do that in the future," I promised, digging into my pocket "but now allow me to pay for the ticket for the cruise."

Putting her right hand up, she shook her head. "You are too fast, comrade. First of all, you need to receive permission from the *raikom*, so fill out all the papers in the package I have given you."

There were so many forms stuffed in there, I could barely hold on to the envelope. "But the cruise starts in October," I pressed, "so I have only seven weeks for the paperwork and the hearing."

"I am sure you will meet all the requirements on time. And now you may go," the woman turned back to her work, severing our conversation.

Over the next few days, all my spare time was dedicated to filling out in pen two copies of the *objectivka*—an enormously lengthy and detailed form. I had to answer questions about my past, my parents, my late grandparents, and even neighbors and friends. I was asked whether I participated in the Great October Revolution, ever served in the White Army, was in the occupied territory during the First and Second World Wars, was ever surrounded by the enemy, or fought in partisan units.

Late into the night, I worked on that damn form, determined to see it through. Eventually, after sharing every minutia of my existence, I was able to answer all the questions in the questionnaire. Now, round two of the horror commenced. I had to obtain a recommendation letter from my employer.

As usual, she was at her desk, filling out a patient's chart. "Lyubov Evgenyevna," I said, trying to hide my trepidation, as she despised new forms, "I need you to sign a recommendation for the cruise." I handed her the paperwork.

Looking up at me, the chief doctor did not take the form. "Vladimir Abramovich, it was your decision, not mine, to express your desire to go abroad. I cannot just all of a sudden, without rhyme or reason, sign this document on my own." She began shaking her head vigorously. "This is too serious a thing! Are you kidding? I do not want to be responsible for your reckless decision."

"But Lyubov Evgenyevna," I replied, trying to keep my tone calm and reasonable. "I have worked with you two years already. You've praised the quality of my work on several occasions, and I received a commendation from the District Hospital. Do you suspect I will run away from the country where my wife and my parents live? I like the country where I was born, and I am not privy to any state secrets."

A popular joke leaped unbidden to my lips, but I suppressed it, fast.

What do you call a Soviet quartet that goes abroad?
A trio.

"I am not thinking anything of the sort," she answered, slight amusement flashing briefly across her wide face. "I am concerned," she went on, seriously, "that on the cruise, where you will be representing our community and Gradieshti Hospital, you might tell—as you periodically do—inappropriate jokes, many of which I do not understand. You might not appreciate it, but the honor of our team is very important to me!"

I couldn't help it, and rolled my eyes. "You think the entire world has nothing better to do than to worry about the honor of Gradieshti Hospital in Moldova, consisting of 50 beds, two sheds, and a horse stable?"

The chief doctor didn't react to my quip. "I do not know what you are talking about. That's enough. Let's hear the voice of our collective during the morning session."

Oh, great.

The next day, when the morning briefing session was almost over, I reminded her about the recommendation.

"Oh, I thought you would forget about that," shrugged Lyubov Evgenyevna, turning to the group. "OK, comrades, our pediatrician, Doctor Tsesis—you know him well by now—is asking us to give him an official recommendation to allow him to go on a luxury cruise to the Mediterranean. Are we going to give him this recommendation or not? Personally—and this is my opinion—I feel he will learn much more if he travels in Moldova or Ukraine instead of going somewhere where nobody knows who he is. What is the opinion of the collective?"

The first raised hand was that of my friend, the surgeon Ilya Sergeevich, who was sure to oppose anything that his lifelong rival favored.

"Oh, come on, Lyubov, let him go," he said genially. "He is young; let him see the world! When he comes back, he will work even better because he will be rested and happy to be here."

"What kind of nonsense are you talking, Ilya Sergeevich?" the chief doctor countered. "Have you thought about the possible consequences?"

For the umpteenth time, their eyes clashed. "I've thought about the possible consequences, and I am ready to vote in favor of a recommendation for the trip by our pediatrician."

"Let me have a word," the hospital's horse groom quickly injected, raising his hand and glaring at me. "Is this doctor better than everybody else here? Why should he go and not I? If he earns too much money and does not know how to spend it, let him share it with me. I suggest that he treats children in our village instead of traveling who knows where."

"He deserves to have all the money he has," my nurse, Svetlana Dogaru, interrupted, coming to my defense. "Why do you make such a fuss? He has a right to spend his money as he wants. Stop your envy!"

"So what?" the hospital driver, Kirill Zandelov, jumped in, loudly. "I had a chance to visit his apartment. Let me tell you, this man is only with us two years, but his apartment has something like a kitchen, wooden floors all over, and running water. All this for only one person! He has enough luxuries here. Why should he go somewhere else?"

Thanks a lot, Kirill.

"You, Kirill, shut up," snapped the gynecological nurse, Magda Petrinesku, who lately had become one of his lovers. "I have told you a hundred times not to poke your nose into other people's affairs!"

"I do not," answered Kirill, visibly annoyed and shifting in his chair away from her, "and I do not envy anybody. I just fight for social justice, that's all."

"If you fight for justice, you better come on time to pick me up, understand?" snapped Magda, leaning toward the driver and preparing to launch into a tirade of complaints.

"Stop resolving your personal issues, comrades!" The chief doctor's reprimand carried effectively over the squabble. "It's late and we need to finish the meeting, so let's make it short."

"Wait, wait. I want to say something," announced the usually quiet Eugene Rachok, the red-faced X-ray technician. "If this doctor wants to go, let him go. I do not mind voting in favor of a recommendation, but for the record, I am not responsible if he betrays our Motherland."

"He will not betray your Motherland," Ilya Sergeevich muttered, shaking his head. "He is too young and naive for that. Stop all this ridiculous discussion. A patient is waiting for me in the operating room."

The chief doctor as usual pretended not to hear the surgeon. "What do you say, Vladimir Abramovich? Will you betray our dear Motherland?" Everyone turned to look at me.

"Of course not. I will betray neither Motherland nor Fatherland. I promise to be good and politically correct. I will not even get close to foreigners. I do not know any foreign languages anyway. If somebody forces me to speak to them during the cruise, I will tell them how we enjoy our free medicine here or I simply might pretend that I cannot hear or talk." I paused, and looked out at some still skeptical faces.

Hmm . . .

"Do not forget comrades that I will bring travel souvenirs for each of you," I hastily added, to smiles and nods.

"OK. If nobody objects, I will sign the recommendation," announced Lyubov Evgenyevna decisively. As she wrote on the form, she couldn't help but add, "I do not think that the District Party Committee will be as indulgent as our collective. I know that if somebody is going to visit a capitalist country, they prefer to send someone who is older than you and who belongs to the party."

With the recommendation in my pocket, I went to the hospital internist, Maria Shtefanovna, for a medical checkup. She thoroughly examined me, but then made it clear that I needed to go to the Tiraspol city hospital to have blood, urine, and X-ray tests, which were also required for the travel. Oh, well, I was going to Tiraspol anyway for the ten photos required by the *raicom*.

It took some searching, but I finally found a photographic studio in the center of the city.

"Why do you need so many photos, young man?" the photographer quietly asked me.

"These pictures are required for a cruise to the Mediterranean."

Putting down his camera, he stared at me, surprised. "Are you kidding? To the Mediterranean? That's very far! Are they going to let you go there? Are you one of ours?"

"Yes, I am Jewish, how do you know?" I replied, a little defensively.

"The same way you know I am Jewish—by your profile." He gestured at his face. "Do not forget that I am a photographer. That's all I do—look at human faces." He picked up the camera, and then shook his head and set it down, again. "Listen to my advice. I am an honest man, and I do not want to take your money for what you do not need. They will never let you go abroad."

"Why do you think that?"

"'Why, why?' If at your age you still do not know why, it is not for me to explain such simple things to you."

"But I at least want to try. Please, take my picture."

"You *really* want to try? You know the people's saying: *Odna poprobovala, semerich rodila.* 'One lady just tried and gave birth to sextuplets.'" Shrugging, he picked up the camera. "OK, look at the lens. The pictures will be available tomorrow." The photographer clicked the shutter.

Finally, a week later, armed with the recommendation from my hospital, the physician's statement confirming my health, and ten photos, I made my way back to the city and to the Tiraspol District Communist Committee again. Now, I had been told, I needed an appointment with the First Secretary, whose permission to go on a commercial cruise was required.

The secretary of the First Secretary, a middle-aged woman wearing carefully applied makeup, sat behind a big table in her boss's waiting room, typing rapidly.

"Sit down, comrade," she offered, not looking in my direction.

To wait in the Soviet Union is as natural as it is in the West not to wait, so I sat and read a book that I had brought along for that very purpose. Three-quarters of an hour of typing flurry passed, and then a stern voice interrupted my reading.

"What do you want, comrade?" she asked coldly, looking through me.

"Comrade Secretary, my hospital's collective gave me a letter of recommendation to go on a cruise trip, and I have come now to receive permission from you to go there," I replied in a subdued respectful tone, handing her the ridiculously thick packet containing every document, all completed and approved.

The secretary shuffled the papers, making sure all the necessary forms were there, sniffled, tossed them in a drawer, and then curtly remarked without looking at me, "Good. You may go now."

"Does this mean I will receive permission to go to the Mediterranean?" I chose each word very carefully, trying not to offend this touchy and overworked servant of the people.

"You may come back here in ten days," she curtly replied. "Then you will be informed of the decision. But now you may go," the secretary of the First Secretary resumed the keyboard attack on her typewriter.

Time was running out until the cruise. Ten long days later, I stood in front of the same maniacally typing secretary. Finally, the woman paused briefly—she could not find the necessary page. I took advantage of this delay to approach and, with the tone of a meek lamb, inquired whether my recommendation had been approved.

"Your name, comrade?" she demanded.

"Tsesis."

"Let me look." She pulled out of the same drawer the same overly stuffed envelope I had given her over a week ago. "Yes, we do have your papers, but the decision about your trip has not been reached yet."

I couldn't take my eyes off of the envelope. "How come?"

"How would I know?" she snapped. "*I* am just a secretary of the Secretary here, and *I* am telling you what *I* was asked to tell. Come here in ten days at ten o'clock in the morning, sharp."

"But then it will be too late for the trip, Comrade Secretary of the Secretary," I protested.

"I have no time to talk with you!" she barked, turning back to the typewriter. "See you in ten days. Have a nice day."

Giving up, I turned to leave. Suddenly, the door of the reception room opened and through it walked the chairman of our *kolkhoz* (and Stalin look-alike), Seraphim Mikhailovich Namashko. He knew me, as I had treated him at the hospital after his unfortunate fall and had attended to his daughter Natasha on more than one occasion. After the first time we had met, he had complimented my work to the hospital's chief doctor, but had also mentioned that he was surprised that I was so serious and not smiling when we had spoken. "Keep in mind," Chief Doctor Oprya had whispered to me, "that the *kolkhoz* chairman gives more credence— I do not know why—to those who smile. I do it all the time for him."

Needless to say, despite my inner turmoil, I greeted the esteemed chairman with a broad smile.

Seraphim Mikhailovich was in good mood. "Hey, doctor, what are you doing here? You should be in Gradieshti taking care of sick children," he said, affably.

I explained the near-hopeless situation to him. "You are lucky," he exclaimed, slapping me on the shoulder. "I came here to see Mirtcha Gerasimovich Mukutsa, my personal friend. Come with me, I will introduce you."

The secretary stopped typing and stood up, pointing at me with obvious disgust. "Comrade Mukutsa is too busy today to have an unexpected visitor. He is waiting for *you*, Comrade Namashko, but not for *that* man."

The chairman would have none of it. "Don't be nervous, comrade," he assured the bristling woman. "I am a good friend of your boss, and he will not mind if I bring another person with me."

The receptionist gave up, and in a minute we were ushered into a sacred place, the site of many marriage counseling sessions with my boss, the grand office of the First Secretary of the Tiraspol Communist Party Committee.

The Secretary was sitting on a leather chair behind a massive desk with three phones in front of him. After both men exchanged handshakes and warm greetings, the chairman of the kolkhoz introduced me.

"Listen, Mirtcha Gerasimovich, this is our village pediatrician. He is a good guy. Takes good care of my daughter. Can you help him?"

"What's the problem?"

"Actually, it's not a problem." Seraphim Mikhailovich answered, stroking his thick, gray moustache. "This guy wants to go to the Mediterranean for two weeks. He will give you no trouble. Nobody else in my *kolkhoz* wants to go there anyway. They do not even know what the Mediterranean is. Don't worry—although he is Jewish, he is a good fellow."

Comrade Mukutsa nodded and punched the intercom on the desk. "Bring me the Tsesis file," he demanded in a commanding voice that sounded like he was a movie actor playing a role of professional revolutionary.

I promise you, I most promptly suppressed a giggle way down deep.

"Believe me, Seraphim Mikhailovich," continued the First Secretary, after reading my file, "I would be happy to sign Tsesis's papers, but I cannot do it. I have a special directive to provide these types of vouchers exclusively to local cadres."

"But I am local cadres," I broke in, speaking politely and still smiling for the chairman, "I was born here. I finished school and then medical school in this republic."

"Yes, I understand," he replied, patiently, "but you know that according to our official affirmative action program, the party requires us to give priority to people of Moldovan nationality. They are the majority in our republic, and they should be the first, right?"

"So I have no chance?" I asked, softly.

"Why be so pessimistic? Let me call the capital and speak with my friend. Maybe he will allow me to give you permission. By the way, your father's name is Abram. Where is he working?"

I gave it one last shot. "Let me get straight to the point, Comrade Mukutsa. My father is a war veteran. He was wounded and has several high military decorations. I think that is enough to show my father's loyalty to our country."

"That's good, that's good," quickly assured the Secretary. "And your mother is also Jewish, doctor?

"Yes, I am a pure-blooded Jew, Comrade Secretary."

"Well, we do not make any distinction among different nationalities," the Secretary said swiftly, giving the chairman an inscrutable look. "You know what? Come to me in five days to receive the final answer. Have a nice day."

"Seraphim, I like your doctor," the Secretary confided, although I was still in the office collecting my papers. "Only one thing bothers me. He wants to be first in our district to go abroad, while I, the First Secretary of the *raicom*, have myself never traveled outside the Soviet Union."

I left, a smile still on my face, but with little hope in my heart.

Five days later, with only three days until the cruise, I stepped into the waiting room of the First Secretary's office. The receptionist immediately noticed me and called out loudly, "Tsesis? No decision. Come back in five days. Do not forget to bring all the documents." My head bowed, I simply left without a word, the sounds of angry typing following me all the way back to Gradieshti.

When I returned to the hospital, the maintenance workers had created a huge bonfire from dry autumn leaves and twigs they had collected on the grounds. Large flames flared and leaped high in the sky. Still clutching the packet of copies of documents in my hand, I approached the bonfire, joining several people who were admiring its wild beauty.

My hand, as if of its own accord, lifted up the papers that had cost me so much time, effort, and dignity to put together over the last month. With all my might, I threw the unfulfilled dream straight into the middle of the bright, crackling blaze.

Farewell, Mediterranean. I do not need you, if to see you I must beg and belittle myself.

Walking back to my apartment that afternoon, Little Pal happily trotting at my side, I realized that I had indeed taken a trip. It was just a longer and much more painful journey than I had ever imagined.

A listener asks Armenian Radio, "What is the easiest way to explain the meaning of the word 'Communism'?"

Armenian Radio replies, "With your fists."

Windmills

———◍———

Two weeks after the bonfire, I'm rolling over and over on the chilly hospital grounds, trading punches and elbow jabs with a belligerent jerk, hot rage driving my fists because the white lab coat I washed last night is now not only smudged but also getting bloody.

Welcome to another day at Gradieshti Hospital. Most were full of the routine of practice and paperwork, but there was always—and I mean always—a chance the unexpected, the absurd, and sometimes the crazy would wander onto our grounds. Those very special days I remember well.

Like this one. At the beginning of a crisp autumn afternoon, I'm making my way across the hospital grounds toward one of our older buildings that has recently been rehabbed, by order of the Republic. It now houses forty transferred syphilis patients, and I have been assigned temporarily to treat them. Last week they revolted and forced two condescending doctors to flee for their lives from the building. I get along with them just fine.

A thin tendril of smoke curls up slowly behind the main hospital building. A heavy, burnt smell has hung heavy in the air for several hours now, since one of our sheds caught fire out back around 4 a.m. and burned to the ground. Wouldn't you know it, we discovered in the ashes the charred corpse of one of the syphilis patients, a quiet fellow who had been known to sneak away for hours at a time but always made it back for his shots of penicillin. Not anymore. Seems he liked to nap in that shed.

Suddenly, I spot a truck driving at full speed through the gate. In the back, a group of men, all in working clothes, are crouched in a circle, looking down.

Instead of driving to the admitting office, the truck screeches to a halt in front of the main hospital building. Seeing me in a white coat, the men in the truck scream and wave wildly at me to come quick.

"Come up to the back of the truck right away, doctor!" shouts a short man as I run up. Later I learned that he is Fyodor Ostapóvich, foreman of this electricians' crew. "One of ours is in critical condition," he exclaims. "He was electrocuted before our eyes. Accidentally stepped on a high-voltage wire, that's what!"

Scrambling up, I see the victim lying on a thin layer of straw on the bed of the truck. Spare tires, wires, and pieces of canvas are scattered around him.

"We've done artificial respiration on him nonstop on the way here," the foreman adds, pointing. Two men are performing the Silvester artificial respiration method, which was very popular at that time. The victim is face up, shoulders elevated to allow the head to drop backward. One of the rescuers grasps the victim's wrists and crosses them over the lower chest. He then rocks forward, pressing on the victim's chest, and then backward, stretching the victim's arms outward and upward. The cycle is supposed to be repeated approximately twelve times per minute.

I kneel in front of the victim and listen for breathing.

Standing close behind me, the foreman doesn't seem to be able to stop talking. "The accident happened in Belogorka village, maybe three quarters of an hour ago," he says, urgently. "The guy stepped on a hot wire and was electrocuted. We pulled him off the wire, tore open his shirt, and began artificial respiration right away. We haven't stopped since. We did all that was possible."

The victim is not breathing. I palpate for a pulse and feel nothing. Spontaneous respiratory movements are absent, and the pupils of his eyes are widely dilated.

"The road to the hospital is full of potholes, so sometimes we stopped for a moment," the foreman goes on, speaking faster and faster. "Right after the accident he was still breathing on his own. But later on, it was not so obvious. His color was becoming bluish, but I am sure he is still alive. The guy has a wife and a child. Help him doctor, quick!" He grabs my shoulder, hard.

Shrugging off his hand, I listen to the victim's chest with my stethoscope and directly with my ear and can hear neither heartbeats nor breathing.

After a few minutes of further examination, I stand up and tell the anxious men that their co-worker is dead. It's time to stop resuscitation.

The men begin cursing and shouting that I am damn wrong.

"It cannot be so. The guy is alive," the foreman yells, indignantly. "He was just alive. You better start helping him!"

"I take full responsibility for my words," I answer firmly and loudly to what is rapidly becoming a mob. "But as unfortunate as it is, your coworker is dead, and we should keep our hands off him because—"

The main door of the hospital suddenly swings open, and from it, accompanied by two nurses, the hospital's chief doctor dashes out, screaming.

Well, good, maybe they will listen to her.

Never doubting her sovereign right to play the valiant heroine in any event, Chief Doctor Oprya runs up to the truck, demanding explanations from the foreman, while totally ignoring me.

"The guy's name is Andriesh Balan. He was electrocuted, and now this young doctor says that he is dead," the foreman exclaims, giving me a scornful look. At his sign, the crew members resume their attempts at resuscitation. "That cannot be. He was just alive!"

Without even looking at me, Lyubov Evgenyevna grabs outstretched arms from the top of the truck and climbs up. Looking quickly over the victim, she turns and suddenly shouts, "You are right, comrade! He is alive! Take him out of the truck and carry him to the admitting room!"

You have got to be kidding me.

Standing very tall on the truck bed, the heroic chief doctor whirls dramatically to the nurses. "Alexandra Petrovna, Varvara Vyacheslovovna, when he is there, *immediately* check his blood pressure, take his tempera-

ture, start an IV, and give him oxygen from two oxygen pillows. Prepare
to give him adrenaline, camphor, lobelin, cordiamin, and strychnine
right away, and do not forget about a hot water bottle!"

Only cupping glasses and a mustard plaster are lacking.

The victim of electrocution is taken down and carried to the admitting office. Hopping down from the truck and shaking my head, I begin
walking away. The foreman jumps in front of me.

"Hey, doctor, who gave you the right?" he snaps, blocking my way.
"Who gave you the right to call the man 'dead'?" he yells, pushing me in
my chest with both hands. "Are you one of those murderers in the white
coats?" His crew starts gathering around us, muttering.

"You are dead wrong. He was not alive when you brought him here,"
I protest vehemently, trying to ignore the now ominous rumble. "And
instead of looking for scapegoats, think about yourself as the one who is
responsible. You, as the victim's foreman, were obliged to provide a safe
workplace."

"That is none of your business. I'll show you how to declare people
who are still alive dead!" the foreman screams, punching me in the face.
Blood splatters on my white coat.

Thoroughly exasperated with him, my quixotic boss, and now a
messed up coat that I will have to wash again tonight, I hit him back,
hard. Soon, we are punching and rolling on the ground, while the crew
surrounds us, yelling and jeering. Suddenly one of the workers breaks
through the mob and tries to pull the foreman away, telling him that the
chief doctor wants to see him immediately in the admitting office.

Within a few minutes, both sporting bruises and bloodied lips, we
stand in front of Chief Doctor Oprya. Looking solemnly down at the
dead electrician, she sighs.

"Fyodor, we did everything in our power," she says to the foreman,
sadly. "We used every available medication, gave him all the oxygen we
had on hand, tried to continue the artificial respiration, gave him all
kinds of shots, but Fyodor, he is dead. Take his body and bury him in
Belogorka."

Brushing roughly past me, the now subdued foreman steps forward
and thanks my chief medical officer for all her efforts to revive a dead

man. His men carry their coworker out, and soon the truck with the deceased electrician rumbles away, taking him home for the last time.

Having tilted another medical windmill, having demonstrated to the world her unbelievable professionalism and extraordinary indispensability one more time, the chief doctor walks away, clipboard firmly in hand. At the door to the admitting office, she pauses and turns.

"Oh, doctor?"

Wiping the corner of my tender mouth, I look over at her.

"Doctor, I must insist that your coat be clean at all times when you are on duty." With a firm nod, she disappears from my afternoon.

As I said, some days at Gradieshti Hospital were very special.

A listener asks Armenian Radio, "What if socialism were built in Greenland?"

Armenian Radio replies, "First snow would become available only through ration cards, and later snow would be distributed only to the KGB officers and their families."

Milk

---⚜---

Two years before I arrived in Gradieshti, the sage leaders of the Tiraspol District Party Committee were inspired to create a cow collective. Their revolutionary decision set in motion a long chain of happenings that eventually ended with me being summoned by local party secretary Lupu to explain why I had taken pictures of . . . milk. Only in the Soviet Union could it all have unfolded in such a predictable, irreducibly socialist way.

Before the District Party Committee's enlightened plan of action, every kolkhoznik family in the "Red Sparkle" kolkhoz had been allowed to own one or two cows, which supplied them with milk and other dairy products. The chairman of the kolkhoz, Seraphim Mikhailovich Namashko, announced at a general meeting that all individual cows would become part of a common herd. The socialist bovines would be managed at a livestock farm, where they would benefit from the latest scientific discoveries, as well as a specially educated and trained staff, led by a veterinarian.

In this "win-win" situation, the owners would supposedly benefit even more by receiving a modest sum for their share of the calculated income of the collectivized cattle. Each family in Gradieshti would also receive two liters of collective herd milk each day from a special mobile milk cistern. All the villagers had to do was carry their jugs to the top of a certain hill on the two-lane asphalt road a little way north of the hospital, where the cistern would be waiting between 6:00 and 7:30 a.m. every day. Just think of the health benefits of that daily morning walk! What a cure for a hangover!

Needless to say, not everyone was enthralled by this new socialist vision. The vocal doubters of the great Gradieshti cow collectivization movement were quickly ushered outside the meeting hall. After possible outcomes for their opinions were made very clear, they converted to the will of the people on the spot.

As with everything in the Socialist Motherland, it all went so well at the start. Within a month, every cow belonging to private owners was relocated to the animal farm. Just as promptly, the kolkhozniks received the promised modest amount of money per cow. As arranged, the milk cistern arrived on time at the designated place on the highway. The driver set himself up at the cistern, opened the faucet on the back of the tank, and distributed to the customers their allotted portion of the precious milk. That portion was hardly enough milk for the average family, but at least it was available. And now people without cows were guaranteed at least some milk.

After two months, unfortunately, the milk cistern simply did not show up one morning. A large group of villagers with milk jugs in their hands waited patiently—I told you we were good at waiting—for a long time but finally dispersed. The next day, they waited in vain again and returned home with empty jugs. Eventually, a group of villagers went to the village council.

"You have to realize, dear comrades, the situation in its entirety," admitted a young deputy of the kolkhoz chairman (not surprisingly, the chairman himself was all-so-regrettably too busy to meet them at that particular time). "Very unfortunately, we all feel the bad effects of drought this year. This is reflected in the amount of milk yield per cow. We understand your predicament and feel your pain, but you ought to understand ours. We are parents ourselves. We know how important it is for you to get milk. But we are behind in state milk deliveries, and nobody can deny that this is the number one priority."

At that point, their cows and now their milk taken forever from them, the incredulous villagers still kept silent. Each standing there knew well from long years of experience that protesting was not only futile but could be counterproductive and dangerous.

"We have not forgotten our moral duty to provide milk for infants in our kolkhoz," the young deputy said, clearing his throat. His face suddenly lit up. "As a matter of fact, at a special session of our collective farm, we came to a very important decision everybody will like: in the center of our village we are going to build a large modern milk kitchen through which we are going to satisfy the milk needs of our children. Because we experience shortages, the limited supply of milk will be dispensed by prescriptions issued by our pediatrician."

And that's how—ta-da!—forming a collective made a nonsensical shortage of one of the most common food items in Gradieshti. And that's also how I became involved in the party's self-created problem. Immediately after arriving, I, a young pediatrician, was promoted to the privileged class of those who controlled an important deficit in the village. Milk could be distributed to families only if I wrote prescriptions for them.

This awesome, completely unnecessary power did not come with special benefits. It did, however, make the new pediatrician a recognizable figure in the community and forced mothers needing a milk prescription to bring in their children for examination more frequently than they would have. As I looked at the children, my nurse Svetlana would hand the parents prescriptions signed by me for a product so easily available before the government had gotten involved. Such an absurdist play, a state-sponsored farce, but we all knew our lines and just kept playing along.

My appointed oversight of milk distribution in Gradieshti made me very aware of the critical need for rigorously clean sanitary conditions in the new "large, modern milk kitchen" in the center of the village. For some unknown reason, however, monitoring the milk kitchen had been assigned to the hospital chief physician and her husband, the epidemiology technician. One scorching August day, I noticed that an inspection of the milk kitchen had been scheduled. Since the matrimonially blessed Opryas were on vacation, I made the mistake of deciding to pay it a visit and impulsively carry out the inspection myself.

The milk kitchen was a small, freestanding brick building with a primitive interior—a medium-sized room with wooden floors and roughly plastered walls and ceiling. Because of the day's intense heat, the door was wide open, so I just walked in and announced myself and the inspection. Two middle-aged, portly women with flushed faces were taken aback at my sudden appearance. Soon, though, the chief of the milk kitchen and her helper shook my hand, and began walking around with me. All of my remarks, critical or not, were met with the same serene smiles.

The whole, much praised "high" technology of the milk kitchen consisted of two large cauldrons. One was for the primitive sterilization of milk by boiling. The other was for mannaya kasha, semolina, one of the most popular foods for young Soviet children. (More than a century after the first milk formula was developed, it was still unavailable in the Soviet Union. All "baby food" in the 1960s was simply milk diluted in different proportions with water for younger children and undiluted for older children.)

At first glance, I thought the milk kitchen was basically clean, but on closer examination, I spied many gross violations of the basic rules of hygiene. Dirty rags, filthy windows, nonsterile cotton balls, and . . . flies. Dead flies floating in each of the cauldrons, not surprising given that the doors were open.

At the end of the inspection, the two smiling women eagerly cleaned off a small table covered with oilcloth that stuck to my hands while I wrote my report on it. I then took out a camera that I often used to document inspection findings. Eyes widening, the women looked at each other and retreated. Intent on completing the inspection and photographing the evidence, I didn't notice that they had decided suddenly to leave me alone.

A week later when my boss and her husband had returned from vacation, she accosted me in the long, linoleum-floored hallway of the hospital. In a stern voice, not looking directly at me, she ordered me to come with her into the physicians' lounge.

"Vladimir Abramovich, employees of the milk kitchen are complaining about your unbecoming, unprofessional, rude behavior," she announced, as we sat down opposite each other at the table.

"I do not understand you," I stammered, completely surprised. "Who complained and why?"

"Nobody ever asked you to visit the milk kitchen," she said, reprovingly. "But you went there on your own and with your questions and your camera practically terrorized both workers there. They are still in deep shock! What kind of professional behavior is this?"

"As a pediatrician," I insisted, "I have every right to inspect the place where children are getting their nutrition, and I am very sorry I did not do it sooner. The people working there are probably good people. I do not have anything against them. But I found there poor sanitation which might be harmful to the health of our village children. And if children start getting sick, we both will be responsible. Let me show you the report and the pictures that I just developed and printed."

Lyubov Evgenyevna sighed and grimaced. With inexplicable displeasure, she quickly thumbed through the report and pictures.

"Well, I agree, these flies do not belong in the milk kitchen," she admitted. After a heavy pause, she sighed deeply again, put the pictures on the table, and looked directly at me. "You went there for the first time and immediately drew up a report and took pictures. Are you a spy? I do not remember anybody in our village ever taking pictures for documentation. Who do you think you are? The police? Do you know that you scared these poor, uneducated women to death? Why couldn't you have expressed your comments to them verbally?"

"Lyubov Evgenyevna," I began, spreading my hands imploringly. "I never met those women before. I did not write my report about them, but about violations of the elementary rules of hygiene, which present a serious danger to our children. I thought you would be happy to address, with me, measures which would protect the health of the village children." I leaned toward her. "Did you not criticize me recently for the large number of children admitted to the hospital with dangerous intestinal infections?"

"You are too young to lecture me about elementary things, Doctor Tsesis," the chief doctor retorted, her face now flushed with indignation. "Before you arrived here, I, as the chief doctor, had protected the children's health for many years. What you really did—you complicated very simple things. Now I, not you, will need to apologize to Comrade Lupu, our party organization secretary, for your actions."

Shaking her head in disbelief, she looked at the door, lowered her voice, and whispered, "Both of the milk kitchen workers whom you so harshly offended are his blood sisters! Do you understand what you did? Specialists like you come here for a couple of years and then leave us, and I have to stay here to pick up your mess. I understand you are young and idealistic. And when I was young, I was also such a fool as you are now. But when the time came, I quickly matured." She thought for a moment and then smiled. "Let's do this: we throw out your report and photos, and I promise that, together with Grigory Nikolaevich, we will put right of all the problems you've found."

"Sorry, Lyubov Evgenyevna," I murmured, now far too aware of what was going on. "I was totally unaware of all the political implications you just mentioned and already sent a copy of the report to the district hospital."

"OH, MY GOD!" shrieked the atheist Communist. "Oh, my God! What did you do? Without talking to me!" Putting her head in her hands, my boss remained silent for many minutes.

She finally raised her head and I stared into desolation. "I am tremendously disappointed in you," she whispered, voice cracking. "In this case, you and your impulsive actions and many jokes are on your own from now on. I will have nothing to do with the way you've acted this time."

For two weeks, I made my rounds wondering when the summons would come. My patients seemed more nervous and eager to talk to nurse Svetlana than me. Finally, at the end of a work day, a car appeared, sent to take me to Comrade Lupu, the local Communist secretary. I quickly grabbed the folder with the necessary documents.

As I entered his small office in the kolkhoz building, Zachary Ionovich Lupu, without greeting me, began sternly, switching back and forth between Russian and Moldovan as he sat behind his desk. "I read your report about our collective farm milk kitchen. It is good that you show interest in disease prevention, but you have to explain to me why it was necessary to write a report and send it to the district hospital, of all places."

I began to explain, and he held up a hand and continued, his tone even sharper. "Nobody says we do not have shortcomings; we are doing our best to eradicate them. Instead of taking time to explain to the employees what was required of them, you frightened and offended them. These people have worked there for years, and you come from nowhere and try to create trouble. Good workers, nice Moldovan women, should be highly esteemed instead of slandered. The head of the milk kitchen said that you invented defects that were not even there. Why muddy the water? You may be our only pediatrician, but, I guarantee, the time will come when you will need something serious from us. I am sure that you are not perfect yourself. I don't want you to be sorry for your actions later."

"Zachary Ionovich, we are both interested in the same thing: the prevention of infections in the child population," I answered, treading very carefully. "We already have plenty of cases of gastrointestinal infections to be worried about. I can assure you, I did not desire to offend anybody. All I am concerned with is to make sure our milk kitchen meets sanitary norms. I appreciate what you are telling me, but look at the pictures. They do not lie." I laid them on the desk in front of him.

As Lupu gazed down at the photos, his stern expression began softening.

"First of all, these filthy rags and crumbs I personally never saw at the milk kitchen, so it could be considered that they are just an accident," he murmured, eventually. "Next, dirty windows. This is, of course, a petty thing; the workers there are very busy. They just do not have time to wash windows. I am sure this problem has already been taken care of.

"Oh, Dumnezeu. Flies, so many flies, in our milk." The secretary shuddered, now dismayed. "This is an oversight, for sure. We must provide fans so they will not need to open the doors because of the heat. My sister told me she needs sticky flypaper from Tiraspol. But now it is summer, and everyone needs it, so it's just not available. We will get it, don't you worry. If nothing helps, I will ask somebody in the District Party Committee to help me with flypaper. We recently had a problem with mice and we found ways to get rid of them."

I remained silent.

The local secretary motioned for me to sit. We looked at each other for a moment, and then he leaned back, a grin almost breaking through. "My sisters who work at the milk kitchen are, shall we say, strong personalities. I have a thousand more important things to do, but they forced me to speak with you. And now we have, and you may go."

And so life went on in the little village, as some things changed, and some did not. The kolkhoz milk kitchen was substantially renovated and became more sanitary. The chief doctor was on guard about my antics even more than before. I never stopped writing absurd prescriptions for milk—now fly-less—until the day I left dear Gradieshti. And at every brilliant Moldovan sunrise, in a large pasture to the south, a determined collective of cows resumed grazing their very best for the good of the people.

Question: What does a Soviet optimist say?

Answer: It can't get any worse!

The Wanderers

———— ✥ ————

The cattle collective of Gradieshti came under serious attack in the mid-1960s, when foot-and-mouth disease stalked the Moldovan countryside. This serious viral illness causes high fever for two or three days, followed by blisters inside the mouth and on the hooves that may rupture and cause lameness, and it frequently leads to the death of the animal.

Because the rampant disease threatened the livelihood of rural Moldavia, the authorities, *kolkhozniks*, and veterinarians in particular were very worried. The chairman of Gradieshti's "Red Sparkle" *kolkhoz* in fact put so much pressure on one of Gradieshti's veterinarians to stop it that the terrified man suffered a mental breakdown. Little Pal and I missed the veterinarian, as he had regularly and with great tenderness treated my three-legged dog.

The Moldovan Ministry of the Interior deployed military troops to attempt to prevent the spread of foot-and-mouth disease. Checkpoints were organized over a large area of the countryside. Vehicles were stopped and the drivers and passengers forced to wipe their shoes with disinfectant cloths. Since these checkpoints were located fairly close to each other, they became a significant impediment against traveling.

The establishment of one of the checkpoints near our village forced a small Gypsy (*roma*) camp to settle temporarily in an abandoned site on the outskirts of Gradieshti. From what I gathered from my patients, Gypsies hardly ever appeared in the village in the past. The Gypsies had been here long before the Communists, but for decades, the Soviet Union had been forcing the traditional wanderers to abandon their nomadic life. By the 1960s in Moldova, it was working as many had settled down, particularly in the north around Soroca (Soroki, in the past).

Off and on during this time, a handful of Gypsies appeared in the hospital's admission room for trivial medical problems. I came to recognize married Gypsy women because they wore head scarves, large earrings, and long, flowing skirts with many layers. Red seemed to be a common color for scarfs and clothes, and I learned that it was considered lucky. Many of the *roma* were multilingual, speaking their own language, Romanian, Moldovan, and Russian. Although I had heard of the prevailing prejudices against the Gypsies, I never witnessed any conflict or intolerance toward them by the villagers.

One muggy evening in July, I was called into the hospital to examine a six-year-old boy from the Gypsy camp. A very worried *roma* family sat on a narrow bench next to each other as I walked into the examination room. The young wife cradled the boy against her chest, speaking softly to him in their language. Next to her, the middle-aged father tightly clutched a horse-whip, which he kept turning over in his hands. Their son was unmistakably sick. He was pale and sluggish, with a haggard face darkened by disease.

They told me that their son, Ephraim Djungo, had been ill for a week, and they had run out of options. At the camp, the boy had been treated like other sick children—given warm milk with honey and a decoction of different herbs. Traditional charms were used as well. These usually effective methods, they told me, did not help the child, and his condition had steadily deteriorated. Ephraim's symptoms included fever, painful swallowing, drooling, a slightly bluish coloration of the skin, bloody, watery drainage from the nose, difficulty breathing, and a high-pitched croup-like (barking) cough. Luckily, nobody else in the Gypsy camp was sick.

Even a very short physical examination of the child confirmed my grave suspicions. Wearing a protective mask and gloves, I used a tongue depressor and right away spotted the classical manifestations of diphtheria: a gray to black covering of the throat, enlarged lymph glands, and swelling of the neck or larynx. After the introduction of mandatory vaccination, severe childhood diseases had been mostly uprooted, but some, such as diphtheria, still occurred in small numbers. Ephraim's parents could not say whether their child had been fully or partially vaccinated.

Continuing the examination, to my deep dismay, it got much worse. I discovered that Ephraim also had a terribly alarming symptom, bradycardia, which is a slow heart rhythm. That meant that the patient had one of the complications of diphtheria: inflammation of the cardiac muscle—myocarditis—a secondary effect of the diphtheria toxins. Prior to Ephraim's admission, our hospital had received its first EKG machine, and it was actually functioning that day. An electrocardiogram performed on the patient showed incontrovertible signs of arterioventricular blockage to a significant degree, which meant that the regular electrical impulse generated on top of the heart did not reach the peripheral heart tissues on time.

The odds were becoming rapidly stacked against their son. Even if he successfully survived the major complications of the upper respiratory tract, if his bradycardia continued to progress, and especially if he exerted himself too much, he might die at any moment from cardiac arrest.

Time was running out, and I had to move quickly that night. Ephraim was immediately placed in a quarantined hospital room and all measures were taken to prevent the spread of this dangerous infection. At the end of the hallway, I saw his parents arguing in their language. The father was gesturing toward the door, clearly imploring his family to leave, while his wife kept shaking her head and looking over at me. Finally, he threw his hands up in their air, grabbed the horse-whip, and stomped out into the night.

Not reacting to the disagreement, I then instructed the anxious mother, who stayed with the child, how to care for her son. Over and over I emphasized that she and the nurses should strictly ensure that under no circumstances should the boy leave his bed, and that he was to receive no visitors.

After ordering intramuscular penicillin and IV fluids, and giving necessary instructions to all who were involved in Ephraim's care, I went to the office to call the District Hospital to arrange transfer of my patient to the Republic's Infectious Disease Hospital in the capital city of Kishinev—the only place in Moldova where antidiphtheria serum was available.

A wave of dread crashed over me as I reached for the phone, as it hadn't been working well all day. Cradling the receiver in a sweaty palm, I listened. Fortunately, that evening the telephone connection happened to be normal. Soon, I was able to get in touch with a physician in Kishinev, who promised to come and transfer the patient as soon as possible, hopefully the next afternoon. An infectious disease consultant would also come to Gradieshti, but again, not earlier than the next afternoon. Worried about the delay but relieved that help was on the way, I returned to the pediatric floor and told Ephraim's mother and nurses the positive news.

The next day on the way to the hospital for early morning rounds, I noticed two horse-pulled carts coming through the gates of the hospital carrying the father and other Gypsies. The men were dressed in darkly colored suits and the women in long dresses with red kerchiefs. I simply didn't have time to speak with them, as I needed to check on the boy.

I was pleased to see that Ephraim's condition had slightly improved—he did not appear as tired and bluish—but his pulse remained slow and even weaker than the day before. Ephraim woke and tried to wiggle out of bed, but he was securely held there by his mother. Her son was in very grave danger, and there wasn't anything I could do but wait for help to arrive hours from now from Kishinev.

Shouts broke out from outside, and I looked out the window. The father was heatedly arguing with Chief Doctor Oprya, who kept shaking her head. The other Gypsies, whom, I later learned, were members of the parents' families, maintained a respectful distance, grooming their horses and sitting in the carts.

One o'clock arrived, and still no medical team from the capital had arrived. Crossing the hospital grounds to the ambulatory, now very concerned, I noticed that the number of Gypsies in front of the main hospital building had doubled. Ignoring my presence as I walked past them, the men and women, also looking worried, talked among themselves in their own language.

Two o'clock. Tired of staring at the entrance gates, I picked up the phone, but it was dead. Frustrated, I slammed the receiver down, hard.

Where are you?

Two-thirty. Interrupting my ambulatory obligations, I went to the pediatric floor to visit Ephraim. He was quietly sleeping while his mother, with worry written on her face, sat tensely next to him.

I then went outside to try to speak with the father, as he was upset at not being able to see his son. He wasn't with the Gypsies. As I approached, a gray-haired patriarch asked for attention, and there was immediate silence. The man pulled a little book out of his pocket and started to pray sincerely and passionately, and the others joined him. I could not understand anything that was said except the name of my patient, Ephraim Djungo, periodically repeated by the patriarch. At the end of the prayer, the patriarch raised his hands to the sky and knelt. The entire group followed, and, before I could understand what I was doing, I was on my knees, too. At that moment, abandoned and afraid, I became convinced that Ephraim was in such a grave, life-threatening condition that only God could help him successfully recover.

At three o'clock that afternoon, the storm broke. The ambulatory door burst open and an orderly came running into the examining room, extremely panicked. Before she opened her mouth, I bolted past her. I ran into Ephraim's room, and found his mother silently crying and clinging to the motionless body of her son.

From the nurse, I learned that Ephraim's mother had gone to the restroom, leaving him for just a minute sleeping and restrained in bed. Ephraim's father, who had been prowling around the building, had finally located the window of his son's room. Seeing him sleeping, he started banging loudly on the window. Ephraim immediately woke up. Seeing his father, he managed to free himself from the restraints and run toward him. He never reached the window. By the time his mother and the nurse ran into the room, the boy had died. The father had stood silently at the window, looking expressionlessly down at his son, and then had turned away.

Later on, the Gypsies quietly entered the hospital, walked purposefully past the protesting staff, and reclaimed with great dignity one of their own. Defeated and weary, I stood in front of the weather-worn main door of the hospital, watching as their horse-drawn carts pulled away. An hour later, at a steady horse-drawn pace measured by the centuries, the Gypsies made their way past an ambulance from a faraway city, broken down and abandoned on the side of the road.

A Frenchman, a Brit, and a Russian are admiring a painting of Adam and Eve in the Garden of Eden.

The Frenchman says, "They must be French, they're naked and they're eating fruit."

The Englishman says, "Clearly, they're English; observe how politely the man is offering the woman the fruit."

The Russian notes, "They are Russian, of course. They have nothing to wear, nothing to eat, and they think they are in paradise."

Death in a Family

—————— ✿ ——————

I've mentioned that when I first moved into my apartment near the Gradieshti Hospital, a delightful family with four boys and six girls lived next door, separated from me by a low picket fence. The mother of the family, Nastasia, proudly wore on her old, unpretentious jacket the "Mother Heroine" medal, which acknowledged her contribution to a higher-than-average birth rate for the family.

Despite enormous family responsibilities and his work as an underpaid *kolkhoz* truck driver, her husband Feodor managed to find time for art, which he created from all kinds of local materials. Feodor welcomed me to help him in the production of his art. We spent an enjoyable time together during which, in a peculiar mixture of Moldovan and Russian words, Feodor shared his secrets for making unsophisticated ceramic and wood dolls, creating miniature pieces of furniture, and building simple picture frames. He never failed to present me with several pieces of art, which I exhibited on my bedside table.

While Nastasia was constantly busy taking care of the household, Feodor was either helping her with the never-ending chores or was creating art objects. He also had a passion, from time to time, of consuming large amounts of homemade Moldovan wine (he could not afford to buy vodka), after which I would spot him sprawled out on a haystack at the back of their house. On those nights, his companions were the family's two goats—the Muntyanus' only truly precious possessions.

Once a month, Feodor took a sackful of his art and hitchhiked to Tiraspol, where he sold it at a flea market. He was quite popular, and many there purchased his works. The money he earned, he never drank away but, as a proud breadwinner, brought back to his Nastasia.

On summer nights, I was a frequent guest at Muntyanu family gatherings in their large backyard. One night, I found Feodor there, surrounded by Nastasia and all their children. Under the intense stares of eleven pairs of eyes, he was assembling a primitive potter's wheel, which he had just brought from Tiraspol.

"I have great news for you, Vladimiru. My cousin from Dubossari visited me a week ago and taught me how to manufacture ceramic jugs of all sizes," he cheerfully informed me, interrupting his efforts for a moment. "Using this device I'm going to make jars and pots, which nobody around here does."

Always faithful to his word, Feodor, after numerous attempts, started to produce jugs and pots of all shapes and sizes, using local clay. Another two weeks passed, and with the help of his brother, Dimitriu—a village stove-maker—Feodor built a primitive kiln for firing his pottery in his backyard.

Before long, Feodor handed me a small jar that he had produced with his own hands. This primitive, thick-walled vessel looked quite decent, and I used it for storing drinking water. Thanks to the material from which the vessel was built, the water remained cool during hot summer days.

A harsh fall with heavy rains and strong winds forced Feodor to halt his hobby, but early the next summer, as soon as the weather became dry and the air warm and balmy, he returned to his wheel and kiln.

After about a month, he welcomed me into his backyard with a gentle smile on his earnest face.

"Great news, Volodya!" he exclaimed. "Last time I was selling my stuff at the flea market, I met a man from Slobodzeya and he taught me how to glaze the earthenware. Believe me, when I learn better how to glaze pottery, I will be the only one for thirty kilometers around who knows how to produce this kind of merchandise!

"Imagine, soon everybody around will buy Feodor Muntyanu's ceramic pots!" he promised with an undisguised satisfaction while filling a little piece of paper with inferior, home-grown tobacco—*machorka*—and rolling it into a *zakrutka*, a cigarette.

"Next week you will see something very special, Volodya," he promised me, expelling a large cloud of smoke from his mouth. "You will be really surprised. Just wait."

For the next couple of weeks, I could see Feodor through the window of my apartment, pouring and manipulating with the help of his cousin different-colored powders with strange, strong odors. Being too busy with my work to join their alchemy business, I had no idea that among the powders they were experimenting with was lead oxide—the main chemical component for pottery glazing.

One early morning a week later, I was awakened by loud knocking on the window that faced the Muntyanu home. Feodor stood in front, together with three of his ten children, all younger than five years old. With the immense satisfaction of a creator, he handed me a clay plate. On the surface of it, I could see the depiction of a typical Moldovan hut with a symbolic image of the sun in the upper part of the design.

A glorious smile appeared on Feodor's composed, prematurely wrinkled face. "Like it, Volodya?" he asked.

"Nice piece of art, Feodor," I answered, turning it over. "Nice hut."

"Hut? Hut? What are you talking about, man! Who would wake you up early in the morning just to show you a hut as if you never saw one before?" Feodor declared, letting a cloud of tobacco smoke straight up into my nostrils. "Look at the surface of this plate, man! Don't you see that it's glazed? Do you see it now? And who did the glazing job, Volodya? It's me, Feodor Muntyanu, a simple peasant, who did the glazing job yesterday evening, which means I can produce glazed pots for sale and that my children and my wife will have more food on the table and clothing and shoes. Can you imagine? They will not be dressed in second-hand torn trash, but—for the first time in their lives—they will wear their own new and beautiful clothing.

"You just watch it now!" he finished triumphantly, waving and walking away.

In a short time, Feodor was able to manufacture a large jug, the internal and external walls of which were generously glazed. Nastasia immediately began to use this object as a container where she stored *borscht*, a soup made with meat stock, cabbage, beets, onions, and tomatoes—one of the main dishes she prepared daily to satisfy numerous mouths. Walking back home after rounds, I heard laughter from their yard more than ever, now. The large, congenial family seemed very happy and hopeful.

Shortly afterward, in the middle of the night, I suddenly woke to a loud banging on the window. One of the Muntyanu children, Procopy, screamed at me that something was wrong with his family. Sprinting to the Muntyanus' hut, I found there a catastrophe. Both parents and six-year old Gregory were lying in their beds in different stages of coma, while the other children were vomiting and suffering abdominal pain. Only six-month-old Yakov and Procopy, who had been staying at a friend's house until coming home late, were unaffected.

Shouting at Procopy to run to the hospital, I examined everyone, spoke to the conscious children, and did what I could. Acute lead poisoning caused by the pottery's homemade glaze had struck Feodor, Nastasia, and their six-year-old son, Gregory, almost simultaneously. They had first developed symptoms of gastrointestinal discomfort that evening: abdominal cramps and decreased appetite. Feodor had then experienced unrelenting generalized seizures, while his wife's and Gregory's seizures were intermittent. The other members of the family were free from neurological symptoms, but they demonstrated signs of acute lead poisoning in varying degrees. Luckily the youngest had been exclusively breastfed, while Procopy hadn't been home that night. Medical personnel and neighbors ran to the Muntyanu home, and quickly carried the family on stretchers to the hospital.

Only the Republic's Infectious Disease Hospital in the capital city of Kishinev was equipped for the treatment of severe lead poisoning. Without delay, accompanied by physicians and nurses, the ten sick members of the Muntyanu family were transferred to the hospital in Kishinev, where they received calcium sodium EDTA, a chelating agent which was the recommended treatment for lead poisoning.

Though all the poisoned members of the family were still alive after their trip to Kishinev, the results of blood tests for lead levels in Feodor, Nastasia, and Gregory were too high to expect their recovery. Three days after admission, having never regained consciousness, they all died. The other children survived and later returned to Gradieshti.

With a tight feeling in my chest, as soon as I returned to my own apartment, I threw out all the ceramic pieces glazed and given to me by Feodor.

The funeral of the three Muntyanus was attended, it appeared to me, by the entire village. The surviving children were adopted by tender-hearted relatives, but they never all lived together again. I made sure that every object that we knew of that had any connection to the lead poisoning was meticulously destroyed.

A few nights later, I turned off the lights and sat in front of the window, as it began to rain, hard. I thought about the dire cost of a poor but joyous man daring to dream of providing his family with a different life through the power of his art. Why him? Why did it happen to such a nice family?

Across the picket fence, a potter's wheel stood motionless in the down-pour. I sat, staring at it, for hours.

Visiting a research institute in biology, Brezhnev inquires about the success of their genetic engineering.

"We are almost sure we are capable of creating a tastier chicken!" a scientist proudly announces.

"Well, were you successful?"

"No one ever caught one to find out," the scientist admits. "But we can conclusively state that the Soviet chicken is the world's fastest."

The Great Chase

———— ⬩ ————

You know, it seems I was always in pursuit of something during those long ago years—to become a doctor; to settle down with Marina in the same city; heck, to just catch up with my whirlwind of a boss as she marched across the hospital grounds. But, I will admit that as a young pediatrician, I was chasing nothing more than my mother-in-law's approval.

While I fought foremen, paraded in circles, photographed flies, and even managed to treat children during all of the excitement in Gradieshti, my wife, who was still in Meteorological College, lived with her mother, Sofia Lvovna, in a communal apartment in Odessa. Three other families shared with them a bathroom, kitchen, storage, and other common areas.

Sofia Lvovna was an energetic woman with expressive dark eyes and a strong commanding character. Her brown hair streaked with gray, she was moderately overweight, as any self-respecting lady from such a city as Odessa was supposed to be. After a divorce, she had single-handedly gave my future wife a disciplined upbringing. To make ends meet, she worked as a cashier in the famous Odessa Opera House.

When Marina married me, my mother-in-law never hid her disappointment with her daughter's choice. She always seemed convinced that her only daughter from the glorious city of Odessa with its famous Opera House deserved more than just a penniless, skinny young man from a small provincial town. I never heard words of praise about me to her neighbors; I was an afterthought in introductions to others.

One weekend, all that changed when I made the long journey to Odessa and back just to earn, finally, my mother-in-law's favor. As with all things Moldovan and all things Vladimir, it proved to be a most eventful round trip.

It began with the latest entry in the litany of unfavorable comparisons and disproval from the lips of Sofia Lvovna. Tired and slightly sweaty after spending long hours in different lines for potatoes, carrots, onions, meat, fish, milk, and bread, she dropped two large, overly stuffed bags on the floor and looked at me. The bags were called "авоська," (*avos'ka*; translated as "just in case" or "perhaps"), a popular Soviet style shopping bag made out of a mesh, woven from strong yarns and used mainly to visit markets and shops. This type of mesh string bag takes up very little space in a pocket or purse, and it comes in very handy when a line suddenly forms for an unknown food item. Getting in line, a citizen might not know what the line is for but still joins it—"just in case."

As we always told ourselves, the foolish capitalist economy in the 1960s spent enormous sums of money for advertising. In our wise socialist economy, merchandise flew off of empty shelves.

"Vova," my mother-in-law said in a voice full of reproach and hint, "I am very surprised. How is it that you work in a village as a physician and never bring anything from there? Look at Lenya Berlyand—you know him well—he is also a village doctor."

Ladies and gentlemen, let's welcome back Lenya Berlyand one more time into our humble home. Nodding automatically, I began putting away the produce, which was wrapped up in sheets of flat gray paper. My mother-in-law did not take a breath.

"His mother told me that he never comes home empty-handed. Why are you so meek? Can't you bring, let's say, a chicken or some eggs from your village? I need to stand on my sore, swollen legs in a long line to buy these products in a store where they are rarely available. Of course, I can buy a chicken or eggs on the "Privoz" farmer market, but for a steep price.

All you bring from your *kolkhoz* are ears of corn and small apples. Who needs them anyway? They are good for animals, not for people. Be a real man! Be a breadwinner!"

As I pulled another almost rotten potato out of the bag and said nothing, I had to admit she did have a point. Soviet citizens spent many hours of their lives in lines for bread, milk, meat, vegetables, and fruits daily. It was normal for any city dwellers—including physicians, teachers, and professors—to visit a village if they had the opportunity, to buy food products that were available there at prices cheaper than in the urban areas.

Before leaving, now acutely aware of my lack of breadwinning qualities, I promised that I would return with chickens and eggs. Sofia Lvovna didn't look convinced. "The main thing, Vova," she warned, "is not to allow the chickens and eggs to become spoiled on the way to Odessa."

Back in Gradieshti the next day, I went in search of chickens and eggs. Following the advice of coworkers, I went to the village council and introduced myself to one Manuel Mikhailovich Gramma, a short stocky foreman at the poultry farm outside of the village.

Gramma was happy to help. "No problem at all, doctor," he announced, congenially, opening his rather short arms. "Whenever you come to us, you will always be welcome. My wife brings our children to your office. So visit my poultry farm and take all the chickens and eggs you want. I am sure you will find someone there to help you catch chickens. Just ask and somebody will give you a helping hand."

A couple of weeks later, early on a Friday morning, one of the hospital drivers returned a favor by driving me the three miles to the *kolkhoz*'s poultry farm. My visit there was the first stage of an incredibly detailed master plan that would end with chickens and eggs in my mother-in-law's grateful hands: On the farm I would obtain the precious cargo and store it in two battered rough-hewn boxes I had secured from the hospital. Then the car would drive me back to the hospital where, for a fee, an orderly in the surgical ward had agreed to help me ready the chickens for transportation. I would then hitchhike, carrying the chickens and eggs, the ten miles to Tiraspol and then take a bus to Odessa. What could possibly go wrong?

The *kolkhoz* poultry farm unsurprisingly consisted of dilapidated and unpainted wooden barracks-like buildings crumbling at the end of a rutted gravel road. The chicken yard was ringed with two parallel rows of boards, warped by time and nailed to little posts set in the soil.

On the walls of the foreman's office hung framed portraits of members of the Central Party Committee, Lenin, Marx, and Engels, all looking down on a filthy tiny room littered with cigarette butts. Dim yellow light somehow found its way through a dusty windowpane, probably not cleaned since being installed. In a corner stood a dusty red banner, similar to what the hospital had received, signaling the highest success in a socialist competition between other *kolkhoz* enterprises.

Manuel Mikhailovich warmly greeted me from behind a desk. Wall slogans appealing for discipline and productivity framed him as he leaned forward and shook my hand.

"Welcome, doctor. I was expecting you after our conversation. Unfortunately, today I am very short of manpower," he confessed, shaking his head sorrowfully. "I never have enough help here. Grab your cartons, and pack the chickens in one after you catch them. And here is some twine to tie the chickens' legs before you put them in the box."

"All the chickens you catch are yours," the foreman continued, now smiling a bit slyly. "Meanwhile, one of my workers will gather some eggs for you."

I walked into the chicken yard, set the boxes down in a spot relatively clear of droppings, and suddenly found myself in a front-row seat to bedlam. Scrawny chickens of different colors were cackling loudly and running in all directions at and from each other. Whenever a chicken caught up with another, lightning-fast it pecked a space between the legs of the bird, and then rushed after another to perform the same action.

How in the world was I supposed to wade into this unending game of frantic peck-tag and catch some? Rolling my eyes, I returned to the little office of the foreman.

"Why are your birds hunting each other? What is going on here, Manuel Mikhailovich?"

"Oh, that. Do not pay attention to it at all. It is nothing special, my friend," he answered casually, smoking a cigarette and leaning back. "You see, we feed our chickens all kinds of grain, but they do not have enough minerals: calcium and magnesium. That mixture of minerals is only prepared somewhere in the Ural Mountains of Russia, and we are here in faraway Moldova. We order the mixture every year, but they don't send it to us."

Putting out the cigarette, he reached for another. "But, listen—did you notice how smart the chickens are? They guessed on their own about recycling the digested minerals of their fellow birds. It's normal."

"But why should they lack minerals if there are plenty of minerals around us? Calcium is abundant in the environment. Why not just add it to their food?"

"Calcium, schmalcium. What calcium?" sneered the now annoyed foreman. "Chickens need special calcium, not the regular kind, doctor. I wish you knew more about chickens."

"You are right. I am not a poultry specialist," I admitted. "But your chickens are spending a ton of energy trying to obtain the recycled minerals, as you call them. Look what they are doing to each other!"

"Go on and catch your chickens, doctor. I have other things to do," the foreman snapped, pointing to the door.

As I returned to the chicken chaos, I spied a *kolkhoznik* walking by, dressed in a faded flannel shirt and patched-up dark gray trousers.

"Excuse me," I addressed him politely in Moldovan. "Can you help me catch some of these chickens?" A brown chicken darted over my foot, cackled indignantly, and then dove back into the churning sea of feathers.

"I do not have time," the worker answered, without stopping or looking at me. "You know how to eat chickens, so go and get them now."

I took a step toward him, still clinging to the hope of help. "But how can I catch these birds when they are running like crazy?"

"First thing is to learn how to run quicker than them," he offered, turning and winking before disappearing through a doorway.

My mother-in-law's expectation of disappointment before me, I took a deep breath and ran after the nearest chicken. Easily evading my grasp, it collided with another, took a quick strategic peck, and dashed away. For the next fifteen minutes, I raced like lightning back and forth across that dropping-drenched yard, hands stretching out, way out, to nab something, anything that had feathers. Finally, stumbling out of breath in the midst of a soft white cloud of downy feathers, I glanced over at the hospital car. Widely grinning, the driver held up a bottle and saluted my failure.

I changed tactics—instead of hunting each fowl separately, I began diving into the densest clusters of them, pouncing like a hawk. If my mother-in-law had witnessed my heroic run-and-jump efforts, I am sure (almost) she would have been proud of the hunter her daughter married.

Rushing to a newly formed group of fowl with my arms spread, I stumbled over something hard jutting out of the ground and fell on top of them. I staggered to my feet, hair and clothes smeared with droppings, but now clutching a chicken in each hand. Yes!

But, oh agony, oh ecstasy: how could I tie their legs if I had no hands free? As I tried jamming one under an arm, it wiggled free and flew out of reach, so startling me that I loosened my remaining grip and lost the other.

Now as covered with droppings and feathers as the yard, I looked down at the fowl foes milling around and thought quickly. On impulse, I took off my shirt and used it as a net. Within a few minutes, I had caught four chickens, tied their feet, and stored them in one of the boxes.

Just then, Manuel Mikhailovich Gramma came into the chicken yard with a worker. The foreman paused, admiring my catch.

"Look at him," he said with respect to the *kolkhoznik*, who wore a kerchief on her head from which strands of hair kept escaping. "Though he's a doctor, he knows how to catch chickens."

"And how do you catch them, Manuel Mikhailovich?" I inquired, still out of breath from the Great Chicken Chase.

"We do not need to catch them," he confided, smirking. "When they are asleep in their henhouse at night, you can take them with your bare hands."

"But how do you nab them when they are outside?"

"Then it's harder," the foreman agreed. "Then we run after them until they get too tired and out of breath to run away from us."

I preferred my solution. With the satisfaction of a hunter, I looked over at the box filled with the precious cargo.

To achieve the objectives of stage one of my bold plan, all that was left now was to pick up a box of eggs.

"Here, take them, doctor," Manuel Mikhailovich told me, delicately handing me the breakable goods. "But be very, very, very careful."

"Of course I'll be careful," I answered. "I realize that eggs are fragile."

"You do not understand, doctor. These are special eggs, these are the '*kolkhoz* eggs,'" said the foreman, winking at me. "Look at them. Their shell is like a sheet of paper. You see, our poultry farm specializes in live chickens, so their eggs are only a byproduct of our activity. As I told you before, we do not have enough minerals to provide calcium in their diet. That's why their bodies cannot produce thicker shells."

"So why, for example, not find some chalk, grind it, and add it to the chicken feed?" I suggested.

The foreman whistled sharply through his teeth, shaking his head. "Well, yeah. As if I have nothing better to do but crush chalk. It is against regulations! You do not realize what might happen to me if the veterinarians disagree with me. This is a collective farm, not my personal chicken coop. As a foreman, my first responsibility is to organize people, to make sure we realize our production, to take care of the buildings, to provide reports to our accountant, to attend meetings, to speak about recent events in politics, and other crap. Everyone does their job here. Do you think I have enough time left to deal with such details?" He stalked away, now muttering and irritated at me again.

Following him into his office, I warmed him up again by setting down on his desk the universal present expected from Soviet medical workers: a small bottle of rectified alcohol with an alcohol content of more than 96 percent.

"Oh, doctor, we love this stuff," murmured Manuel Mikhailovich, caressing the bottle. "It relaxes and softens the soul right away."

Carrying two boxes full of chickens and eggs, I returned to the car. The foreman intercepted me before we drove away, smiling and handing me an old oilcloth through the car window.

"To avoid a bad experience with those delicate eggs, you better take your time and wrap them well," he suggested, now amicable again.

Back at the hospital, after the chickens had been plucked and dressed by the orderly, I repackaged the eggs and placed them back into one of the boxes. After that, I put each box into a specially prepared large mesh shopping bag (*avos'ka*).

I trudged out to the two-lane asphalt highway outside of Gradieshti, tightly holding on to the mesh bags. Waving down a passing truck. I was ready to climb up onto the bed, but the driver, a young man with sharp blue eyes and a nice-looking face, invited me to join him in the cabin. Passing through a handful of foot-and-mouth disease checkpoints, we chatted about his forthcoming wedding and my adventures with the chickens. Eventually, the truck slowed and stopped at an intersection, still about a mile from the bus station in Tiraspol. Smiling ruefully, the young driver admitted that the bus station was out of his way and he was behind schedule.

The bus would be leaving soon, so I began running toward the station, holding the mesh bags as far out as possible on both sides so I wouldn't bump and break the eggs. By that time, I didn't have a clue which bag held what.

Do you know how difficult and tiring it is to run that far with arms outstretched and carrying cargo in each? An expectant mother-in-law waiting impatiently at the end of the race does provide motivation, though.

The bus was jammed full and ready to depart when I staggered on board, red-faced and gasping. I was forced to join other standing passengers crushed together in the aisle. With one hand, I managed to grab an overhead strap; the other clutched both large mesh bags.

From the minute the bus set off to Odessa, I swear it hit every pothole. It shook wildly and bounced, as those of us standing kept bumping into each other. Tightly squeezed between two young blue-collar workers who were dramatically recounting the latest soccer match by our Soviet national team, I became very alarmed, as both were gesturing energetically and constantly hitting the mesh bags.

Carefully, so as not to offend their feelings, I asked the ardent fans several times to calm down, and they sincerely tried. However, they would soon forget my entreaties and become animated again.

We were about halfway to Odessa when one of them, when vividly reenacting a blocked goal, raised a hand suddenly and collided with one of my mesh bags, hard. I lost control and loudly shouted, "Осторожно, яйца!" which means, "Watch my eggs!"

Everyone on that jam-packed bus stopped talking and just looked at me. After a moment, some passengers began giggling, some smirked, and others pointed at me and started whispering.

That's because, dear reader, the Russian slang word "яйца" means both "eggs" and "testicles," or—for simplicity—"balls." Very soon, snippets of conversation reaching my ears revealed that the distinguished pediatrician from Gradieshti had been just collectively awarded the title "this young man who protects his balls."

The bus lurched and bounced onward, as I now tried not to look at anyone. Finally, after the next stop a seat next to me became vacated, and I sat down, ready for a nap. My neighbor, an intelligent-looking middle-aged woman with large horn-rimmed glasses perched at the end of a powdered nose, leaned over and formally introduced herself as a high school teacher of anatomy.

"Young man, I want to tell you something very important," she said, in a lecturing tone. "I understand you have problems with, pardon the expression, your testicles. You appear to be a civilized man, so I am shocked why you should announce your private—if you know what I mean—problem to the entire group. It is totally inappropriate and unbecoming of you."

In vain, I tried to explain that it was all a misunderstanding, but the teacher did not listen. She continued her lecture, raising her voice to include everyone around us in her impromptu classroom.

"I'm an experienced woman in many ways and you are lucky to encounter me. I would not have started this delicate conversation, but I want to save your young life. You see, my late husband was an administrator in the theater and once he told me 'Honey, can you look at my privates; they appear to me to be larger than usual and one of them is bigger than the other.'"

I closed my eyes, willing her to stop. She was just getting going.

"Let me tell you, young man, that I put on the same glasses I wear today—I never misplace them—and closely inspected the area in question. My husband was right. We waited to see a doctor because we don't trust them, but were finally forced to because his testicles had swelled as big as oranges. This doctor had no idea what was happening to him.

He told my husband to wear looser drawers and prescribed for him pills, soaks, and *sitz* baths with French mustard and vinegar. Nothing helped. His testicles continue to puff up until my husband died.

"On the autopsy they found he had a cancer of his genitalia," she announced, louder than ever, "and nobody could ever diagnose it. And now, young man, I want you to go straight to a good doctor without delay. You need to nip it in a bud. If you have cancer this will save your life." She then pointed at my crotch. "Watch your balls!"

Having delivered her lesson, the teacher sighed deeply, closed her eyes, and went to sleep. When she began snoring, someone sitting behind me shook my shoulder. I turned around and saw a woman in her seventies, looking kindly but concerned.

"Young man," she said, not softly, "I listened to that other woman and have to tell you that she is dead wrong. My husband all his life had large balls. Now he is an old man and is still strong as an ox. Pay no attention to what this woman told you. What does she know about them balls?"

Unable to summon a single word in reply, all I could do was nod, turn back around, and close my eyes again. By the time the bus reached Odessa at twilight, two more elderly women had offered me free advice for treating my obviously afflicted family jewels. I just sat in my seat, hands wrapped around the two mesh bags and nodding. From the bottom of one of them, a long, booger-like thread began trickling toward the floor.

Miraculously, two eggs survived, as did all the chickens. The next day, my mother-in-law for the first time ever praised my abilities as a family breadwinner to her communal apartment neighbors.

A few days later, I caught the bus back to Tiraspol. The bus experienced an unexpected delay due to mechanical problems, and I arrived in the city three hours late. I had counted on hitchhiking the remaining ten miles to Gradieshti, but I soon discovered that the foot-and-mouth disease checkpoints were closed for the night, meaning that traffic to my village would be permitted to resume only the next morning.

I had three choices: walk back to downtown Tiraspol and hope to find a vacant hotel room, sleep on a bench in a bus or train station, or take advantage of the pleasant weather and walk for a few hours to Gradieshti.

I cheerfully started hiking home from the closed checkpoint, after conscientiously wiping the soles of my shoes on sawdust that was soaked with disinfectant solution intended to kill the foot-and-mouth virus.

It was a beautiful warm evening. The asphalt of the road was cooling down after a hot day, a fresh breeze blew agreeably on my face and through my hair, and the excited singing of cicadas filled the air. Twilight gradually approached as the sun touched the horizon. The road was so quiet and peaceful without traffic that time seemed to have stopped. With comfortable leather shoes on my feet and only a light bag in my hand, walking was a pleasure. Humming the melodies of favorite songs and whistling to birds winging their way to a night's sleep, I strode briskly toward home. The road was mostly flat but occasionally crested a low rolling hill.

The sun faded and the cloudless sky lit up with bright stars. Luckily, thanks to the rising moon, I still had enough light to see the way ahead. Polished by automobile tires, the smooth surface of the road reflected the moonlight. The wind blew at my back. On both sides of the road, ears of wheat rustled, and from somewhere distant came the muffled barking of dogs—many of them.

More than an hour passed. On the right side of the road I could see familiar hills and the silhouettes of military radar installations. To my satisfaction, I had already hiked half the distance to Gradieshti and was not tired. Not in a hurry, I found a broken tree trunk on the side of the road, sat on it, and pulled from my little bag a sausage sandwich my wife had packed for me. I began eating the sandwich, nibbling from time to time on a peeled cucumber.

There was a sudden rustling noise to my right, and a medium-sized, mongrel dog appeared. It approached anxiously and then stood expectantly in front of me, occasionally licking its muzzle. I pulled out my othersandwich and began gradually sharing it with the stray.

I resumed walking, and the dog—sometimes darting ahead and sometimes falling behind—ran alongside. Feeling comfortable, I pulled out and turned on a small Spidola shortwave radio. I listened to melodies on the popular "Mayak" station and then switched to the illegal Voice of America. Here, on a deserted road, I was not afraid of being denounced to the authorities.

About two miles outside of Gradieshti, in the moonlight, I could make out the familiar outlines of the hamlet where lived the large Funar family, whose children were my patients. The transistor radio sounded the popular lines of the "March of Enthusiasts" performed by the Red Army Choir: "We do not have any barriers in the sea or on land."

The dog abruptly stopped, straightened its ears toward the hamlet, and began growling. Perplexed and now cautious, I continued walking ahead. The dog stared in the night, growling, and would not move.

What was happening? Peering quickly at the trees and bushes on both sides of the road, I could see nothing in the darkness except wide, dark space. Taking a few steps forward, I invited the dog to do the same, but it stood anxiously rooted to the spot.

Something was definitely going on. Turning off the shortwave, I searched frantically for a piece of wood to defend myself from a yet unknown danger. A thick stalk of corn, which had probably fallen out of a truck during the day, was all I could find.

The dog stood tense and lifted its right paw for a moment, then turned and ran into a wheat field. I had no choice but to continue my slow journey home alone.

Soon, I grasped how truly and deeply I was in trouble. From the hamlet, I now heard the loud and angry barking of a pack of dogs rapidly approaching. I froze in place, not knowing what to do. It was useless to scream—no one would hear me anyway, and it would probably further infuriate the dogs. Running would also provoke them, and there was no tree in sight.

Meanwhile, the barking and growling drew closer and closer. Terrified, not knowing what to do, I continued to stand motionless in the middle of the road, clutching the tall cornstalk. About a hundred feet away, a pack of large dogs appeared in the moonlight, running toward me.

Right then, I remembered my father. When I was a child, he had shown me how to deal with an attacking dog. More than once when we had met aggressive strays, he would assume a peculiar semisitting position, leaning forward in a squat with buttocks protruding from behind. The animals always fled. He explained that the dogs became confused by the strange, changed shape of the human body. I would never have believed it if I hadn't seen it several times with my own eyes.

The son imitating the father, I assumed the same position in the middle of the road and waited, trembling.

Attention riveted on my impending mauling by wild dogs, I didn't notice a car turning on to the highway from a narrow road that split two nearby wheat fields. The Volga's lights illuminated me in full semi-sitting pose as it pulled up close. A back door opened, and the smell of stale wine wafted out. Howling, the dogs raced into the arc of headlights right toward us.

The driver shouted to me in Moldovan, "Hey, you! What are you are doing here in such an interesting posture in the middle of the night? Do you think the highway is a restroom?"

Two drunken passengers inside the car loudly laughed at his joke.

Yelling, "Let's move! Let's move!" I dove through the door as a large German shepherd leaped past the front of the car and tore one of my pant legs. The passengers quickly grabbed my arms and pulled me in as the driver stomped on the gas pedal, and the car peeled away.

Inside a tipsy man and two women passengers smiled at me. When I told them I was walking home to Gradieshti, one of woman smiled at me.

"Well, if you really want us to take you there, then you should drink with us," she declared, emphatically pouring a glass of wine from a cut-glass carafe and handing the drink to me. Without objection, I drank the contents in one gulp.

A few rounds later, they let me off at the gates of the hospital. Little Pal, who was lying on the porch, met my unsteady and weaving approach with a graceful thumping of his tail. Plopping down wearily next to him, exhausted from a long weekend of chases over too many miles, I began petting him and gazed up at the stars. My faithful dog stayed put and fell sleep. At long last, so did I.

An old man is dying in his hovel on the
steppes. There is a menacing banging on the
door. "Who's there?" the old man asks.

"Death" comes the reply.

"Thank God for that," he says, "I thought it was the KGB."

KGB Daughters, and Why Not to Treat Them

———— ✥ ————

O nce upon a time, there was a valiant, bold KGB major who became the chairman of the "Red Sparkle" *kolkhoz* in Gradieshti. This chairman, whose name was Seraphim Mikhailovich Namashko, was a most important and busy man. Most villagers glimpsed him only when his chic black Volga sped past them in a cloud of dust, driven by a discrete personal chauffeur. None of them owned such a magnificent vehicle, but what of it? They were all blessed to be equal in what they owned or didn't own, as the chairman and his secretive friends many times reminded them.

Those good, hardworking socialist citizens sometimes spied the chairman in the backseat of his shiny black car, in deep conversation with someone else. Who? It was better not to know. That's because the people of the village in their hearts feared him. Their leader didn't know that, because they always smiled at him. The people all knew that the chairman liked it when they smiled. If they didn't, he became very unhappy. Soon, so would they.

Before long, as the tale goes, the chairman fell in love with and married a secretary who worked in the main office of his *kolkhoz*. Capitolina Artemovna, a stout woman of the people, immediately accepted the trappings of her new, most glorious position. Who could fault her off-the-rack, imported clothes? Or the newly discovered sharpness of tone with the villagers, including former friends? Fortune had smiled upon the new wife, more than any other woman anyone knew.

The happy couple moved into a beautiful large house made of bricks, and surrounded themselves with a wall so wonderfully tall that no one could look in on and disturb their tranquility. There, assisted by a fierce and loyal servant, they talked on a phone whenever they wished and bathed in hot running water every day.

Six years before, the good chairman and his wife were blessed with the birth of the most beautiful daughter in the village, Natasha. As a dainty child of privilege in a worker's paradise, she always wore cute, colorful clothes made by other, less fortunate workers who sadly lived far outside of the enlightened Socialist Motherland.

Then one day, a dark chapter opened for the happy couple. The little princess became ill, for three days running a high fever, causing her father and mother such great distress. They became so sad. Before anyone knew it, practically the whole village became swept up in a collective effort to make their daughter healthy. Most importantly, everyone yearned for her most important father to be happy once more.

During the morning hours of my work one fall day at the outpatient clinic, Lyubov Evgenyevna Oprya suddenly burst into the examination room. She was out of breath and red-faced.

"What are we going to do, Vladimir Abramovich?" the chief doctor wailed, grabbing my arm.

"We will work for the benefit of our Socialist Motherland!" I snapped and saluted, by now being accustomed to her surprise visits.

"Do not joke, and be serious for a change!" admonished my boss. "The fact is that our Natasha is sick."

"Which 'our Natasha' are you talking about? There's more than a handful of them in Gradieshti."

"Did you just fall from the sky?" the chief doctor exclaimed. "Natasha, the daughter of Seraphim Mikhailovich, our collective farm chairman! She is sick! Her father called me early this morning. Yesterday evening, for the second day, her temperature was close to 104° and her legs were quite aching. This morning her temperature was 103°!"

Grabbing a patient chart, I shrugged and began turning away. "Well, she most probably has a cold. Everybody has it around this time. I will be happy to check her out in the clinic anytime."

"You are probably out of your mind!" my boss exploded, grabbing my arm again and whirling me around to face her. "Do you really expect that the Namashkos will bring their child to the clinic with such a high temperature? That's not how we do it here. Don't you understand that Natasha Namashko is a special patient?! Her parents are very busy people, and we are obliged to respect them and visit their daughter at home."

"How can I? My schedule is busy," I replied calmly, pointing to the door. "You see out there that my waiting room is full of patients. Natasha has been sick for a couple of days, and her symptoms are no different from other children."

"Stop being silly!" Lyubov Evgenyevna objected, now bristling with indignation. "Listen! I will personally take care of your patients. You go straight to Natasha. The hospital car awaits you outside. Don't forget to greet the hostess nicely—no jokes!—to take your shoes off when you enter the house, and to put on your best doctor gown. Our chairman's wife keeps her home meticulously clean. Everything there sparkles.

"And now listen to what I am telling you," she went on, in a quieter, conspiratorial tone. "Do you remember the special conference I went to a couple of weeks ago? I will tell you secret information, but you must not share it with anybody. The Chief Infectious Disease Specialist told us that two cases of wild polio have been diagnosed in Moldova. Since Natasha has a fever and she complained that her little legs were hurting, I told Seraphim Mikhailovich about it. Remember, he is a former KGB officer, and I should not hide secrets from him. He got scared listening to my information, but I do not regret it. I could not hide my knowledge about the recent cases of polio in Moldova from him."

Why in the world would she tell him that? Thanks to vaccination, polio has practically disappeared. He's going to be alarmed about nothing.

I left immediately, clearly grasping that my boss had managed to brew another mess, and now, without batting an eye, was sending me to deal with it.

Within a few minutes, I was knocking on the door of the chairman's grand brick home. The family domestic servant, Madalina, opened the door and glared at me for moment. Reluctantly, she let me in. I removed my shoes, sat down in the chair offered to me, and awaited the very special patient. Very soon, Capitolina Artemovna, dressed in a chic satin Chinese robe, entered, holding the hand of her daughter.

Upon seeing me, Natasha immediately disliked my white doctor's gown, for some reason. "No! I want the doctor to leave our house!" she cried, slipping from her mother's grasp and running into another room. For the next ten minutes, I could hear the fashionably dressed mother in the adjacent room soothing her pitifully sobbing daughter and urging her to agree to an examination.

There was nothing to do but wait. Madalina, who sat opposite me, looked me up and down like a ravenous German shepherd. *Was there anyone in the village she liked?* Rather than stare back, I stood up and took in the many photographs hanging on the walls. Along with family photos, there were pictures of a stern Seraphim Mikhailovich in the uniform of a KGB major and also equally formidable in civilian clothes.

Capitolina Artemovna finally carried Natasha back into the living room. The mother held her daughter in her expansive arms while the little one sobbed, her wet nose buried in her mother's shoulder.

"Doctor," Capitolina Artemovna said firmly, "I promised my daughter that the examination will be very quick."

Before the examination, Capitolina Artemovna, with Natasha in her arms, escorted me to the sink to wash my hands. Under her close supervision, I meticulously washed my hands in the kitchen under running water, with a big piece of laundry soap. Upon returning to the living room, the mother handed me a piece of cotton soaked in vodka, and demanded I wipe the bell of my stethoscope with it before touching her daughter.

And then, a very enjoyable examination began. Natasha, whose temperature was still high and who still had pain in her leg muscles, expressed her extreme displeasure through sobs, frowns, and constant fidgeting. Inspection of the throat—the most unpleasant part of a doctor visit for any child—I put off until the very end.

No amount of persuasion could force the child to open her mouth. Natasha sat on her mother's lap, teeth tightly clenched. Capitolina Artemovna and I pleaded with her again and again to open her mouth and say "Ah-h-h," but she just shook her head and defiantly refused.

Right then, her father entered the room noiselessly in his soft boots. Hands on hips, dressed smartly in tunic and breeches, the chairman rapidly became impatient with our efforts.

Stepping forward, he looked at me with great reproach as I smiled at him. "Just look at you, doctor," he said disdainfully, stroking his gloriously full gray moustache. "I wonder what they taught you at your medical school. You do not even know how to unclench the mouths of your patients, and I, the chairman of the *kolkhoz*, need to teach you how to do it. Lucky for you, I worked for the special service where we easily and without wasting precious time did a procedure on those who tried to resist us."

"Madalina, bring me a clean tablespoon," he ordered the servant, not even looking at her. "And you, Capitolina, take Natasha on your lap, put her legs between your knees and hold them tight. Learn, doctor!"

Leaning down, the father tightly compressed Natasha's cheeks on both sides between his thumb and forefinger. Ignoring the loud screams of his daughter, he quickly inserted the flat end of the tablespoon between her teeth, pressing the tongue down. Despite the cascade of tears, I was able to get a good view of Natasha's throat and announced with supreme confidence that everything was in good order.

"You see, doctor, though you recently graduated from medical school and I did not, you still have many things to learn," my instructor patronizingly informed me, returning the tablespoon to Madalina. "The method I just demonstrated to you we used to call the 'KGB hold.' Remember it; it will be useful for you to know in the future."

"You bet I will remember," I enthusiastically assured the chairman, giving him an even broader smile.

The examination completed, Madalina took the whimpering Natasha into another room.

"In medicine there are no absolutes," I said to the parents, when we were alone. "But in Natasha's case, I am sure you should not worry too much about anything serious regarding your daughter. It is definitely not polio. The muscle pain in her legs is produced by her flu-like condition. It happens quite frequently. Another reason not to worry is that Natasha has received full vaccination against polio for her age."

The chairman's face became red and he advanced toward me, now clearly outraged. "But why did your boss scare my wife and me to death with all this polio business?" Seraphim Mikhailovich shouted.

"Isolated cases of polio indeed occur in extremely low numbers, but they are caused by the wild virus and are the exception to the rule, not the rule," I replied, keeping my voice calm and looking the former KGB major steadily in the eyes.

"Whatever you say, pal. But keep in mind that if you are mistaken, you are going to be in big trouble," the father spat, dark threat in every word.

"I understand your anxiety, and I promise to examine your daughter twice a day if necessary until her full recovery," I replied swiftly, packing the medical bag as fast as I could. "You can send your car for me any time. But I am sure everything will be all right. Just listen to how much fun Natasha is having now playing in the other room."

"We *will* see you tomorrow, doctor," Seraphim Mikhailovich stated laconically as I fled his house, still smiling.

After two days of uneventful visits to the Namashko residence, and Natasha recovering nicely, I was surprised to find the chief doctor nervously waiting for me in the doctor's lounge, early in the morning of the third day.

"Listen, Vladimir Abramovich," she began in a choked voice, twisting a pencil in her hands as I walked into the room. "We need to work out a clear plan of action. An hour ago Seraphim Mikhailovich came to my house. Both Capitolina Artemovna and he are scared because Natasha continues to have a high temperature at night. Plus, she still has pains in her legs and she had a severe headache last night. Do not take it personally, but her father thinks you are too young and inexperienced to be trusted to handle such a serious situation. He was astonished earlier this week when he had to teach you how to open Natasha's mouth for examination."

Sure, maybe it would help if all pediatricians were trained by the KGB.

"Seraphim Mikhailovich used a lot of profanities in our conversation," the chief doctor admitted, looking very pale, "which I accept because I am a devoted Communist like him and because he is very nervous. We need to help him out. We must do something."

"But I have no doubt that all his daughter has is a viral upper respiratory infection, just like everyone else," I said reassuring to my frightened boss. "Last night, when I was leaving the Namashko residence, Natasha was running and jumping around the house just like any healthy girl. If it were polio, she would have dangerous manifestations of the disease by this time, but she shows absolutely nothing."

"To be honest, it is difficult for me to understand your logic, Vladimir Abramovich. Don't you understand that your patient might have a nontypical form of polio?! You are ignoring the fact that polio exists in Moldova. Do you have enough experience to take full responsibility for Natasha's health condition? And do you have any idea what might happen to both of us if something goes seriously wrong with his child?"

We both visited the Namashko residence, a few hours later, first performing the required rituals of shoe removal, hand washing, and wiping of the stethoscopes. We then anxiously waited in the living room for the patient's arrival. Seraphim Mikhailovich was not home. Soon, Natasha, disgruntled and half-asleep, appeared in the living room, accompanied by her mother and Madalina.

As I expected, her physical examination showed no changes—none—since the last time I had seen her, yesterday. Unfortunately, Lyubov Evgenyevna Oprya began wringing her hands and expressing deep concern about "lethargy"—well, yes, that was because the patient was not yet fully awake.

"I am sure that something is going on," Lyubov Evgenyevna interjected excitedly several times, making everyone even more nervous. She leaned forward, and I did not like the all-too-familiar conspiratorial gleam in her eyes. "I did not say it before," she went on, dramatically lowering her voice, "but now I will tell you in confidence: we, the hospital chief doctors of the republic, were notified at a recent meeting in Beltsy that there is an increased number of cases of meningitis among children in Moldova."

Great, just great.

With the meningitis scare, my boss performed the cheapest trick in an unscrupulous physician's book—conjuring an alibi of horrendous disease in case of unforeseen complications. Once I asked one of my colleagues why he always shamelessly exaggerated the patient's condition. "And why not? It costs me nothing," was his cynical response. "If they get better, I am seen as a miracle worker. If they don't, then everyone blames the unstoppable disease, not me."

To put it in the simplest language, my boss was covering her behind.

"Capitolina Artemovna, may I contact your husband immediately?" the chief doctor appealed to the hostess, a most somber expression now playing on her wide face.

"Of course, of course," answered the dismayed mother, quickly.

"Seraphim Mikhailovich, this is Lyubov Evgenyevna," my boss started the telephone conversation, crisp and authoritative. "The pediatrician and I just finished Natasha's evaluation. Of course, it is encouraging that her condition has not changed much, but what I personally do not like—and Vladimir Abramovich agrees with me one hundred percent—is that Natasha still has headaches and that she looks lethargic this morning. The problem is that a week ago at the conference in Beltsy, we, the hospital chief physicians were informed—confidentially of course, but to you, I can disclose this—that in two villages in Moldova at least two preschool children have died of meningitis.

"After our thorough discussion here, we came to the conclusion that with such unfortunate circumstances, we must insure we are on the right path, and we both advise that Natasha should have a consultation with a reputable child neurologist at Tiraspol City Hospital. I am ready to accompany you when we go there."

The chairman's response made Lyubov Evgenyevna first straighten up, then get to her feet. Her eyes widened and face fell as she stood at attention.

"Yes, Comrade Chairman. Yes, Comrade Chairman. Right you are, Comrade Chairman! I understand you, Comrade Chairman," she said obediently. Then, as if it was a fragile piece of glass, she carefully placed the handset on the cradle.

"Seraphim Mikhailovich," she said to us carefully, with deep meaning, "is on his way here. He is *very* unhappy. He wants to discuss this issue with us. He does not trust Tiraspol."

Within minutes, through the door carefully opened by his loyal personal chauffeur, the chairman of the *kolkhoz* stomped into his house. Everyone sprang up as Capitolina Artemovna ran toward him, wringing her hands.

"Seraphim, dear, what are we going to do? We must save our baby," she cried, holding her face in her hands. "Children are dying from meningitis all around, and Natasha is lethargic!"

Her husband menacingly stepped closer to me and Lyubov Evgenyevna. We both tried very hard to smile at him.

"Explain to me, Doctor Oprya!" he shouted, the spittle now flying. "Explain to me why my daughter's condition becomes worse every day! Tell me what prevents you headless white robes from helping my child. Do you want to be punished for neglecting my daughter's health? Do you? Is this some kind of sabotage?"

"Seraphim Mikhailovich, please calm down, I beseech you. As one Communist to another, I assure you, we are doing everything possible," Lyubov Evgenyevna replied, remarkably not fainting. "Natashenka gets the most expensive tinctures, vitamins, nasal drops, and antibiotics. Her blood tests are not bad either."

"You know nothing," the father waved dismissively. "One of you could not even examine the child's throat without my help. Forget about it. My driver is brighter than both of you, and on the way here he gave me excellent advice which I am going to follow now." Standing even taller, he glared at us. "My daughter *will* see an eminent specialist from Kishinev. I want him here, is that clear? You, Lyubov, go to the hospital and call the specialist from there. Use my name and tell them we need a pediatric consultant urgently. Got it?"

"Seraphim Mikhailovich, maybe it is better to take Natasha to nearby Tiraspol? Right now Natasha is not sick enough to call a consultant from the capital." My boss spoke reasonably, her gaze never leaving his.

"Do what I told you to do and don't contradict me! 'No' means 'no,' Communist Oprya!" barked the *kolkhoz* chairman. "I cannot understand you. Are you trying to tell me that, after all I do for the Motherland, my child does not deserve a consultation? Go and make the phone call, Lyubov! In the meantime, I am going to speak with my friends at the Central Committee in Kishinev.

"Right now it is 10 a.m.," the chairman concluded, glancing at his watch. "The specialist should arrive here early in the evening. Period."

As soon as our car arrived back at the hospital, Lyubov Evgenyevna popped out like a cork from a champagne bottle and, shuffling rapidly on short legs, ran to the phone in the doctors' lounge. Overhearing her conversation with both a physician in the capital and a nurse from the Sanitarnaya Aviatsia (Medical Air Flights)—an air ambulance service providing emergency specialist consultations and medical evacuations—I was astonished to learn that my patient, Natasha Namashko, was critically ill and needed immediate attention. Potemkin village on fire!

Lyubov Evgenyevna, looking much less frantic, carefully put the handset down and turned to me. "You see, Vladimir Abramovich," she began, in full lecture mode, "once again I have to do your job. When I was a young professional, no one ever helped me. But look at how I am spoiling you here. The consultant from Kishinev will arrive in Tiraspol at 1 p.m. on the San-Av airplane. Our hospital car will meet him there and bring him here to the hospital. After the specialist is done with the consultation, our car will take him to the Tiraspol railway station. At eleven o'clock in the evening he will take a train to Kishinev. Did I miss anything?"

The plan was indeed excellent, except that the specialist didn't arrive at Gradieshti Hospital until seven o'clock in the evening, five hours later than expected. The specialist from Kishinev was Dr. Gleb Markovich Shereshevsky, who used to teach childhood infectious diseases at the medical school where I had recently studied. He was strict but fair, never missing a chance to lecture us medical students about professional ethics.

When he saw me, he nodded and smiled warmly as if we were old friends.

"Contingencies. In Kishinev we had an unexpected thunderstorm," he breezily explained to Lyubov Evgenyevna and me. "Flight delayed twice. Nothing could be done about the weather."

"What a pity," Lyubov Evgenyevna acknowledged. "We need your opinion about a young patient. Vladimir Abramovich and I are afraid of missing the early stages of polio or meningitis. Fortunately, this girl does not need to be in the hospital."

"Oh, that's nothing unusual," the consultant answered impatiently. "Let's see the patient, now. After my consultation, I must rush back to Kishinev. Tomorrow I have a *very* busy day."

"Do not worry, doctor," promised the chief doctor, energetically. "It will not take much of your time!"

"Well, that's fine," Gleb Markovich commented, looking at his watch. "In that case, I'll be just in time for my train."

"And we're ready of course any time," Lyubov Evgenyevna said coquettishly and cheerfully. "Wait for a minute, please. I will notify the patient's father, the chairman of the *kolkhoz*, Comrade Namashko, that we are on our way. I am sure he will be extremely delighted to hear the news."

Gleb Markovich and I were chatting about events in the news when Lyubov Evgenyevna returned from the office. Deep disappointment was written on her face.

"I have unpleasant news, Gleb Markovich," she said slowly, catching her breath. "We have to wait until tomorrow morning to visit the chairman of the *kolkhoz*'s daughter. I feel very sorry, Gleb Markovich, about the delay. I assure you that we will provide you with royal accommodations in one of the hospital's rooms far from the patients. You will be so comfortable there, you will not want to leave us."

Gleb Markovich was shocked. "What do you mean I cannot examine the patient right away?" he exploded. "It's only seven thirty! I was in such a hurry and spent three hours traveling here, and now I must wait until tomorrow? Is that so? Tell me why we cannot examine the patient immediately and be done with it. That way I would be able to be back in Kishinev on time. I'm an associate professor. I am a respected specialist and researcher. I have my plans, my schedule. In Kishinev I was assured that—"

"Doctor Shereshevsky, you must understand our side of the story! I am sure you're a father yourself," retorted Lyubov Evgenyevna with an air of offended righteousness. "The poor child and her family were expecting you all day and their nerves have gone to pieces. The poor child needs rest! The girl was extremely tired and nervous, and her parents have put her to bed. Her father told me that tomorrow morning at nine o'clock Natasha will be ready for the visit. Meanwhile, I wish you good night, dear doctor."

But my former teacher was not willing to giving up. "Thank you, but I must be back in Kishinev tonight," he insisted, furious. "Suppose she were not at home but in the hospital now. Would it make any difference whether she was asleep or awake? I know who her father is. Just because he is such a big shot, I have to spend an extra day in your village? Are you kidding me? I have my responsibilities. Where's the phone? Let me talk personally with your chairman!"

"Oh, no! For your own sake, this is not advisable for you to do at all!" exclaimed Lyubov Evgenyevna, now genuinely scared. "Sera-phim Mikhailovich is a very busy man. Not only he is the chairman of the *kolkhoz*, he's also a hero of labor. We must treat him with great respect."

"So what? I also have my medals. You—not he—are the chief doctor of the hospital! His business is the *kolkhoz*, but your business is health!"

"Yes, I am the chief physician of the hospital, but in case you do not know," the chief doctor whispered, looking around, "he is not only the chairman of the collective farm, but he also happens to be a former major of the KGB."

The very busy and loudly demanding Doctor Shereshevsky from Kishinev stopped abruptly and stared at us. A few minutes later, our consultant obediently followed an orderly, who showed him where he would spend the night.

At nine o'clock the next morning, a motorcade consisting of Doctor Shereshevsky, the chief medical doctor, her deputy, and I drove to the large brick house of the chairman of the *kolkhoz*.

Next to the house stood the crème de la crème of village society: tall and lean Comrade Lupu, the local party secretary with his wife; the head of the village council; the head of the kindergarten; and the chief of the Gradieshti Cultural Center, Valeriu Raylyan, whom, I am confident, was mentally composing just the right slogan for the occasion. They had all decided to visit by "the call of their hearts" to learn the opinion of the consultant about poor Natasha's health. Deep concern and sorrow were written on mournful faces. Since the hosts did not allow them into their home, the only way they could demonstrate their devotion to the chairman of the *kolkhoz*'s daughter was to stand patiently outside.

The secretary of the local party greeted our medical team as if he were the impromptu group's representative. "Thank you so much for coming, doctor," Comrade Lupu said, pumping Doctor Shereshevsky's hand and studiously ignoring us. "You are our only hope. Tell us what you need, and we will be glad to satisfy all your requests."

Shaking his head and rolling his eyes at me, my former teacher walked with us into the house of the patient. Under the stern supervision of Madalina, we removed our shoes, put on white robes, ritually washed our hands, and took our places at the table where everybody spoke in whispers.

"Is this all really necessary?" Doctor Shereshevsky murmured to me. I simply raised my eyebrows and smiled at him.

Soon the bedroom door opened, and the star of the occasion entered, dressed in pajamas and accompanied by her worried parents. On this day, Seraphim Mikhailovich's appearance more than ever resembled the late leader of all times and all peoples. All that was lacking was Stalin's smoking pipe.

As soon as the parents had dryly greeted those present, Lyubov Evgenyevna, in a mellifluous voice, asked Capitolina Artemovna about Natasha's health.

"Thanks. Natasha is better today," her mother curtly replied, eyes only on the doctor from Kishinev. "Her temperature was normal. She did not complain about pain in her head or legs, and she was more playful this morning as well.

"I did everything you told me, Lyubov Evgenyevna," she continued. "Wrapped an alcohol compress around her neck, rubbed her chest with alcohol, applied a mustard plaster to the soles of her feet. A lot of work, but Madalina helped me."

"Wonderful, wonderful," my boss replied, eagerly smiling at the chairman, who said nothing. "I am glad it helped her."

"Excuse me, Lyubov Evgenyevna, but you are an obstetrician-gynecologist, not a pediatrician," intervened Doctor Shereshevsky, looking puzzled and glancing at me. "Why were the medical orders coming from you?"

"Oh, what are you talking about?" Lyubov Evgenyevna responded with a disarming smile. "I did not interfere with Natasha's treatment at all. Having my own children, I was simply sharing my experience with Capitolina Artemovna."

Doctor Shereshevsky quickly performed a physical evaluation of the patient. Confronted with the presence of unusual guests, Natasha was not capricious and meekly obeyed the commands given to her. When it came time for the examination of her throat, she dutifully opened her mouth and produced a loud "Ah-h-h."

Gleb Markovich once more reviewed the basic laboratory results, made a note in the patient's record, rolled his eyes again at me, and then turned to the parents.

"Allow me to congratulate you, "he proclaimed, cheerfully. "There is absolutely nothing I can add to the treatment of your daughter. Natasha suffers from a flu-like disease complicated by a prolonged but slight involvement of the muscular system. There is not a smidgen of suspicion of polio, meningitis, or anything else serious."

"Well, thank you for the good news, doctor. In that case, I do not understand why Lyubov Evgenyevna frightened us with the possibility that Natasha might have had polio or meningitis," replied Chairman Namashko, his stony expression apparent to all of us.

"Dear Seraphim Mikhailovich," my boss immediately broke in, clearly relieved. "I repeat once again, I was providing friendly advice, nothing more, nothing less." Laughing slightly, she nodded toward me. "All the time, Natasha's attending physician was Dr. Tsesis."

"I am out of time and will speak with you later, Dr. Oprya," retorted Chairman Namashko. He turned toward the consultant, looking at him closely. "Do you *guarantee* Natasha does not suffer from polio or meningitis, doctor?

"I can guarantee you that," Gleb Markovich, replied with an understanding smile. "After one more day at home, your daughter may safely return to normal activity."

"Well, in that case, we are over this problem," concluded the father, rising to his feet. "I must go, comrades. People are waiting for me in the office."

Before leaving, the chairman ripped a sheet of paper from his note-book, wrote something on it in pen, and handed it to my former teacher.

"Thank you for the good news, doctor," he said. "Here is the phone number of my friend at the Central Committee. Call him and tell him who you are. This man will be useful to you."

No one said a word as we doctors filed past the village delegation, still standing in the yard, and got back into the car.

"This Sanitary Aviation call was absolutely unjustified!" Dr. Shere-shevsky hotly, indignantly, and loudly lectured the chief doctor as we rose toward the train station in Tiraspol.

"Think about it! Only because this man is the chairman of the *kolkhoz* and former KGB does he have the nerve to demand—practically without a reason—a consultant from Sanitary Aviation!" Doctor Shereshevsky continued, heatedly. "You better believe me, I am not going to let it go! I am a man of principle. Be assured! First thing tomorrow morning, I will write a report about this unjustified visit. The Minister of Public Health of the Moldavian Republic, Nikolai Andreevich Testemitsanu, was one of my best friends in medical school. If necessary, I will speak personally with him! Just think what this unjustified visit cost: ambulance, airplane, train, car, travel!"

A month later, during a medical conference in Kishinev, I stumbled upon Gleb Markovich Shereshevsky between sessions. After we warmly greeted each other, I asked him what had happened with the report he was going to write about his visit to Gradieshti.

"Yes, I wrote a detailed report," my former teacher answered evasively. "When an answer had not come in a week or so, I called the chief of the Sanitary-Aviation service. He responded that he had read my statement but did not think any action was necessary since the case was not a typi-cal one. And he told me that our socialist economy is rich enough not to worry about such an episode."

Gleb Markovich suddenly grinned mysteriously and his eyes bright-ened. "You won't believe this," he said confidentially, lowering his voice, "but unexpectedly my trip to Gradieshti had great results. Do you re-member how Comrade Namashko asked me to call his friend in the Central Party Committee of the Moldavian Republic? Indeed, I did. Imagine, after I conveyed greetings from Seraphim Mikhailovich to this comrade, all of a sudden I became very popular among very interesting people. For example, last night I was asked to come to the house of the Minister of Commerce. Actually, it was nothing urgent. The one-year-old daughter of the minister was cutting her teeth, but her parents were afraid of missing something more serious.

I never knew that connections could be so useful. I waited five years to install a telephone in my communal apartment, and now, thanks to my new friends, I have my own personal telephone line. You think that was all? No! You might not believe me, but they promised me that in a couple of years I would have the chance to buy my first car. Please, send my warmest greetings to Chairman Namashko and his wonderful family!"

Waving, my former teacher walked away in good spirits, returning to a life now better because of happenstance and personal favor. As for me, I returned to my little apartment, made the rounds at the hospital the next morning, and never again set foot inside of the chairman's stupendously sanitized house.

And so the villagers rejoiced that their little princess had returned to the full sunshine of perfect health. As the chairman's black chauffeur-driven car roared past them, they smiled as they wiped spattered black mud and dirt from their dull worn clothes. He was happy and so were they all, once again.

An American is visiting the Soviet Union. He's taking a train from Leningrad to Kiev and listening to his handheld radio when a Soviet man leans over to talk to him.

"You know, we make those better and more efficiently here in the Soviet Union," he says.

"Oh?" Says the American.

"Yes," the Soviet man responds. "What is it?"

The West Meets the Best

---⟨∅⟩---

The day the Americans came to Gradieshti, I vowed to see and hear for myself whether the promises and reports I listened to in secret on the Voice of America broadcasts were really true.

They were.

I was an educated professional, and socialist doctrine expected me to perform some kind of community work in Gradieshti. When asked about my preference, I offered to lead an English study group of teachers and high school students once a week in the evening. The only foreign language taught at the school was French, so its administration was keenly interested in my offer.

One late afternoon, while I was working in the doctors' lounge, I received an unexpected personal telephone call from no one else but Zachary Ionovich Lupu, the secretary of the local Communist Party organization, whom we have met a number of interesting times in this story.

"Hello, doctor Tsesis," Comrade Lupu began with gusto, "I have a special assignment for you. As you well know, our *kolkhoz* "Red Sparkle" is one of the wealthiest and most advanced in our district. We are the recipient of a high honor: an American delegation—seven people—will arrive tomorrow to visit us and to learn secrets of our success."

Pausing, he continued in a lower voice. "Now, this is only for your ears. I want you to know that the guide for this group, Dmitry Zorin, is a KGB officer. He speaks Russian and Moldovan, but not English. The group's official interpreter unexpectedly caught a bad cold, and I was told that you teach English to the villagers. I have already spoken with your chief physician; she has canceled your work in the ambulatory tomorrow and you will be able to spend the entire day with our guests. Ready?"

Well, this was completely unexpected, and welcome. I had never before met a single foreigner and always was looking to do so. Also, I would have a unique chance to listen to real American English. I quickly answered that I was indeed ready, but not sure my English was adequate for the task.

The Communist secretary told me not to worry. "Don't let it bother you. Members of the delegation were notified you are not professional translator. They will forgive you."

The next morning, exactly at 9 a.m., a small bus, driven by none other than the personal chauffeur of the *kolkhoz* chairman, arrived to the hospital's main entrance. Taking my seat, I introduced myself to everyone in Russian and English.

Besides me on the bus were eight passengers. Dmitry Zorin, the official guide of the group and KGB officer, was an ordinary-looking, muscular man in civilian clothing in his forties. He had fair skin, mid-length auburn hair, and hazel eyes. Not forgetting who he was, I tried to keep a respectful distance and communicate with him as little as possible. He did the same but out of contempt.

The Americans were two professors and five students (three boys and two girls), all from the same agricultural college in California. Jerry Wilson, the head of their delegation, was in his fifties, tall with gray eyes, and sporting precisely cut short blonde hair. He had an angular face, impressive eyes, and smooth cheeks. His fellow professor, Rudolph Zell, slight shorter, was fairly thin and quite tan. He had blue eyes and short, curly dark brown hair. Both professors were bareheaded and dressed in jeans and dark cardigans. The students, certainly instructed beforehand to be as invisible as possible, were quiet and communicated mostly among themselves.

It did not take me too long to realize that Professor Wilson was an ardent supporter of the Soviet experiment, never missing an opportunity to express his admiration for socialism. On the other hand, Professor Zell did not miss a chance to insert an acidic remark about our way of life from time to time. Throughout that day, I wondered why these two opposites traveled together and what the rest of their trip in the Soviet Union must have been like.

The entire visit worked to Potemkin perfection: as ordered and scripted as possible, with anything perceived to be lacking always on order or scheduled to be built.

Even with the windows rolled up, we on the bus could all smell the *kolkhoz*'s pig farm before we reached it. Expecting our visit, the farm's supervisor and his two assistants were nicely dressed for the occasion, greeting us as we disembarked with wide smiles. It was obvious to me that the workers had done their best to clean inside and outside of the building.

Professor Wilson could not stop admiring all that he saw, especially the fat snorting pigs feeding cute piglets, as if he never saw such a picture in his own country. In the meantime, Professor Zell began a running commentary, intended for his senior partner only, about poor light, ventilation, absence of a heating system, poor window insulation, and, of course, the omnipresent filth. Eventually Professor Wilson made a few negative remarks to the hosts. Their response was—as anticipated—that the shortcomings were only temporary and would be corrected in the next week or two. Everything had been ordered and was on their way.

Passing cornfields on the way to the central dairy farm—another triumphal source of our *kolkhoz*'s pride—the Americans noticed many young people dressed in urban clothing working in them. They tore corncobs from the stalk of the plant, pulled out leaves and silk from them, and then threw the cleaned corncobs to large piles on the ground. Some people were working; others were lying on the plant beds made out of yellowish corn stalks. Many of the boys were smoking. I spotted only a handful of *kolkhozniks*.

"Those are students from Tiraspol. They are here to help this *kolkhoz* harvest the corn," loudly explained Dmitry Zorin to the Americans, with my translation. He was met with nods.

The KGB officer then turned to me and confided in Russian that the highlight of today's agenda would be a meeting between American and Soviet students in the Gradieshti Cultural Center. "This important meeting is the main reason why I needed you," he said. "From the moment the Americans came under my supervision, they asked to meet with local people. In our business, we should be cautious; initially I was planning a conference with *kolkhozniks*, but how could I be sure they will not say something wrong? Fortunately, I learned about the students whom you just saw. Let the Americans speak with them, I thought. We'll have the right questions and answers. We need to present ourselves in the best light. Yesterday, I spent the whole day with these students selecting and preparing them for the meeting."

He concluded with a simple admonition: "Watch carefully how you translate."

When we arrived at the central dairy farm, just as had happened at the last stop, the supervisor and his assistants—all dressed in freshly pressed white lab coats and white caps—warmly met the delegation. As we toured, I must admit that I had never seen such a clean farm. The Americans nodded their heads in approval when the supervisor enthusiastically recounted the successes of the dairy farm and its bright prospects for the future.

At the end of presentation, Professor Wilson invited everybody to join in applause, but Professor Zell held up his hands and insisted on a few questions.

"Mister Supervisor, no doubt you all are working hard to achieve your success, but I wonder how you protect your cattle from excessive high and low variations of temperature? How do you provide water for the animals? How do you wash them?"

"Oh, that's very simple," answered the supervisor, smiling benignly. "What you see here, comrade foreigner, is nothing more than an old building. Our *kolkhoz* "Red Sparkle" currently builds a modern dairy farm with all the improvements we need! It will be operational very soon."

Looking at the still-skeptical American professor and stern KGB officer standing behind him, the supervisor swallowed nervously and continued, speaking faster. "As Communists, we never rest on our laurels. We already have a plan to eradicate drunkenness and lewd behavior, especially among cow caretakers. The City of Tiraspol pipe plant made a commitment to help us with the construction and to provide our farm with diesel fuel for engines. The furniture factory, another sponsor of our farm, promises us to give funds for fodder for them—for our beloved cows." I did my best to translate at a slower speed.

Professor Zell turned to me, clearly annoyed. "Doctor, please ask this dairy farm supervisor why he tells us all this gibberish." Dmitry Zorin did not take his eyes off of us as we spoke in English. "That's crazy! What does this drunkenness, lewd behavior, a pipe manufacturing plant, and a furniture factory have to do with the dairy business? Ask him!"

All of sudden, Professor Wilson slid over to the side of his fellow professor, looking tense. Starring down with his gray eyes, he hissed, "Rudolph, you better shut up, you son of a bitch! If you do not stop your provocations, I will make sure you will never receive another permission to come to the Soviet Union. Do you understand? You better shut your mouth! Do you want an international scandal? Is that you want?"

"But, Jerry, where is any common sense? Is that a madhouse or a dairy farm? I only wanted to—" Professor Zell fell silent at the sight of the glowing eyes of his partner.

Dmitry Zorin expressed his satisfaction when I translated an edited version of that whispered conversation to him.

"Good for you, Professor," he said squeezing and shaking Wilson's hand. "I am proud of you!"

The good socialist supporter from California beamed.

The next stop on our Potemkin tour was the *kolkhoz*'s kindergarten, where its director and two educators greeted us with lush bouquets of flowers. Dmitry Zorin proudly explained to the Americans that kindergartens in the Soviet Union were free of charge, news greeted favorably by all of the delegation.

After walking through a few classrooms, everyone was invited to the main hall to listen to the toddlers' chorus. The children lined up in a semicircle, with those better dressed, I noticed right away, ushered to the first row. However, one ambitious four-year-old boy in the third row pushed his way to the first and now stood right in front of the Americans, very pleased with himself. The problem was that the boy's clothes were old, wrinkled, and obviously not as clean as his neighbors.

While the children were preparing to sing, one of the American students took a small camera from his trousers, ready to take a picture of the charming little group. When the kindergarten director noticed the camera lens aimed at her charges, among them the shabbily dressed boy, she yelled "No, no, no! Take it away!" Grabbing two of the welcome bouquets, she shielded the misplaced boy from the foreigners with flowers.

Snatching the camera, Zorin angrily reminded Professor Wilson that one of the conditions of the trip was to take pictures only when it was permitted. In turn, Professor Wilson scolded the student for trying to take pictures.

The children sang and then everyone left, not entirely happy. The boy in worn clothes picked up a bouquet at his feet, looking confused, as we walked out.

After a generous lunch at the Village Cultural center, we met seven Soviet students—four girls and three boys—in a conference room. Dmitry Zorin introduced everyone at the round table. Warning that the time was limited because the delegation needed to leave Gradieshti very soon, he asked the Americans to start their round of questions. I stood by to translate everything. Professor Wilson asked the first one.

"My delegation and I, personally, are happy to meet with you," he said, all smiles. "We all are from an agricultural college in California. And where are you from?"

"We all are first- and second-year students from Kishinev Music Conservatory," answered the Komsomol leader, Leonid Kuznetzov, a young man with blue eyes and blond hair.

"Excuse me, young man," Professor Zell, now surprised, raised his hand. "Did I understand you correctly: are you really all students of the music conservatory?"

"Yes, we all are musicians," Leonid proudly replied, looking only at him.

"It is very nice you came here to help with crops," the professor continued, with compassion, "but what kind of extraordinary condition forced this *kolkhoz* to ask help from musicians? After all, you are representative of a special profession where it is critical to have your hands intact and to practice daily. I play piano and know well how important it is not to lose musical skills."

"I do not understand what you mean by 'extraordinary condition,'" the Komsomol leader smoothly objected. "Like hundreds of thousands of students all over the country, we come here to help the agricultural workers. This is completely normal. Soviet agriculture needs our help because, thanks to our modern methods, the size of crops increases every year. The villagers do not have enough manpower to harvest such bumper crops by themselves. That's very simple."

Professor Zell pressed his point. "So, in this case, did you bring musical instruments with you to practice here?"

"But we are here only for four or five weeks," quickly replied the student, now becoming a bit nervous.

"What about your hands? I suppose you should be very careful about them? I am asking you as a musician myself."

"That's not a problem at all; it was taken into consideration from the start. Corn is not rough to deal with. Students from the engineering school, for example, are digging potatoes this year, which is a lot dirtier job. Besides, the collective farm representative assured us that we soon will be getting special gloves. They are on back order."

"Do you enjoy your work?" an American student named Paul asked, looking at the Soviet students.

"Oh yes, we are having a great time," a young girl answered in Moldovan, smiling, "and we are happy to be here to help!"

"But how do you know that your help is really needed? What if they deceive you?"

"How can you ask such an outrageous question?" the girl replied, looking puzzled. "As members of the Komsomol, we never doubt the words of our Communist leaders. It's our ethics, which you, obviously, cannot understand."

Dmitry Zorin's face expressed deep satisfaction. He felt like a conductor of a well-tuned orchestra.

"How much are you going to be paid for your noble contribution?" another American student inquired.

"We are not materialistic! We trust whoever is in charge will compensate us generously. However, I belong to a group of students, who do not want to be paid at all," the girl replied, with some indignation. "I just told you: we are here not for money but to respond to the Komsomol call!"

"Yes, she is right," the Komsomol leader, Leonid Kuznezov, confirmed, nodding. "In our society, we all help each other. And, honestly speaking, we are surprised that you do not practice the same in your country."

The back-and-forths were heating up, and I was having increasing trouble keeping up with the translations. Fortunately for me, Professor Wilson then attempted to switch to a gentler, slower conversation.

"We do provide help to people in need but in many other forms. We have plenty of welfare funds in the United States. It is true we are not helping our farmers the way you are, but in our country farms are private enterprises. Our farmers are only happy with large crops. Additionally, many of them are receiving governmental subsidies." The socialist sympathizer nodded to the room, encouragingly.

His attempts to calm the exchange completely failed.

"The difference is that you help them with all kind of handouts, but we are doing it with our own work and we are proud of our socialist mentality!" snapped Leonid, defiantly looking for approval from the KGB guide.

"But people who are getting necessary help in the United States are grateful and do not think of it as handouts. It is mostly for those who suffer temporary hardships," interjected Stephan, another American student. "For many reasons, in my country many fewer people are involved in the agriculture, and they do not expect help from an outside working force. If a farmer cannot take care of his farm appropriately, he hires help or simply buys additional equipment."

Out of the corner of my eyes, I noticed Dmitry Zorin inclining his head slightly to Cornelia Plamadeala, a pale and slender woman with shoulder length hair and light green eyes. She was probably an informer at the conservatory. In a low, inviting voice he murmured to her in Moldovan, "Plamadeala, make it hot for them!"

"It is difficult for you to understand our country because our agriculture suffered tremendously during the Nazi invasion," Cornelia began, every word uttered in a ringing, chanting voice. "While America hesitated to be involved with Germans, my country fought to defeat the enemy and lost many more lives than yours. Do not forget it: it was the Soviet Union that saved the entire world from the fascist plague!"

When I translated the last statement, the previously silent Professor Zell stood up.

"Let's be fair!" he yelled. "My father and my older brother were wounded at the Battle of Normandy, and my uncle was killed at the Battle of El Alamein. Besides, I am an agriculture expert and I know firsthand that we provided to your country valuable assistance with food, military hardware, and other materials during the war. It was called the Lend-Lease Program and it was an important help to your Army and to your citizens at the time of the war with Germany. Nobody can ignore it!"

After I translated, Dmitry Zorin, his objective achieved, now tried to appear to be reasonable. "Allow me to comment on this issue," the guide said, looking intently at the standing American. "Nobody is saying here that America did not participate in the war. This student simply wants to emphasize that the merits of our country largely exceeded the contribution of the other allies in the final victory over the Nazis. We are extremely happy to have here our dear American guests, and we want our countries to live in peace and friendship always. I only would like to point out that it's a real pity that the United States of America, unfortunately, disseminates aggressive propaganda against Soviet Union. Please, do not take it personally, but—and I will be honest with you—we don't like it."

"I am a teacher and an honest man," responded Professor Zell, pointedly turning his back on his fellow professor. "I am an educated man. I wrote several books, I read newspapers, I listen to radio and watch TV, and, I have not read not heard any evidence of aggression against your country from the United States. We want to live in peace no less than you do. I really do not understand why you accuse us of aggressive intentions!"

"It's your turn, Urbanski." Zorin turned to a young man with straw-colored hair.

"I do not understand why you do not see something that is so obvious for us!" Urbanski threw at the visitors. "Yes. It's obvious. We have in the USSR unlimited supply of raw materials, and the capitalists in the United States are dreaming about our riches. Our newspapers report it regularly. Look at what happened with Alaska! You bought this territory practically for nothing and you know how profitable Alaska is for you! In my opinion, it's time to return Alaska to us. What is fair should be fair!"

His latter remark visible agitated all of the Americans, so much that Professor Wilson sternly ordered his delegation to calm down. "We are guests here and we want to have peace and quiet while we are in this country," he lectured them. "Let me respond."

"Dear Soviet friends," he started, "we understand your frustration. It is true that our country is ahead in many areas but do not feel bad about it. I am sure that it is only a question of time, before the Soviet Union catches up with us. We admire your achievements in the cosmos and the word "Sputnik" is known to every citizen in the world. You have a privilege to live and work in a socialist system, which, as I personally believe, is the most advanced. Please, do not have any doubts that in another five or ten years you will overtake and surpass the United States. I think that your five-year plans are a work of a genius. I do not believe that my country will ever raise its hand against Soviet Union, and I am telling you that as a man who openly supports socialism. You can sleep comfortable. Let's fight together for peace and be friends."

"We also want peace," Komsomol Leader Kuznezov responded swiftly, savoring every word of his well-memorized speech. "But if you really want peace, why do you interfere in everything going on in the world? Our country is a country of creators and heroes! Your country is a country of consumers and hucksters! You think you are the best in the world, but what about the treatment of minorities in America? In our schools, our teachers teach us in detail about the numerous injustices in your country."

Professor Zell leaped to his feet again, face red and hands shaking.

"Let me tell you young man. You are either brainwashed," he said with a high-pitched trembling voice, "or totally, totally . . ."

He could not finish because his colleague and boss Professor Wilson grabbed his arm. "For God's sake, for God's sake, I beseech you, Rudolph. Please, stop it! Shut up! Do you want to have an international scandal in this village, whose name we do not even know? Please, sit down! Calm down and remember that I did you a big favor by recommending you to be a part of my delegation. This young jerk is totally wrong, but you forgot we are not at home where we can speak our minds freely."

Pale as paper and breathing heavily, Professor Zell, his lips tightly pursed, reluctantly took his seat.

"Translate for me immediately every word they just said," Dmitry Zorin ordered me. "Do not miss anything!"

I told him that Professor Wilson strongly demanded his colleague to stop arguing and asked him to restore peace. Naturally, I did not mention "young jerk," and myself added that Professor Wilson was upset that his colleague was tired and did not have enough sleep.

Dmitry Zorin sat quiet for a moment and then began his closing remarks, reminding everybody in a fatherly tone that we were friends, and that we should like each other and learn how to coexist. "Our countries are the greatest countries in the world," he concluded, "and we should understand how to respect each other for our mutual benefit."

The meeting over, the Americans gathered on one side of the room while I joined the Soviet team on the other. Shaking hands with the students, Dmitry Zorin was eminently satisfied. "I told you guys," he confided smugly to Leonid and his friends, "these Americans are so stupid, it's simply disgusting. We visited today two farms and you should see how we pulled the wool over their eyes. They are naive like small children and don't know how to defend themselves. Well done, fellows! It only proves how important is to prepare well for this kind of discussion."

As I approached the Americans to shake their hands in farewell, I overheard Stephan speaking softly to Paul.

"I wonder, if they are so altruistic and devoted to their socialist ideals, then why when we were in Moscow and Leningrad that all the Russians we met were begging us for American dollars and for American jeans?"

Of course, they were not fooled. Looking over at my self-congratulatory comrades, I wondered, not for the first time, whom was really deceiving whom. In a few days, the Americans would board a plane to return to a free country and to reclaim lives their people had built without interruption for nearly two centuries. Yes, their world had its challenges and complexities, but all seven of those students and professors were free to criticize or commend their way of life however they chose.

They would leave behind six Soviet students and a KGB officer who, when the triumphal laughter and smirks faded, would continue to live in a country where they would be free to say only what their government would allow them to say.

He laughs best who laughs last.

A man walks into a grocery store with a notebook.
"Do you have sausage?" he asks the clerk.

"No."

He makes a note. "Bread?"

"No."

He makes another note. "20 years ago, they would have shot you for making notes like that," says a woman waiting in line.

"No bullets either," he writes.

The Incredibly Shrinking Crop

---⚜---

The second spring in Gradieshti, tired of foraging for practically nothing in the stores, I vowed to grow my own food. Finding a meal was not always a problem, especially when you were a doctor on call. According to the established tradition in country hospitals, a physician on duty was entitled to "take a sample" of the food prepared for patients in the hospital. In practical terms, a special table for the physician stood in a corner of the hospital kitchen covered with an old wrinkled oilcloth, where different dishes from the limited menu of the hospital were served. Such hot meals were a lifesaver during a busy work day. It saved me scavenging in depleted stores for decent food and then cooking what little I could find in my little kitchen.

My food options at other times were not good. The only grocery store close to both the hospital and my apartment was nothing more than a small, miserable, one-room hut, perpetually leaning to one side. Year-round, the assortment of food products was limited to dark bread, cabbage with signs of damage, onions, potatoes, and sometimes—but not often mind you—carrots of poor quality. Of all products, the most rotten were guaranteed to be the potatoes, where more than half needed to be whittled down to tolerable slivers and chunks or just thrown away. During the summer, melons and watermelons were piled in a large heap on the floor in a corner. Some were ripe, some green—buying one was as chancy as a lottery ticket. Dark Moldovan soil still clung to everything I carried out of the grocery lean-to, requiring extensive scrubbing at home before preparing food. The store clerk, dressed in her peasant clothing, explained to the customers in a bored voice that they should take into consideration that the vegetables were cheap, so they shouldn't worry about what was given to them.

Yeah, I could probably do better.

A better-stocked grocery store stood in the village center. There it was possible to buy fish and meat in cans, macaroni, dry peas, kidney beans, bread, and hard candy. Sometimes they sold sausages but with a high fat content. Always available and in unlimited quantities, of course, were vodka and bottled Moldovan wine. To buy such items as meat, high-quality sausage, and different kinds of cheese, however, it was necessary to find a way to get to Tiraspol and back.

My four-mile round trip walk to the grocery at the Gradieshti village center was not only time-consuming and especially tiring on the package-laden trip back, but it was also horrible when it rained. The dirt-and-gravel road turned into a liquid mush, with pedestrians like myself splashed with muddy water and droplets by passing cars. Crossing from one side of the road to the other was especially difficult. Because there was no drainage system, even walking in rubber boots didn't help much. On more than one occasion, clinging clay mud pulled the boots right off my feet.

One day, looking back at boots still attached to the middle of a swampy street, I swore there had to be a better way.

I began close to home, full of optimism as always when trying out a new, brilliant Vladimir idea—grow my own fresh vegetables! One early spring, I obtained from my friends and acquaintances tomato, cucumber, onion, and garlic seeds, along with seeds for different sorts of flowers. I found a suitable piece of land just next to the building where I lived, dug it up, and turned it into a garden. My three-legged canine friend, Little Pal, enjoyed participating in this work, especially when I started to plant the seeds. He honestly tried to help me dig holes with his single front paw and two back ones. I regularly rewarded my assistant with a piece of sausage.

Now all we could do was tend to the garden and wait. In case you were wondering—yes, I did sing with vigor as I planted, just like when I worked in the cornfields as a student. And no, the little garden was not located near the outhouse or latest cesspit in the backyard.

My little agricultural initiative was only the beginning. During a morning briefing session a few weeks later, the head of the hospital labor union (an organization whose function I never truly figured out in three years) announced that the physicians, as representatives of the rural intelligentsia, would have the opportunity to receive a small plot of land outside the village to grow their own corn or potatoes.

Immediately, we physicians, and for some reason, several representatives of the hospital auxiliary staff, went out to inspect the site. It turned out that the field was a long way from the hospital; without transportation, I would not be able to get there. And that was the least of the challenges. How would I be able to prevent my future crop from being stolen? Finally, did I really have the time and energy to pursue this agricultural gift?

As I began walking over to the chief doctor to refuse the generous offer, a man I hardly knew, the disinfector technician Michai Marinovich Nyagu, approached with a wide, friendly smile splitting the maw of a half-toothless mouth. Putting his hand on my shoulder and grinning as if he were my closest friend, he addressed me graciously in Russian and Moldovan.

"Well, doctor, are we taking this plot?"

Looking at him, startled, I took a step away from his touch—and his breath. "What do you mean 'we'? And who is taking the plot?"

"C'mon, doctor, we are not going to pass up such a great opportunity," Nyagu urged, gesturing toward the field. "I live not far from this place, so I'll help you take care of the field. I'll plant it with the best seeds, I'll work the land, I'll take care of the plants, and when fall comes we will have plenty of corn for ourselves and to sell. All we need is several good rains."

Such a hard-to-refuse offer ignited my imagination and determination for fresh vegetables, which had already been kindled by the little garden.

I told my half-toothless, newly appeared friend that I would accept his offer on two conditions: that we would work the land together, and that when the time came to sell our crops, we would share revenues on a fifty-fifty basis.

"Michai Marinovich, from your experience, can you tell me how much money we might expect to make when we sell the produce?"

"*Măi doctorule*, doctor, why do we need to discuss such details now?" he answered smoothly with a little smile. "Aren't we partners now? You are a doctor, a learned man, and I am only a laborer. We work at the same place, so how can we mistrust each other? I started working at the hospital probably when you were still at school. Ask anybody about me. Everybody here knows me. I suggest that after you pay for the seeds, I will do all the work on the field, and you will get half of the harvest. Satisfied?"

"In that case, all I want is a quarter of the crop," I said, and we shook hands to seal the deal. I felt I had joined those noble people who, with their hands, fed the rest of humanity.

Agriculture occupied my mind so much that late summer that I started dreaming about it. In one such dream, I saw my business partner, Michai Marinovich, comfortably seated in a horse-pulled cart in the front yard of my apartment building. His semi-toothless face radiated confidence and reserved manliness. Leaping off the cart, he carried into my apartment bag after bag filled with cobs of corn. Soon my room was filled with my portion of the crop.

"Enough, Michai Marinovich. Stop bringing these sacks. Enough! I am running out of space," I implored him in the dream.

"No, doctor. An agreement is an agreement," he responded, bringing me the next sack of corn. "Take it. And this is not all! I'll be back in an hour with another cartful of corn. I am an honest man."

Such hopes and expectations! But then, alas, it all changed near the end of August. One morning after the briefing session, when some of the staff were waxing eloquently about their latest harvest from the collective field, the disinfectant technician stopped me in the hallway. Head down, he mumbled that excessive drought was hurting the corn and that it was possible that my portion would amount to only half a cart.

Drought? None of my coworkers had mentioned it. But still, a half cart was a great prospect, so I smiled and replied that I understood. Looking relieved, my business partner scampered off.

On my way to the briefing the next morning, I stopped in to look at my thriving garden and instead came across a complete disaster. Only a miserable stubble of lonely rootlets remained, all surrounded by the unmistakable traces of a horse's hooves. My faithful dog was as much in shock as me, wining and periodically looking at me with pain as we sadly and slowly made our way to the hospital. Poor dog. Poor me.

Arriving at the morning briefing session, I soon discovered that no one was sympathetic. My friend, the hospital surgeon Ilya Sergeevich Petresku, shook his head, not even trying to hide a condescending smile. "What is the matter with you?" he scolded. "*Everybody* knows that the hospital horse grazes on the hospital grounds at night."

I immediately walked over to the hospital groom and coachman. "Arseny Prokopevich," I complained, "what are we going to do? The horse you are in charge of trampled my entire vegetable crop."

Arseny Prokopevich stared at me without emotion. "First of all it is *our* horse. It's a hospital horse," he said, flatly. "And second, you are lucky the horse has not destroyed your garden before. Is it news to you that horses like fresh feed?"

I could not disagree with the groom's impeccable logic.

By this point, I dreaded seeing the technician, as his near toothless mouth always brought bad news. Two weeks later, pleading a fungus infestation, my business partner, Michai Marinovich, unexpectedly cut his obligation toward me to only one bag of corn. At the end of September, the disinfectant technician sorrowfully reduced my share to half of a bag.

One late afternoon in early October, I saw through the front window of my apartment a horse-pulled cart approaching my building. On the crossbar of it sat my benefactor and business partner, Michai Marinovich.

At long last! *Something* fresh had survived this dreadful harvest! I was sure of it! I ran out onto the porch and gazed eagerly at the cart.

Which was empty.

Jumping down, Michai Marinovich pulled out from under the crossbar a bundle made from a peasant kerchief. Cautiously pressing it to his chest, he climbed the stairs.

"You kept asking me about the harvest," he began, after we had gone into the apartment. Perched on the edge of a chair, he looked distressed. "This was not a good year for corn at all, doctor. Not at all! As I told you—drought, fungus, damage. Almost everything perished. Yesterday

I harvested all I could and got exactly five cobs of corn. So sad. My wife dried it, ground it, and from the corn flour prepared for us mamaliga. Since we are partners, I brought your personal portion on this plate— half of the mamaliga. The other half of it is for my poor family." Uncovering the dish, he handed it to me and stood up.

I had to say it. "Michai Marinovich, how is it that all of our employees' harvests were great, nobody complained, and yet we and we alone were so unsuccessful?"

"They are lying. Everybody's crop failed like ours," he muttered, opening the door. He paused and turned. "Although you are a doctor and I respect you, let me give you a piece of good advice: Do not ever get involved in something you have no idea of." He left, loudly slamming the door behind him.

As the cart pulled away, I set the mamaliga on the table, and put water on the noisy kerosene Primus stove to boil. Twenty minutes later, I sat down to dine on a summer's worth of diminishing returns and one big lesson learned.

A man came home and found his wife in bed with a stranger. Furious, the man shouted, "You, good-for-nothing, look at what you're spending your time for, while at the corner store they're selling eggs and they have only three boxes left!"

A Frosty Farewell

---◈---

The secretary of the local Communist Party organization, Zachary Ionovich Lupu, was such a happy man, lately. He had pleased his faithful and dependable wife, Rodica Ionelovna, by making sure that a new, decent grocery store was built near the center of Gradieshti. It had taken three years, but was certainly worth it. The new store was solemnly opened in an official ceremony attended by the *kolkhoz*'s leading figures and their spouses. At that special occasion, we all filed through the store, admiring the relatively wide assortment of dairy, meat, and produce. A sturdy, double-locked door protected the valuable merchandise after-hours. Particularly awe inspiring was the store's special pride—a large, walk-in refrigerator, a previously unknown piece of modern technology in the district.

The store also brought Comrade Lupu particular pleasure because of one of its clerks, whom he had personally hired. The gorgeous Camelia Kodreanu, whom we have already witnessed in conversation with the secretary when I verbally accosted him about handrails, was eternally grateful for being rescued from the outdoor drudgery of *kolkhoz* labor. On the days that she worked, Comrade Lupu was a frequent, lingering guest in the store.

Well, given the difficulty of hiding anything for long in the village, soon everyone began speculating and whispering about the party secretary and the clerk. Certainly, it was an established truism in Gradieshti that the handsome Comrade Lupu loved women even more than he loved the Communist Party. As the gossip grew, Rodica Ionelovna, after a serious conversation with her husband, very politely asked Zachary Ionovich to stop his frequent visits to the store. He did not object. Immediately afterward, the clerk's husband, the tractor-racing, muscular Dimitriu Kodreanu, reminded an equally intoxicated Zachary Ionovich at the end of a party that Camelia was married to him. Although he had a healthy respect for the Party secretary, he would not forgive him if he continued to see his wife. Everybody in the village knew Dimitriu had a wild temper, especially when he was drunk and something concerned his wife, so Comrade Lupu was quick with the assurance that he would stay away from her.

He kept the promise for a couple of weeks, while Dimitriu remained watchful, but eventually gave in to temptation again. Even in a village, passion is passion, and he had become obsessed with Camelia. For her, it was very difficult to break off a relationship with the person whom she had to thank for liberating her from the slavery and severe hardships of rural work. And, he was rather handsome, to boot. Unlike Dimitriu, the Party secretary retained every one of his front teeth.

One Friday night, the Kodreanu brothers met on the two-lane highway near the hospital for another epic night of tractor racing. Ivan, concern making the scar on his face especially prominent, caught up to his brother and without preamble shouted that Lupu was in the new grocery store, after-hours.

Swearing, brother Dimitriu sped off, driving as fast as he could to the village center. As Ivan faded slowly from sight, Dimitriu became immediately aware of two problems with his bold plan: on a large, crawling tractor, his chosen method of approach would take some time. Second, everyone, from the hospital staff, to the *kolkhoz* chairman, to the short foreman with little arms drinking late at the poultry farm would hear every tire-turn of his inchworm advance into the village. Nevertheless, the aggrieved husband stayed in his seat, took another swig of vodka, lowered his head, and vowed revenge.

I later learned that Zachary Ionovich Lupu had indeed been at the store with Camelia that evening, drinking homemade wine he'd brought with him, which he kept pouring from a bottle into two glasses. Assuming her husband was tractor-racing with his brother, Camelia did not refuse the drinks; beside, the wine was personally manufactured by her benefactor who also happened to be a very important man in the village.

One thing led to another along the often-short road to intimacy. In the midst of growing heaven and harmony, the couple heard the sound of a loud tractor motor approaching. Neither of them doubted that it was Camelia's jealous husband, and that they were in deep trouble. How would they justify being found together in the closed store behind double-locked doors? The couple shook with fear, gulping from the wine bottle and not knowing what to do. The party secretary was convinced that, despite his special position in village life, he could very soon be mercilessly beaten. As terrible, his non-Communist behavior would become known to his wife and—more importantly—to his party bosses.

At that moment, Camelia came up with a brilliant idea, to which her lover just had to agree.

"Listen, Zachary, my Dimitriu will kill us both if he finds us here," she fearfully gasped. "But we should not panic. I will let you inside the walk-in refrigerator. When he sees that everything is all right and leaves, I will let you out again. It should not take long."

Each lover swallowed another big gulp from the bottle of wine, as the tractor engine became silent, right in front of the store door. A tense silence ensued. Camelia dashed silently back toward the pride of the store—the walk-in refrigerator—opened its door wide, and shoved the inebriated Comrade Lupu and his unfinished bottle of wine through it. Closing the massive door of the refrigerator as softly as she could, she then raced to open the store to let her husband in.

"Where is he?" Dimitriu thundered, brushing past her brusquely.

"Where is whom?" asked Camelia, as innocently and surprised as she could on the spot, following her husband deeper into the store.

"Where is your friend Lupu?" he barked, reddened eyes sweeping every aisle, every pile of produce.

"You're crazy, Dimitriu. He is not a friend of mine and he might have been here, but I didn't see him. I was busy all day long with my customers. If not for Lupu, you wouldn't have your new tractor, right?"

"I guess you're right," her still-excited but increasingly bewildered husband grunted, pausing and scratching the back of his head.

"Now let's go home, Dimitriu, and we'll have our dinner," said Camelia, soothingly. She now reasoned that as soon as she could get away, she would slip back to the store and let Comrade Lupu out of the refrigerator.

As they walked out to the tractor, Camelia slammed with vigor the door of the shop, so relieved that everything was going as planned.

On the way home, excuses raced through her head to get her back to the store as soon as possible. She comforted herself with the thought that her elder friend—an iron Communist—would be able to withstand the lower temperature.

What the poor schemer had forgotten was that today was the birthday of Dimitriu's mother. When the couple opened the door of their house, they were surprised to see all the Kodreanu relations gathered and already fully celebrating the heralded occasion. Everyone there insisted, in good ole Gradieshti style, that they take seats at the table and drink a toast to the health of Dimitriu's mother. One toast then followed another, and there was no way Camelia could refuse a single one, lest she be accused of disloyalty to the family.

When the dinner was over, Camelia was significantly drunk. Still clinging to a tendril of urgency, she managed to slip away and run back to the store. Standing in front of barred windows and a solid door with double locks, she discovered to her absolute horror that she had left the keys inside.

Racing back home to find a spare key in one of the drawers, she discovered Dimitriu preparing to go to sleep. Tired and still quite inebriated, Camelia decided to take a small nap until Dimitriu fell asleep. Then she would find the key, scoot back to the store, and rescue the party secretary.

When Camelia opened her eyes, however, it was daylight outside and her husband had already left for the *kolkhoz*. Shrieking, she frantically searched until she tracked down the spare key. Heart beating wildly, she sprinted to the store. With trembling hands, she unlocked the double locks, rushed to the walk-in refrigerator, and yanked opened its door.

Zachary Ionovich Lupu, esteemed local party secretary, sat peacefully, leaning against the back wall, his frosted eyelids shut. His frozen fingers were curled around an empty bottle.

Picturing her husband's furious face, Camelia somehow dragged the frozen man from the refrigerator, and then ran to summon the village militia officer.

I was in the admitting department of the hospital, taking care of a young patient, when the doors burst opened and the corpse of the honorable citizen Zachary Ionovich Lupu was quickly rolled in on a stretcher and taken immediately to a smaller room. Racing alongside the thawing secretary was the militia officer, the distinguished chairman of the *kolkhoz*, and my boss, the hospital chief doctor. When I tried to push open the door to the room where the corpse now laid on a couch, Lyubov Evgenyevna grabbed my hand and abruptly ordered me to leave and forget everything I had just seen.

In the Soviet regime, the sudden death of a Party secretary, even a local one, was considered a political catastrophe. Although the death was dealt with in utmost secrecy, the truth was impossible to conceal. Through hints and tips, I soon learned what had happened and expected terrible consequences for poor Camelia.

I was dead wrong. The final authority in the region, the First Secretary of the Tiraspol District Party, guided by political considerations, declared a different outcome. The life of a party secretary, he reasoned, should be dedicated to the bright ideals of Marxism-Leninism rather than the attraction of young, beautiful ladies. Accordingly, the official explanation for Zachary Ionovich's death was a heart attack, which he suffered when he happened to be walking past the grocery store.

His wife, Rodica Ionelovna, when promised a generous gift from the district Communist Party and a relatively decent pension for the rest of her life, did not object to the official version of her husband's death. Moreover, from all accounts, she gradually started to believe it herself.

The most incredible turn of events was that Camelia survived, unscathed. Dimitriu left her for awhile but very soon was persuaded by his one-of-a-kind beautiful wife to return home. Rather than being deported to Siberia or the far north for manslaughter, Camelia continued to work in the store, where, together with her coworker, she was put in charge of food distribution. Her husband continued racing his brother on late summer nights, loving her as only a tractor driver can.

A KGB officer is walking in the park and he sees
and old Jewish man reading a book. The KGB
says, "What are you reading old man?"

The old man says. "I am trying to teach myself Hebrew."

The KGB says. "Why are you trying to learn
Hebrew? It takes years to get a visa for Israel. You
would die before the paperwork got done."

"I am learning Hebrew so that when I die and go to Heaven
I will be able to speak to Abraham and Moses. Hebrew is
the language they speak in Heaven," the old man replies.

"But what if when you die you go to Hell?" asks the KGB.

And the old man replies, "Russian, I already know."

One Joke Too Many

It's the beginning of March 1967, and my three years of obligatory work at Gradieshti are winding down. My medical diploma from Kishinev Medical School just arrived by mail, signaling that it's time to begin exploring options and preparing to leave. As I navigate towering snowdrifts on both sides of the path leading from the hospital to the ambulatory clinic, my next career steps are all I can think about.

I have to admit it—I am not in a big hurry to leave the village. Yes, it is achingly primitive, drunk, and full of eccentrics and self-important petty bureaucrats, but Gradieshti—with all of its strange corners and twists and turns—has become known and comfortable to me over the years. I now can tell its stories and choose with ease which streets are the least muddy and rutty on rainy days. I have forged memories and shared experiences with friends and coworkers, each deepening our conversations and awareness of each other as we sip the newest homemade *must*. After three years, I have earned the respect of many parents and seen for myself the difference I make every day treating their children. People of Gradieshti, I know that I will never really be accepted as one of you, but you have come to know my face, benefit from my purpose, and have become my friend.

My reverie is interrupted by my friend, Eugene Rachok, the red-faced X-ray technician and listener to many of my jokes. Eugene's standing off to the left in front of a transformer booth muttering something under his breath.

"Hello, Eugene," I call, stopping. "What's up, whom are you talking to?"

"Whom am I talking to is none of your business, pal! Today is my birthday but not even a dog wished me a happy birthday. But what do you care!" he shouts, red-faced and slurring his words.

"Come on, my friend," I say, smiling and stepping forward, arms out. "I definitely care. I wish you a happy birthday from the bottom of my heart. I see you have already enjoyed a couple of drinks for the occasion. Be careful, it's slippery today. Don't drink more."

"It's none of your business how much I should drink!" barks the X-ray technician, now clenching his fists and full of menace. "Nobody tells me that I am drunk. For your information I am a former army sergeant and who are you, excuse me? I will tell you who you are: you are a city kike and I hate you kikes. Did you hear me?" His face is now flushed deep red and his body begins to shake.

He can't stop spewing pent-up hatred. "Everybody knows that during the war your people were holed up in the rear enjoying good life and making big money doing all kinds of filthy machinations, while my father was spilling his Ukrainian blood for the country! You Jews are dirty parasites of the society, and you should be thrown out! Kikes are polluting the world all over! Go to your Israel, vermin!"

My first reaction is disappointment rather than anger. Rabid anti-semitism has crawled its way into the peaceful place where I worked and called home. It has curled up in a man I thought was a friend.

"Shame on you, despicable creature! Go home and sober up," I say to him firmly but as calmly as I could. "My father was a combat officer, was wounded and decorated with high military awards. Jews are neither better nor worse than anybody else on this planet and they were always good citizens of this country!"

"Dirty kike!" spits out Eugene.

That's it. "Shut up, scum of the earth!" I roar, now enraged. "You are a rabid dog obsessed with Jews and you don't exist for me anymore, piece of crap!"

My adversary glares at me, eyes burning with a wild hatred I have seen in the past.

"I will never forgive you for this," he mutters. "I won't let it go. Be thankful you are alive. You will hear from me yet. Wait, kike, you will see!"

Turning around and trying to walk steadily, Eugene trudges off to the highway and his home.

I would've disregarded his drunken threats, but whenever the X-ray technician met me afterward at the hospital, he always had a contemptuous smile on his reddened face. It was clear that this man was up to something nasty.

Four days later, during morning rounds, I ran into my boss, Chief Doctor Oprya. Creeping toward me, eyes wide open on her round, anxious face, she looked around nervously and hissed, "What have you done, Doctor Tsesis! What have you done?"

"Nothing special, Lyubov Evgenyevna," I replied casually, looking down at a patient chart, by now thoroughly used to her drama and overreactions.

"Oh, 'nothing special,' so you know nothing!" she whispered, sharply. "Just you wait, and you will know *everything*! How many times did I tell you to stop your stupid clowning, but your problem is that you simply cannot keep your mouth shut." Wildly shaking her head, she was clearly dismayed and frightened. "Anyway, remember this: I have nothing to do with whatever you said or did! This is all I wanted to tell you." Nodding firmly, she turned heel and marched away.

OK, now I was nervous.

An hour later, a nurse's aide ran up to me, terrified and sputtering that I was supposed to pick up the one hospital phone in that corridor.

I picked up the receiver and was assailed by a man's curt voice. "Doctor Tsesis, Lieutenant Kurshitovsky speaking. Tomorrow at 11 a.m. sharp, we expect you at the Committee for State Security (KGB) in Tiraspol, Room 205. Clear?"

"Yes. But what is the reason?"

"This is not a telephone conversation," the lieutenant snapped. "You will be informed when you come in." The line went dead, as I became convinced that the X-ray technician had found a way to denounce me to the KGB.

I had every right to be scared. In the 1960s Soviet Union, where judge was also jury, where defense attorneys were scared of their own shadow, the KGB always had the last word in deciding what to do with anyone who became their "client." They could decide and do . . . anything.

The next day, right at eleven o'clock in the morning, with shaking hands and racing heart, I opened the door leading to the large vestibule of the Tiraspol KGB. I couldn't help what came to mind as I stepped in:

> Listener to Armenian Radio asks: Why are doorknobs of KGB buildings more worn out on the outside of the main door than on the inside?
> Armenian Radio replies: Obviously because people who enter the building rarely leave it.

In somber silence, on a pedestal stood a gigantic bust of Felix Dzerzhinsky—the founder of Cheka, now the KGB—sternly looking down at me.

I heard the sound of approaching soft steps.

"Whom are you here to see?" demanded a young officer, wearing the blue colors of the agency.

As he took me down an interminably long corridor to Room 205, soldiers with menacing faces kept jumping out like marionettes from hidden niches in the walls. My guide kept waving them back to their stations.

In room 205, a young KGB captain with a moustache and a blond bush of hair on his head, sat behind a long table, staring down at a thick folder in front of him.

"Sit down," he ordered, without looking up at me and emphatically pointing to the chair before the table.

I obeyed.

"Nadezhda Matveevna, you are accused of sabotage and political subversion against the Soviet Union!" he growled intimidatingly, still not looking up.

"But Comrade Captain, allow me to say I am not Nadezhda Matveevna," I answered immediately, almost stammering.

The captain looked up, surprised.

"Oh, you are not her, and you are not even a woman," he concluded swiftly, without a shade of embarrassment and beyond reproach. "Oh, yes, now I remember. You are Doctor Tsesis. We called you to let you know that we are very displeased with your behavior."

"What am I accused of?" I asked as calmly as I could. "Why did you call me?"

"Not you but I ask questions here," the captain interrupted. "First of all, you must address me as Captain Lungu, and secondly you should know yourself why you are here."

"But I do not know," I replied, doing my best to look innocent and bewildered.

"Are you some kind of a Zionist?" he demanded, straightening up and glaring.

"I have no idea, what that means, Captain Lungu," I answered, now really puzzled.

"Why are you so upset when someone mentions your ethnicity?"

"I am sorry, I still do not understand you, Captain Lungu."

The phone rang and captain picked it up. In a very soft voice, he began discussing with the caller something that appeared to be important. Unexpectedly, his features softened.

"OK, where were we?" he asked me in a lower tone of voice, hanging up.

"I think you were talking about my ethnicity, Captain Lungu."

"Oh, that. I am too busy for that subject now. My wife just called because our son is sick. Let's go straight to the point. We received reliable information that you are spreading anti-Soviet jokes. Do you admit it?"

Oh, no.

"Sorry, but I have no idea what you are talking about, Captain Lungu," I protested.

"Oh, so you do not admit your guilt! Maybe you want to hear a recording of some of your so-called jokes, ah?"

I remained silent, willing my hands not to shake.

"Remember, this time we brought you here just to warn you. However, next time you will be punished according to the letter of the law!"

"Thank you. I understand."

"Good. You can leave now," he ordered, dismissing me with a wave. The captain then paused, and looked hopeful. "But . . . wait a minute. I spoke with Doctor Oprya. Your boss hoped nothing would happen to you because she does not have a replacement; she said you are okay. So, listen: my son is teething and did not sleep all night. My wife does not know what to do with him. As a baby doctor, what do you recommend? Oh, by the way I forgot to offer you a cigarette."

Politely refusing, I offered advice for what to do for the baby's condition.

"Thank you. It makes sense. I like you. Now you really can leave."

"So is my case closed?" Feeling a tremendous relief, I just had to ask before leaving the room.

"I am definitely done with you, and I hope you will show more respect for the system that protects Soviet citizens. The only one thing that will remain is the record of your visit, that's all."

"Wait a second! Does this mean that now a dark spot will "decorate" my reputation?" I asked. "Can something be done? People tell these innocent jokes all the time!"

"Don't ever repeat what you just said!" he exclaimed, alarmed. "Such jokes are subversive and obviously you are not too stupid to understand it. They can destroy our society. Even if you were my relative, I could not wipe out this incident from your personal file. We are a serious organization and we maintain good documentation."

"But will my case ever be closed?"

"Why should you worry? We have thousands of open cases, but as you know, people are alive and well—at least a majority of them. For your information, the KGB records are preserved forever."

I left the KGB building, relieved but also worried about the permanent record of my KGB questioning. When would it surface again and hurt me? When a parent became angry because a child did not get well?

As I made it to the highway to hitchhike home, my father returned again to help me. I remembered my parents mentioning once that in 1937 and 1938, during the worst of Stalin's purges, as soon as my father would hear the hint of a possibility of being entrapped in the new wave of persecution, they would quickly pack up and simply move to another district. Personal political files were not transferred between districts, so my parents kept moving.

Catching a bumpy ride back to Gradieshti in the back of a truck, my path became crystal clear. In a month, I would be free to move to Odessa, where my wife lived. In all likelihood, if I did, my personal file would stay right here. The size of our country was also its weakness: the left hand of Soviet government on all levels didn't know what the right hand was doing, and so I became determined to squeeze past both.

Right then and there, the dear village that I had grown so fond of lost its young pediatrician. In the spring of 1967, as the hills of Moldova rolled past, I knew it was time for good-bye.

A delegation of foreign Communists came to see a Moscow kindergarten. Before they came, the kids were instructed to answer every question by the visitors with just one sentence, "In the USSR everything is the best in the world."

The visitors came and asked their questions:

"Children, do you like your kindergarten?"

"In the USSR everything is the best in the world!" the kids shouted.

"And what about the food you get?"

"In the USSR everything is the best in the world!"

"Do you like your toys?"

"In the USSR everything is the best in the world!"

At that, the smallest boy in the group started crying.

"Misha, why are you crying? What happened?"

"I want to go to the USSR!"

Endings

I saw the chief doctor the next afternoon, while working in the doctor's lounge. Standing next to each other, we exchanged tense whispers.

"Thank you very much, Lyubov Evgenyevna," I said, softly. "It was very important that you put in a good word for me to the KGB officer. Believe me, it was nothing but a misunderstanding. They thought I had said something wrong, but I proved my innocence and had a great conversation with the captain. I learned a lot."

"Really?" The chief doctor was suspicious.

"Oh, yes. Holy truth! Honestly!" I confirmed resolutely.

"I never know when to believe you, Vladimir Abramovich," said my boss, rolling her eyes.

Suddenly, the happiest smile lit up her wide face. "Whatever really happened, today I will believe anything you say because it is the best day of my life," she continued, her voice rising so that others in the lounge could hear us. "I am overcome with joy since my beloved Communist Party and my beloved government of Moldova Republic have honored me with a title of Honored Doctor of the Republic!"

"Congratulations," I exclaimed, shaking my boss's hand "I am so happy for you! No words!"

"Wait—this is not all. Can you believe it? I am also to receive a medal 'For Merits in Socialist Labor.' And this is still not all! In my honor the road from our hospital to the highway will be named 'Lyubov Oprya Road.' That's forever! In my honor! Unbelievable!"

By this point, my boss was excitedly gesturing and nearly jumping up and down. She then stopped, eyes narrowing, and put her hands on her hips. "And, please, do not tell me that it's one of the dirtiest roads in the village. I know it without you saying it! But just wait, sooner or later they will fix it. After all I am a woman, and we have our ways!"

"Congratulations again, Lyubov Evgenyevna!" I exclaimed enthusiastically, winking at the crowd now watching and listening. "But maybe in front of the hospital they should install a bronze statue of you with a child in your arms! That truly will be spectacular! People from all over will come to see you embodied in metal!"

Hey, I had given notice and was leaving in a few weeks.

"You and your stupid jokes! You still did not learn your lesson," Lyubov Evgenyevna sniffed, retaining her proud humility, though a little smile did play at the corners of her mouth. "I am not Stalin or Lenin to have a statue. For your information, to honor me, authorities are planning a big party in our Village Cultural Center. And, by the way, I did not forget about you. As you are leaving us soon, I asked that you be allowed to sit next to me on the podium. It will be something like a farewell party for you."

The chief doctor then told us that the keynote speaker at her ceremony would be the commander of the Tiraspol Military District, General Kolpakov.

"A real general, unbelievable!" she cried, clapping her hands and laughing. "I never thought that I, a simple peasant's daughter, would turn out to be such an important personality. Even my husband, who, as you know, can be a stubborn ass, after learning this news now behaves like a sober lap-dog. People might think I am crazy, but last night I had a dream that I saw Comrade Lenin resurrected and he shook my hand. I am so happy!"

"Lyubov Evgenyevna, what does the commander in chief of the military district have to do with your gala?"

"To tell you the truth I do not know myself," she replied dismissively, waving her hands. "They told me that it is a military secret. But what difference does it make to me if I am getting a medal! I'm in seventh heaven!"

For the next few weeks, Gradieshti threw itself into preparing for the big festivity at the Village Cultural Center. Rumors abounded that a fleet of chic black automobiles would deliver a large team of guests, including party officials, numerous representatives of press, and General Kolpakov himself with his entourage. Ripped flags on the administrative buildings and old portraits of Communist Party leaders generously soiled by generations of politically incorrect and disloyal birds and flies were replaced with new ones. Creative propagandist Valeriu Raylyan outdid himself with new rhymed slogans. Shouting from large posters around the Village Cultural Center were a litany of inspirational proclamations:

LYUBOV EVGENYEVNA IS OUR PRIDE AND LIGHT, OUR PATH TO COMMUNISM IS STRAIGHT AND BRIGHT.

DOCTOR OPRYA, WE ADMIRE YOU, OUR DEVOTION AND LOVE ARE VERY TRUE.

GRADIESHTI'S CHIEF DOCTOR IS OUR HOPE AND LIGHT, WITH HER HELP WE ARRIVED AT GLITTERING HEIGHT.

Interestingly enough, the gala would take place on my last day in the village. Once word got out that I was leaving soon for Odessa, I spent many an evening at the home of friends, accepting well wishes, souvenirs, and, of course, toasts. In fact, that there were so many farewell dinners and drinks that I looked forward to the relative peace and sobriety of my last full week in Gradieshti, when I was scheduled to be on call after hours.

That final week of being on call went by uneventfully, until the last night, which was a Saturday. Around eleven o'clock in the evening, two orderlies knocked on my door, shouting that there was an urgent need to be at the maternity ward. The hospital's obstetrician-gynecologist, the chief doctor, and her husband were out of the village, taking a vacation before her award ceremony. Without knowledge of what this new challenge might be, I ran after the orderlies, my heart pounding. At my side, Little Pal trotted gamely on three legs.

Racing across the hospital grounds under a full moon, I was startled to hear loud music. In front of the maternity building, two large bonfires lit a fairly large crowd of festively dressed local people. Everyone laughed and drank; some danced the ethnic dance "Moldovenyaska" to the music of a five-man orchestra: accordion, violin, trumpet, clarinet, and, of course, drum. Not understanding what was happening, I entered the maternity floor and asked the nurse on duty, Valentina Stepanovna Vorona, what was going on.

"Oh, doctor, it's a wedding!" the middle-aged nurse explained to me joyfully and with a big smile, as if they occurred everyday on the hospital grounds. "I am surprised you did not hear the music before. They have been here for a couple of hours already, but I did not want to wake you up until the bride was ready to give birth. The wedding started at the groom's house at eight, but the bride—her name is Carmen Anghelescu—danced so hard that she developed strong uterine contractions. The guests loaded the bride on a horse-pulled cart and brought her here at ten. The entire wedding party followed the bride. They've brought a barrel of wine, food, bottles of vodka. They even set up their own tables and chairs!"

Did I really expect anything different on my last night?

Beckoning me onto the large porch ringing the maternity building, Valentina Stepanovna pointed to a man in the middle of the courtyard, dancing with a flower in his jacket lapel. That was the happy father of the soon-to-be-born baby. The groom was a nephew of Costica Gavrilovich Dimitrescu, head of the *selsoviet*, or Village Council. His uncle was among the participants, drinking with his friends to the health of the happy couple.

We went back inside, and prepared to deliver the baby. The music outside was muffled in the delivery room, where Carmen Anghelescu, the bride, lay on her back with high pillows under her head. Beautiful and very attractive, she happily smiled between contractions, still euphoric due to the symbolic amount of wine the bride had consumed prior to her admittance. A table with sterile surgical instruments was set up at the side. At Carmen's insistence, her snow-white bridal dress was placed on a separate stool in the back of the delivery room. Contractions were strong—the baby was expected to be delivered very soon.

Listening to the joyful and uplifting music and merry shouts from outside, I shuddered at the thought of possible complications during delivery. If something bad happened, the families of the bride and groom would show me no mercy.

Before that night, I had never delivered a baby without the supervision of a specialist. Now, without even a spare moment to refresh my memory of the basic knowledge of how to deliver babies, I thought I could only rely on help from heaven. Washing my hands, I thought quickly back to the course on obstetrics in medical school. All I could definitely recall were the hundred unexpected complications that might occur during birth.

"Doctor, what's happening to you?" From a long ways away, I heard the gentle voice of Valentina Stepanovna. "Look at you. You are all pale and almost shaking. You don't have to worry as long as I am here. I've worked here for many years and delivered countless babies. I call Lyubov Evgenyevna to deliver a baby only if there is something really extraordinary. Everything is going according to nature's plan. There is no need to worry."

She nodded in the direction of the middle-aged orderly, who had just brought a warm blanket. "Anastasia's mother was a midwife. If you ever have a chance to speak with her, she will tell you how she delivered at home every new member of her large family."

I was happy to be surrounded by such competent experts and tried to smile at them, but my mind dwelled on possible mishaps. What would I do if labor suddenly ceased, if the mother developed serious bleeding or high blood pressure, or if the fetus's cardiac activity started dropping?

Be a captain on a ship. I tried my best to calm the geometrically expanding number of fears by remembering my brother's wise advice. Taking a deep breath, I stepped forward.

Together with my experienced nurse, I helped the young mother go through the stages of delivery. Soon, she forgot she was a bride and moaned and cried like any other village woman in her situation. Suddenly, somebody outside banged on the heavily curtained windows, demanding explanations for the screams coming from the delivery room. We ignored the hammering and shouting, which eventually stopped.

However, it was only the beginning. A minute later, the unlocked door of the operating room swung open, and Carmen Anghelescu's parents appeared in the doorway, bringing with them the thick smell of alcohol.

"What's going on with you, Carmen?" the mother asked her daughter tenderly.

"Mama, leave me alone! You're bothering me!" gasped the future mother, between her moans and screams.

"My poor child. I brought you something to help you with the pain," slurred the caring father. Raising a glass filled with dark red liquid, he stepped forward. "Have some wine, my little baby."

The nurse and orderly rushed at the parents, ordering them to leave. As he turned away, the bride's father held out the glass of wine and loudly asked if I wanted to drink with him.

Time passed. With each minute, it became clearer that we were dealing with a normal delivery, and I began calming down. In the due time, the cervix fully opened and a future obedient Moldovan citizen began the journey from the darkness of uterine life to the light of the outside socialist world. The mother's moaning and screaming gradually stopped, as she delivered the hairy head of the baby, his body, his arms, and finally his legs.

It is an incredibly exciting moment in the delivery room when a baby is born and takes the first breath. Holding the wet body of the newborn in one hand, with the other I gave a slight slap to the buttocks. The baby let out the most beautiful sound in the world—the shrill cry of new life. The cry was strong, healthy, and reassuring.

Then—in those days before ultrasound technology—came another fascinating moment: the announcement of the baby's sex. Over the years, I have noticed that people in the delivery room actually compete with each other over who will first proclaim the sex of the baby. It did not fail to happen this time either. Before I was able to make my own announcement, Anastasia loudly exclaimed, "It's a girl!" The recently dancing bride, Carmen Anghelescu, had become a legitimate, happy mother.

After Valentina Stepanovna combed the hair of the newborn, I took the baby and brought her close to Carmen, who lay with her eyes closed. She opened her eyes and gave her daughter a long look, touched her face and body, smiled for a moment, and then closed her eyes again, immediately falling asleep. She deserved the rest.

Wiping the baby's umbilical cord with iodine, I cut it with a pair of scissors and placed the baby on the specially prepared table. While the nurse waited for the mother to deliver the placenta, together with Anastasia, I cleaned the baby's upper airways with a bulb syringe, dried her body with a towel, put silver nitrate solution in her eyes for infection prevention, weighed and measured her, and then wrapped her in swaddling clothes.

Looking down on the little one, I was in seventh heaven. Such a sense of sublime inspiration coursed through me, a feeling familiar to anybody who has witnessed the appearance of a beautiful new life. Giddy with relief, I then did something that I had never done before and have never since.

Securely holding in my hands the infant, and accompanied by Valentina Stepanovna and Anastasia, I stepped out on the porch in front of the maternity ward. The wedding guests were still eating, drinking, and dancing to the loud music of the orchestra. With my dramatic appearance, holding the bundle in my hands, everyone became silent and the music stopped. Lowering their drinks, the party-goers stared at me and the bundle in my arms. The only sound was the crackling roar of the bonfires.

Never again in my life has there been such profound interest in what I was doing. Raising the swaddling-wrapped newborn, I loudly announced to the excited crowd that the bride and groom had just become the parents of a fifty-centimeter charming girl, weighing three kilos, two hundred grams.

The crowd burst into cheers and applause, and the festival became even louder. After showing the baby girl to her father and to the grandparents from both sides of the family, I handed her to Anastasia to take to the nursery. Passed from member to member of the exuberant families, I was showered with kisses and hugs but managed to deftly parry dozens of toasts.

In the middle of the crowd, I ended up in front of Costica Gavrilovich Dimitrescu, the head of the *selsoviet* and uncle of the groom. Usually discreet and brandishing an impenetrable expression, tonight he was cheerful and talkative. He shook my hand and hugged me tight.

"You, doctor, did well today, and we like it!" He shouted loudly. "Though you are not a Moldovan, still you are a good man!" His proclamation was met by cheers.

Grinning, I stepped back onto the porch and returned to the maternity ward. *Maybe I will never be one of them, but tonight I came pretty damn close.* Behind me, the good people of Gradieshti continue to drink, hug, and kiss each other, boisterously celebrating late into the night not a socialist paradise, but just themselves.

Gradieshti hadn't witnessed such a spectacle since it had decided to throw itself a May Day parade. Bold banners and slogans hung from every corner; loudspeakers mounted on poles trumpeted revolutionary and patriotic songs. In the square, old women in kerchiefs and long skirts were selling toasted sunflower seeds, corn on a cob, and saccharine sweetened lollipops.

Admission to the Communist gala honoring the chief doctor at the Village Cultural Center was by invitation only. The hall was nearly full and alive with chatter, the audience clearly excited and eagerly anticipating the ceremony. Their mood was sparked by the brassy fireworks of a genuine military band, courtesy of General Kolpakov. The first three rows were packed with the hospital staff: the chief doctor's husband, Grigory Sergeevich, sporting a new suit that was at least one size larger than needed; my faithful nurse Svetlana Dogaru; my friend Doctor Petresku and his wife; and nearly all of the other physicians, nurses, and auxiliary personnel. Everybody was dressed in their best and unusually sober.

The distinguished guests filed onto the podium and sat down. As expected, the center seat belonged to the General, his shining uniform resplendent with more medals and decorations than his chest could accommodate. Next to him sat Lyubov Evgenyevna Oprya, her face flushed and electrified by the moment. To relieve her inner tension, she periodically sipped water from a glass. To my boss's right was an empty chair. I assumed, since she had promised, that the chair was intended for me.

I began climbing the podium steps and was immediately blocked by a threatening, muscular man in civilian clothes.

"Where do you think you are going, citizen?" he demanded, scowling.

I began to explain, but the man grabbed my arm.

"Get out of here!" he bellowed, "These seats are only for the dignitaries on the list, and you do not belong here!" He then unceremoniously escorted me back to the floor.

As the front rows were completely filled by my colleagues, I made my way to the back and sat down. I was a bit sad that no one has saved me a seat, especially since it was my last full day in Gradieshti. Right then, however, Nurse Svetlana and three visiting nurses stood up and, smiling at me, made their way to the back row and sat down next to me.

The meeting started with the anthem of the Soviet Union smartly played by the military band. We all stood at enthusiastic attention, staring forward and visualizing in front of us the enticing, yawning heights of Communism.

A stream of dignitaries then lavishly praised Chief Doctor Oprya as a woman with a vision and a dream. My boss, according to them, raised the quality of the healthcare in the Tiraspol District to now unparalleled heights. Waves of applause followed each proclaimed praise, waking up those not fully dedicated listeners who were nodding off. I clapped loudly, so delighted to learn on my last day that my boss's ardent revolutionary fervor was only matched by her towering medical prowess. On the podium, the beaming Lyubov Evgenyevna Oprya blossomed like a big, round, Communist flower.

In the front row, a surgeon grimaced and looked away.

The big moment arrived; the commander in chief, General Kolpakov stood up with vested authority and pinned to the chief doctor's jacket a large, shining medal "For Merits in Socialist Labor." At that instant, the honoree became pale and probably would have fainted, if not for the firm fatherly embrace of General Kolpakov. Gently holding her in his arms, the general leaned down and, with gentleman's gusto, greatly sped up her recovery by giving her a juicy, prolonged kiss on the mouth.

This unquestionable sign of fatherly affection regrettably produced an angry response from the honoree's husband, Grigory Sergeevich. "Even now this woman cheats," he grumbled loudly in Moldovan, lifting a baggy sleeve and pointing in her direction, "For a medal, my wife would sell her Motherland."

In a moment that she would no doubt relive for years, the fully recovered Lybov Evgenyevna Oprya then stood up and expressed her immeasurable devotion to the Communist Party and its Central Committee, which had allowed her to become "a real human being." She recalled a precious childhood in Gradieshti "herding sheep, milking cows, feeding pigs, and collecting and spreading manure for the glory of the Socialist Motherland." (round of applause)

The socialist preamble over, it suddenly got very interesting, as the chief doctor of Gradieshti Hospital launched into impassioned praise for the Soviet medical system and what we doctors accomplished here every day. That, dear reader, became a tirade for the ages.

"Today, as an Honored Doctor of the Republic I want to offer my own ideas for further advancement of healthcare," she began, rather quietly. "As you know, last year with a delegation of leading rural physicians, I went for a week to Paris. There we had conferences and visited hospitals. The Frenchmen wanted to impress us with their achievements in medicine, but, Comrades, French hospitals are not better than our city hospitals and their medicine is incredibly wasteful. They have a lot of technology but it is too expensive. Waste, waste, waste! Their medical laboratories are unnecessary large and stuffed with equipment for tests you never heard of and could not even pronounce! The cost for medical imaging is astronomical. And guess who pays for it? People like you and me. That's the real ugly face of capitalism: first they introduce all kind of new tests and procedures and then use them as a money making machine."

Believe me, it got even better. I leaned back and prepared myself for a very special twist-and-turn journey through a labyrinth of socialist reasoning.

"You should see how quickly they examine their patients! In and out of the examining room! One French physician told me that she believes that even a meticulous examination of the patient with pneumonia gives her less information than a simple chest X-ray." Snorting, the chief doctor shook her head and looked down at her staff sitting in front. "In our rural hospital, we treat pneumonia day in and day out, even when our X-ray machine is broken. Did you ever hear of anybody dying from a broken X-ray machine?"

The only result I know of for certain from our broken X-ray machine, boss, is that a certain bigoted technician has too much time on his hands.

"Now, take a heart attack patient. In our country, any dedicated physician can safely make this diagnosis by looking at the patient's history, examining the patient and ordering a couple of blood tests—if available, of course. But look how they deal with it in France! So wasteful! They place this patient in an intensive care unit and perform on him a battery of expensive tests. In Gradieshti," she proclaimed proudly, puffing up even more, "we do not have an intensive care unit but we don't need it. Our nurses are watching such patients like hawks and our patients successfully recover in the span of several weeks of strict rest. Wait until we repair our new ECG machine! Then we will be even more effective!"

At this point, the chief doctor bristled, started shouting, and began wagging a finger.

"In France, they know *nothing* about our usual procedures, such as leeches, determination of gastric juice acidity, duodenal intubation, and colonic, when we cleanse accumulated waste from rectum and colon. Imagine! I asked recent graduates of Paris Medical School about these procedures, but they looked at me like a sheep at a new gate. Later, they consulted their smart books and had the nerve to tell *me* that these procedures were long outdated and replaced with more effective methods!"

I pitied the poor French doctors, speaking to a living fossil and striving to remain polite about it. But Gradieshti's Honored Doctor of the Republic wasn't through.

"Those French physicians are so infatuated with their technology that they use hundreds of antibiotics, while we need only ten! Doctor Petresku and I are able to perform almost all surgeries in Gradieshti under local anesthesia, while in Paris they use general anesthesia even for small problems! Our hospital rooms hold six or eight patients, sometimes more, while theirs often have one or two sick people in a room. Patients in these separate rooms are isolated, without a friend in the world, while the poor nurses are forced to run from one room to another to satisfy patients' needs. Many hospital rooms have individual washrooms! We have one washroom on each floor and nobody complains! See how important are the rules of our socialist economy?"

And then, the ranting, fist-shaking chief doctor was signaled by someone in the general's entourage to wrap it up, quickly.

"Soviet medicine is the most advanced in the entire world! We are the best! Our pediatrician Doctor Tsesis has told me about the Dead Sea in Israel, where they treat people with local mud. We have more mud here than we could handle. So, I have a great idea. Comrades, is Gradieshti worse than Israel? I will do my best to build here a modern, first-class mud bath center for the treatment of all kind of diseases. Our Gradieshti mud will be internationally renowned!"

Well, it is certainly known to every piece of clothing and pair of shoes I own.

The hall exploded in applause for one of their own. Blushing furiously, the chief doctor nodded and sat down, glancing over at the general's entourage.

And then, we all were privileged to see and hear the real main event: General Kolpakov, a heavy set man in his early seventies, with distinguished high cheekbones and gray shining hair, rose to deliver the keynote speech . . . dog drunk. His voice was shaking, and his cheeks and nose seemed to flame redder with every garbled word he shouted. From the back row, I could see the villagers shifting a bit and glancing at each other.

"Dear comrades," General Kolpakov said, slowly, little eyes fixed on the audience with a stern expression.

So far, so good, Comrade.

"As a military man with a wide combat experience let me tell you, Lyubov Petrovna—oh, sorry, Evgenyevna—that although you are a Moldovan lady, you are a real Soviet patriot. Let's give her a good round of applause!" Everyone obeyed, and Chief Doctor Oprya blushed again.

The drunken senior military officer then glared at the sea of faces in front of him. "Comrades, you might ask what General Kolpakov is doing in your godforsaken village!"

The hall became dead silent. Around me, no one moved or spoke, as everyone just stared at the podium. The general seemed oblivious. The nervous glances of his staff, however, darted around a now very different audience. On the podium, the chief doctor's gaze was riveted on her shoes.

"Comrades, I used one of your outhouses and it is a real shame! I almost broke my leg and suffocated there. Comrades, your electricity is awful! Last night I was unable to read a newspaper because the light was blinking and disappearing all the time!"

No one clapped. Each one in that hall knew all too well the truths of their lives being shouted at them.

This time, the distinguished guest noticed. Clearing his throat and turning away from too many appraising eyes, the sweaty General gave a sign and the band began to play "International." At that instance, he began to weave and stumble. Two watchful soldiers ran out from backstage and gently tried to lower the General into his chair. Like a Phoenix rising from the ashes, he stayed on his feet, shook his fist, and in a now subdued voice muttered, "Hooray, comrades!"

Looking at her fellow villagers imploringly, the chief doctor began applauding, loudly. Gradually, everyone began playing the game again, and joined in.

Early the next morning, I closed the door of the little apartment for the last time, carrying the same two pieces of luggage I had lugged into Gradieshti three years ago. At the foot of the stairs stood my friend, Ilya Sergeevich Petresku. Shaking my hand and smiling, he handed me a small object wrapped in a white napkin.

"Take it, Volodya. It is a farewell present to you," he murmured, reaching down to scratch behind Little Pal's ears. "It brought me ten minutes of glory, and now will bring you good luck too."

Not understanding, I carefully unwrapped the napkin. It was a fork.

Followed by my three-legged friend, whom my friends had promised to care for, I walked out to the two-lane asphalt driveway to hitch a ride to Tiraspol. Setting the luggage down, I looked around at a rolling landscape, a little gray village, which soon I would know no more.

A horse-drawn cart approached, driven by a *kolkhoznik* wearing a traditional headdress. The cart pulled up and came to a halt. The driver, clutching a large whip, jumped down from the crossbar and walked towards me.

"*Bună dimineața, doctorule* (Good morning, doctor)," he said in Moldovan, gesticulating with the whip.

It was Vasile, the father of my former patient Nikushor Trokalov, who had collapsed and died at school. The same father who had attacked me and Nurse Svetlana at his son's wake.

"What are you doing here?" Vasile asked, looking at my luggage.

"I am leaving Gradieshti for good," I replied, carefully.

"Why?"

"It's time, that's why."

The weathered *kolkhoznik* nodded. "I understand. I understand. We all seek what's better."

Clearing his throat, he then looked at me, closely. "Listen, doctor, it's good I met you here. My wife was mad at me and I myself did not feel good. Don't be sore at me, doctor. You see, I was drunk and very upset at my son's wake. That's all. You forgave me, doctor, right?"

Not waiting for my response, he shook my hand, climbed back on the crossbar, and cracked his whip. The cart began moving away but then stopped. Above the *kolkhoznik*, a large, peeling poster proclaimed COMMUNISM IS YOUR ROAD, TAKE ON YOUR STRONG BACK A HEAVIER LOAD.

Somberly looking back at me for a moment, Vasile opened his mouth to speak. Shaking his head slightly, he turned around, cracked his whip once more and, with the hardened dignity of generations of Moldovan field laborers, continued on his long, difficult journey.

Epilogue

———⚜———

I returned to that quirky, unforgettable village only once, in 1969. The chief doctor and the surgeon, still waging their eternal war, welcomed me enthusiastically.

Five years later, as Marina and I prepared to leave the Socialist Motherland for good, we were visited by my old friend Petresku. Still waiting for his dream car, the good surgeon quietly took me aside and asked for my help in leaving the Soviet Union. There was nothing I could do.

Three decades later, after the fall of the Soviet Union and Communism, Marina and I flew from the United States to Odessa, where we had lived and worked for many years after Gradieshti. During a very pleasant visit with my wife's former coworkers at the Odessa Maritime Academy, I needed to use a washroom. The only toilet on the entire floor, which in the old days had always been open, was locked. A student passing by explained that I needed to go the faculty office and get the key from the secretary.

The restroom was in worse condition than it had been in thirty years before when we left the Soviet Union. No toilet bowl—just a hole in the floor, around which had been sprinkled strong-smelling chlorine powder to hide the stench. The faucet was old and rusty. The sink was wobbly and water hardly drained from it.

Carefully, so as not to hurt anybody's feelings, I shared my surprise about the primitive condition of the washroom with Marina's former colleagues.

"Vladimir, be thankful for what you see. It could be much worse," murmured a professor, my wife's former boss.

"But why is this public place, which serves the entire floor, locked?"

"People are stealing everything, even if it is screwed to the walls or to the floor."

"Even faucets?"

"Everything. Faucets, sinks. Two days ago we had a new faucet, but somebody stole it and now we have the old and rusty one."

Plus ça change, plus c'est la même chose. The more things change, the more they remain the same.

VLADIMIR A. TSESIS, MD, was born and grew up in the Soviet Union, and became a pediatric doctor there. In 1974 he emigrated to the United States, where he continued to practice for another thirty years. Presently he is retired and lives in River Forest, IL. His books include *Children, Parents, Lollipops: Tales of Pediatrics* and *Who's Yelling in My Stethoscope?*

CPSIA information can be obtained
at www.ICGtesting.com
Printed in the USA
BVOW08s1106200117

474047BV00004B/130/P